It's Elementary

A Parent's Guide to K–5 Mathematics

by
Joy W. Whitenack
Laurie O. Cavey
Catherine Henney

NATIONAL COUNCIL OF
TEACHERS OF MATHEMATICS

more4u
www.nctm.org/more4u
Access code: IEG14309

Copyright © 2015 by
The National Council of Teachers of Mathematics, Inc.
1906 Association Drive, Reston, VA 20191-1502
(703) 620-9840; (800) 235-7566; www.nctm.org

Library of Congress Cataloging-in-Publication Data

Whitenack, Joy W.
  It's elementary : a parent's guide to K–5 mathematics / Joy W. Whitenack, Laurie O. Cavey, Catherine Henney.
     pages cm
  Includes bibliographical references.
  ISBN 978-0-87353-701-8
  1. Mathematics—Study and teaching (Early childhood) 2. Mathematics—Study and teaching (Elementary) 3. Education—Parent participation. 4. Homework. I. Cavey, Laurie O., 1968- II. Henney, Catherine. III. Title.
  QA135.6.W4794 2015
  510—dc23

                                        2015019008

The National Council of Teachers of Mathematics is the public voice of mathematics education, supporting teachers to ensure equitable mathematics learning of the highest quality for all students through vision, leadership, professional development, and research.

Printed in the United States

For the children and teachers who have inspired us

Contents

Preface

Maybe you were a math whiz in school, but you've been confounded by your third grader's math homework. Or maybe you struggled with math, and you want your child to have a better experience. Whatever your reason for buying this book, we wrote it for parents like you who want to support and participate in their children's math education with insight and intelligence. As parents you have a vested interest in your children's education. You want to provide them with every opportunity to be successful in the classroom and in life. You know that if a child is to thrive in our tech-driven global society, his or her ability to understand and use mathematics is more important than ever. You also realize that although your children are learning the same topics you did in school, they are often presented very differently. With the wealth of research reported over the last several decades, it is likely that there are many new ideas about teaching and learning mathematics that you are not aware of. Becoming better acquainted and more comfortable with these ideas and practices will help you help your children.

Mathematics is all around us, and your children experience it in and out of the classroom every day. When you help your child figure out how much more money he or she needs to buy a toy or trinket, you may not give it a second thought. But you may worry about how to best help your child be a successful math learner. You may wonder—

- what you can do to encourage your child as he or she does math homework;

- if you should show your child how to solve a problem;

- how your child thinks about and solves problems;

- if there are games, workbooks, or other resources that you should buy so your child can practice math skills; and

- how your children encounter mathematics in and out of the classroom.

In this guide, we talk about these and other concerns that you may have about your children's math education.

The information in this book is targeted to parents of children in kindergarten through the fifth grade. As we thought about what we wanted this guide to do—help provide parents a better sense of their children's mathematical worlds—we realized it would be too big a job to cover all the areas addressed in K–5 schoolrooms. For instance, we do not talk about topics in the elementary curriculum such as geometry (e.g., learning about shapes in kindergarten, classifying shapes in fourth grade), statistics (e.g., making survey questions, collecting and analyzing survey data in third or fourth grade), and so on. Instead, we focus on number sense and the four operations because it is usually these topics that first alert parents to just how differently math is now taught—and sometimes alarm them. They are also among the foundational math subject matter that children learn, and on which they continue to build as they study more advanced concepts in middle and high school.

The central content of the book is organized into an introduction and eight chapters:

Chapter 1: Understanding Today's Mathematics Classroom

Chapter 2: Mathematical Processes and Skills

Chapter 3: Number Sense

Chapter 4: Working with Whole Number Operations

Chapter 5: Understanding Fractions and Decimals

Chapter 6: Working with Fractions

Chapter 7: Mathematics at Home

Chapter 8: Connections to Middle School and Beyond

The introduction sets up the framework for the content of this book—our four guiding principles. We use these principles to underpin our discussions of various mathematical topics, and we make connections between them and the ideas we address in the chapters. You can use the principles as a way to better understand your children's mathematical worlds. As you get started, we suggest reading and making sense of them one at a time. These principles will also help you nurture the creativity and reasoning that children naturally exhibit with mathematics. While all four principles play a part in some chapters, individual chapters focus on particular ones. The chart on the following page indicates the target principles for each chapter.

Chapter 1 provides information about teaching and learning mathematics in the 21st-century classroom. We address what students are expected to do to be successful in math class, and discuss how the teacher supports student learning. Some of the strategies that the teacher uses will be familiar while others will be new to you. Other topics, such as assessment and curricular materials, are also highlighted.

Principles	Chapter 1	Chapter 2	Chapter 3	Chapter 4	Chapter 5	Chapter 6	Chapter 7	Chapter 8
Children do impressive mathematics. It is essential to understand their work to grasp how children think about and approach mathematics.		✓	✓	✓	✓	✓	✓	✓
Parents must be aware of the expectations for students in today's mathematics classroom.	✓	✓	✓	✓	✓	✓		
The mathematics classroom children experience today operates very differently from the one their parents remember.	✓	✓				✓	✓	
Understanding mathematics requires children to make connections among mathematical ideas.		✓	✓	✓	✓	✓		✓

In chapter 2, the math processes and skills that children develop during elementary school are examined. Several processes get particular attention: solving problems, explaining and justifying solutions, and using models (i.e., representing mathematical ideas with pictures or diagrams). We also focus on two important skills that children develop: 1) knowing basic facts for addition, subtraction, multiplication, and division, such as $7 - 4 = 3$ or $4 \times 3 = 12$, and 2) knowing how to efficiently compute (e.g., adding two-digit numbers). Researchers and educators consider these processes and skills to be crucial to children's development of mathematical understanding. If children are to make sense of the mathematics they are learning, they must become proficient in using these processes and skills.

In this chapter we also recognize that mastery of skills is a key factor in a child's overall success. In line with the positions taken by professional organizations and the research community, we believe that skills and processes go hand in hand, so as subjects related to mastering skills are discussed, we keep in mind the vital role that procedures and routines play in developing skills and methods that become more automatic over time. "Practice makes perfect" is as true for math as it is for any other activity, and we talk about its role in helping children remember what they already know and understand.

Chapter 3 addresses a range of topics, from early number ideas and the counting strategies children use to chunking methods (e.g., $15 + 13 = 15 + 5 + 8 = 20 + 8 = 28$) that are related to number sense and other topics covered in the K–5 mathematics curriculum. We also turn our attention to our Hindu-Arabic numeration system because understanding it is essential for students grappling with the concepts surrounding place value. And we discuss how learning basic arithmetic lays the foundation for studying algebra in high school. It may seem out of place to talk about algebra in a book focusing on elementary mathematics, but our point of view is that as children solve problems and explain their thinking, they begin to see patterns and develop more general thoughts about numbers and the operations that can lead to opportunities to explore basic concepts related to algebra.

Chapter 4 highlights how children make sense of the four whole number operations: addition, subtraction, multiplication, and division. Children's work samples are used to illustrate the ways they reason about and develop more efficient methods. We also use work samples to discuss the mathematics that children wrestle with as they make sense of and solve problems.

Children's beginning study of fractions and decimals and their use of intuitive ideas as they explore them are the focus of chapter 5. These ideas include the use of pictures or diagrams to depict these new numbers and how children make sense of them. We also address how important it is for children to develop fraction and decimal number sense.

Adding, subtracting, multiplying, and dividing with fractions are the core topics of chapter 6. Many of the ideas about whole numbers that were previously discussed are extended to fractions as we explore how children think about and reason about these four operations. We should note that not all students formally study division of fractions by the fifth grade, but the topic is covered because children begin to make sense of division of fractions well before they are officially introduced to it. Decimals and how students can work sensibly to solve problems with them are also touched upon.

Math can be fun—really. In addition to providing suggestions for talking with your children about math and helping them with homework, chapter 7 takes a look at how you can be a smart consumer of educational materials, including games and online resources.

The study of mathematics is all about making connections, and so chapter 8 addresses how the ideas discussed in previous chapters extend to students in middle school and high school. To illustrate this point, we examine a problem that children may initially work on in first grade and then follow its track through different grade levels.

Each chapter includes several features that give more information about the topics under discussion:

> **Classroom Vignettes,** usually at the beginning of a chapter, focus on children's mathematical work in the classroom. We use these anecdotes to further illustrate some of the key ideas addressed in a chapter.

> **Taking a Closer Look** highlights the different mathematical ideas behind children's work. We also briefly discuss how the children's methods are related to the topics discussed in the chapter.

> **Reader's Challenge** is a feature that pauses the narrative so the reader can think about key concepts and practices or solve a math problem. Later on in the text, we discuss these questions and provide answers to the problems.

> **Do You Know?** offers additional information about an education concept or issue with which parents may be less familiar.

What's the Math? spotlights some of the formal mathematical ideas that are addressed in the text. We discuss how children's informal methods and ways of reasoning are related to the concepts that mathematicians and others in the scientific community use.

Things to Remember summarizes some of the key ideas that are discussed in a chapter.

Things to Do provides suggestions for how parents might use the information in the chapter to support their child's math journey.

Resources that we have found helpful are listed at the end of each chapter. These resources are not the only ones available. The intent is to provide a selective list of materials for parents to use, either to learn more about their children's mathematical worlds or to use as activities.

The topics in chapters 3, 4, 5, and 6 are often presented in the same order in which they appear in K–5 curriculum. If you are interested in a particular topic, you can read selected chapters or sections without taking away from the overall intent of the book.

Last but not least, we have included a glossary of math terms at the back of the book for easy reference. Some, such as *model, situation,* and *argument,* will be familiar because they are commonly used, but here they are defined within a mathematics context. Other entries may stir a vague memory from your own school days, while a few may be totally new to you. For the most part, this is the vocabulary your children are learning and using every day in math class.

Our hope is that *It's Elementary* gives you the resources you need to effectively and happily play a part in your children's math education in the classroom and at home.

Acknowledgments

It's Elementary: A Parent's Guide to K–5 Mathematics is a collaborative project that is the result of our work with mathematics educators, classroom teachers, and children. We would like to thank the many mathematics educators whose work has framed the ideas in this book: Nancy Anderson, Deborah Ball, Virginia Bastable, Thomas Carpenter, Suzanne Chapin, Paul Cobb, Elizabeth Fennema, Constance Kamii, Susan Nickerson, Maggie Lampert, Jill Lester, Catherine O'Connor, Deborah Schifter, Ed Silver, Margaret Smith, Judith Sowder, Larry Sowder, Leslie Steffe, Mary Kay Stein, Thomas Romberg, Susan Jo Russell, John Van de Walle, Grayson Wheatley, and Erna Yackel.

We are also extremely grateful to NCTM and its Board for the opportunity to take on this writing project. We particularly wish to thank our editor, Maryanne Bannon, for her help throughout the entire process, from editing the manuscript to coordinating the details for the printed book and e-book.

Finally, we especially wish to thank our families, spouses, loved ones, and friends for their patience and unyielding support.

Joy Whitenack
Laurie Cavey
Cat Henney

Introduction

It's likely that when you were in elementary school learning math, your teachers emphasized knowing the standard procedures necessary to get the right answer. Today mathematics educators are concerned with creating opportunities for students to learn mathematics with understanding. Why do teachers concern themselves with "understanding"? It is not enough to know how to do something. The real power of mathematics is achieved by knowing both how and why. For example, when you were in elementary school, you probably learned how to divide decimals using a set of procedures (called an algorithm) to perform the division. Knowing how to follow those procedures to correctly divide decimals was an important skill to develop. In real-life terms, it has likely contributed to the way you quickly decide which size container or brand to purchase at the grocery store. And that's just one small instance of how solving problems and deriving correct answers is important in everyday living. Being able to explain why the algorithm works is just as important. When students learn to explain why certain procedures work, they are better prepared to apply what they know when they face new mathematical situations. And this ability, enabled by understanding, can carry over to confronting the ever-changing conditions of life, too.

Research and Good Mathematics Teaching

Alan Schoenfeld, a professor at the University of California, Berkeley, has spent decades conducting research on students' mathematical thinking. He has found that students' ability to solve problems is jeopardized when their opportunities for learning focus solely on memorizing procedures. But you might be wondering, "Is it reasonable to expect my child to explain why algorithms work?" or perhaps, "Isn't it the teacher's job to explain why things work?" Yes, it is the teacher's responsibility to support students in understanding why things work, and teachers regularly explain and clarify ideas to do this. However, research indicates that students learn mathematics better when given opportunities to talk about and explain mathematical ideas. By "better" we mean children retain their knowledge instead of forgetting it right after taking a test. They can apply what they know in other mathematical situations, develop critical thinking skills, and be motivated to learn more. Focusing on understanding is simply the right thing to do for students.

Current methods for teaching mathematics are informed by the huge body of research on students' mathematical thinking that has accumulated over the last fifty years. Researchers have investigated many aspects of learning mathematics, including the evolution of counting strategies, operations with numbers, fraction and decimal ideas, reasoning with data, and so on. One result of this work has been the development of standards for teaching mathematics, such as the *Common Core State Standards for Mathematics*, published in 2010, and the National Council of Teachers of Mathematics's *Principles and Standards for School Mathematics*, published in 2000. It is research on student thinking that shapes these standards, which outline what mathematical teaching and content is appropriate for different grade levels. A more recent development guided by research is a series of papers, called progressions documents, which describe how student ideas on a particular topic, such as multiplication, develop over time (http://ime. math.arizona.edu/progressions/). In "Taking a Closer Look at Connections" (below), we continue this conversation by looking at how students' ideas about numbers develop and become more sophisticated during the elementary school years, illustrating this point with examples of student work from various grades.

Another large body of research examines how different teaching methods and practices affect students' opportunities for learning, including the following:

- ◆ The kinds of questions that teachers ask
- ◆ The use of problems that involve real-world situations
- ◆ Different ways to structure collaborative groups
- ◆ How to manage classroom discussions
- ◆ Effective use of hands-on materials such as base-ten blocks and other tools like calculators

What researchers have discovered is that good teachers regularly pose challenging yet accessible problems that can be solved in several ways. They do not assume that students necessarily understand all that is presented in class (either by the teacher or other students), even when most students seem to be following along. Rather, good teachers make it a habit to ask students questions, encouraging them to share their ideas and ask their own questions. Thus, good teaching is largely about creating a classroom environment (or culture) where students are comfortable sharing their ideas and asking questions, and where students know that learning to understand mathematics requires wrestling with tough questions. Good teachers know that learning mathematics is more than "getting the right answer" to a problem; it is about the process of making sense of problems and seeing one's ideas fit with the ideas of others. The best teachers know how to create a classroom environment that makes it possible for students to do so.

The Four Principles to Understanding Children's Mathematical Worlds

To help your children be successful math learners, there are four principles to embrace and accept as you take this journey into and through their mathematical worlds:

1. *Children do impressive mathematics. Adults, parents and teachers, must realize it is essential to understand the different strategies children might use to reach a solution. By doing so, adults can grasp how children think about and approach mathematics, and be in a better position to support children's learning.* Children can reason about ideas, invent methods for solving problems, explain their thoughts, and so on. They also can use pictures and other models to think about and to represent many ideas. Although they may not solve problems or reason about ideas the way adults do, they have insightful ways to engage in mathematics. Children not only develop well-constructed ideas but also build new connections among those ideas all the time. Children are capable of vividly and accurately explaining their thinking about concepts and giving mathematical reasons for why they chose the solution approaches they did to solve a problem. Even if their answers are incorrect, the solution might be a reasonable estimate and, more critically, it might show their understanding of important underlying mathematical concepts.

2. *Parents must be aware of the expectations for students in the 21st-century mathematics classroom.* Ask most parents what they want for their children in school, and the answer may be some variation of "Do well" or "Get good grades." But what does a child actually have to know and do in order to achieve such goals? Because a highly technological and constantly evolving culture like ours demands flexibility as an attitude and a skill, stating rules by rote and mindlessly following procedures to solve problems will not be adequate for future success in life—or figuring out the latest electronic game. The modern math classroom requires children to be mathematically flexible enough to think through problems to find a solution. And to be flexible in math, children must understand the procedures that they use and the concepts behind those procedures. A familiar example may help. You were most likely taught to solve problems such as $1\frac{1}{2} \div \frac{3}{4}$ by inverting the divisor—$\frac{3}{4}$—and then multiplying the two fractions to arrive at $\frac{12}{6}$, or 2. You probably have no difficulty solving this type of problem correctly. However, what does the answer of 2 tell you? It is larger than either of the

two numbers you started with. How can that be? In today's classroom, children are expected to explain why this procedure works and what the numbers in the problem mean. While there are some very sophisticated mathematical ideas behind this procedure, such as understanding how multiplication and division are related, children can explain it in their own terms if they've seen and experienced such explanations in their classrooms. Part of the process of helping your children is to observe how they solve problems and note what they seem to understand.

3. *The mathematics classroom children experience today operates very differently from the one their parents remember.* For instance, when you visit your child's classroom, you notice that the students are engaged in activities unlike those you participated in during math class. Students often work together as teams to complete assignments. The teacher does not tell students how to solve problems; instead he or she asks students to solve problems with several classmates, to agree on a solution, and to be prepared to present their work to the whole class when it comes together for a discussion. For these exchanges, the teacher expects students to explain their solution methods and to give reasons why those methods make sense.

   Whole-group discussions are significant in today's mathematics teaching and learning environment. These guided conversations give students a chance to hear about other classmates' thinking, to make connections among the various ideas, to refine them, and so on. This is just one of many arrangements and instructional strategies teachers use to manage discussions and to plan for and meet the learning objectives they have for their students. So while your children's math experiences may be very different from your own, they are designed to allow them to solve and reason about problems and to connect new ideas with those they already know. By understanding the new ways in which your children engage in mathematical learning, you will be better prepared to participate in that learning, from helping with homework to playing math games.

4. *Understanding mathematics requires children to make connections among mathematical ideas.* Children develop understanding of mathematics by recognizing how ideas are related to one another. For example, the way a child understands subtraction often involves thinking about addition because every subtraction problem can be stated in terms of addition; for instance, if you want to determine what you get when you subtract 4 from 9, you can think about what number added to 4 gives you 9. Your child is also encouraged to make connections among different representations—a crucial part of understanding mathematics. To solve problems involving decimals, for example, children must be able to represent decimals using base-ten

blocks, rectangular diagrams, and a number line as well as use formal decimal notation. Knowing how to move flexibly among these different representations is a key indicator of a student's understanding of place value, fractions, and number sense. Homework and math games are natural opportunities to talk about different mathematical ideas and how they are connected to each other.

 TAKING A CLOSER LOOK at Connections

Young children think about the same concepts that older children do, albeit those ideas become more refined as they progress through the elementary grades. For instance, children might explore ideas related to multiplication at various grade levels using different information to determine a solution. Consider the following problem:

If there are 7 children in our room, how many eyes are in the room?

Younger children might count each of their friends, pointing to each friend twice, to count the number of eyes. A first grader might draw the following solution to the problem:

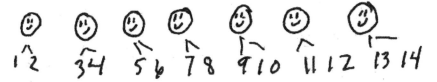

Fig. 0.1. A possible first-grade solution for "How many eyes are in our room?"

Hank, a second grader, not only skip-counted by twos to find the number of eyes but provided an equation documenting his solution:

Fig. 0.2. A second grader's solution for "How many eyes are in our room?"

A third grader might explain that each child has 2 eyes and there are 7 people, so 7 groups of 2 eyes is 14 eyes and $2 + 2 + 2 + 2 + 2 + 2 + 2 = 14$.

Older children may use this information to solve a more challenging problem:

How many eyes are in the room if there are 28 children?

One child reasoned that there are 14 eyes in each row of 7 children because 7 × 2 = 14, and inasmuch as there are 4 rows of 14 eyes (14 + 14 + 14 + 14), there are 4 groups × 14 eyes, equaling 56 eyes.

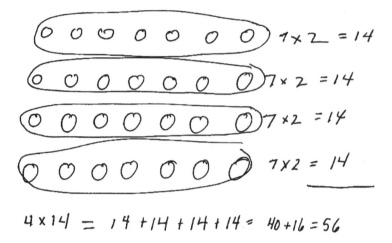

Fig. 0.3. A possible fourth-grade solution for the number of eyes of 28 people

In our examples, the younger children counted or added to find the total number of eyes. Hank, the second grader, made connections between addition and multiplication and began to explore multiplication. And finally in the third and fourth grades, children seemed to understand how they could think interchangeably about addition and multiplication to solve the problem.

Remarkably, children across the grades consider many of the same relationships, but those ideas become increasingly advanced as they continue to make connections among those ideas. You will notice in the following chapters how similar concepts surface from time to time across the elementary grades and how these ideas become increasingly more challenging. It is vital for children's continuing success in math that they make sense of concepts early on so they can continue to build on those ideas to develop an understanding of the mathematics they are learning.

Things to Remember

◆ The power of mathematics is knowing *why* as well as *how* a procedure works.

◆ Children do impressive mathematics. By understanding the different strategies they might use to reach a solution, adults can better grasp how children think about and approach mathematics.

◆ Parents must be aware of the expectations for students in today's mathematics classroom.

◆ The mathematics classroom children experience now operates very differently from the one their parents remember.

◆ Understanding mathematics requires children to make connections among mathematical ideas.

◆ Before reading on, think about the four principles. Do they make sense to you? Can you see how they work together to give you a window into your child's mathematical world? Do you recognize how they can be used to guide your own actions as you support your child's math learning?

◆ Think about how you make sense of and solve problems or make decisions at work and at home. Do you talk about the issue with other people to get ideas? Do you think about a similar situation that you have successfully resolved? Do you make a list or a diagram of various options? Noticing how you solve real-life problems can help you connect to the problem-solving strategies your children use to learn math.

Understanding Today's Mathematics Classroom

Mr. Tafero's fifth graders are multiplying 23 × 18. Once everyone has finished the problem, Mr. Tafero asks students to explain their answers. One of his students, Shauna, says that she knew that 8 × 3 = 24, so she wrote the 24 underneath the 18. And she knew that 10 × 20 = 200 and wrote this number underneath 24. She then added 200 and 24 to get her answer of 224 (fig. 1.1). As Shauna goes through the steps to her answer, Mr. Tafero records what Shauna says even though she has incorrectly solved the problem—she forgot to multiply 8 × 20 and 10 × 3.

$$
\begin{array}{r}
23 \\
\times\ \underline{18} \\
24 \\
\underline{200} \\
224
\end{array}
$$

Fig. 1.1. Shauna's solution for 23 × 18

After Shauna explains how she solved the problem, Mr. Tafero asks if anyone has another way to solve it—a question he often asks students, whether the first answer is correct or not. Paulo, another student, says he has a different answer, and it is a lot larger than Shauna's answer. He asks if he could show his picture on the whiteboard. At the board, Paulo draws a large rectangle and divides it into four smaller rectangles (fig. 1.2).

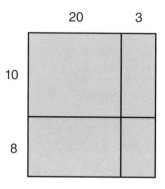

Fig. 1.2. Paulo's drawing

He writes 20 and 3 above the rectangles and 10 and 8 to their left. He multiplies 8 × 3, 8 × 20, 10 × 3, and 10 × 20, describing his actions and writing the partial answers (subtotals) in each of the corresponding rectangles (fig. 1.3). Paulo explains that he then added all four partial answers to get an answer of 414.

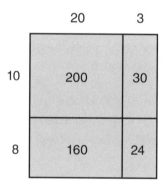

Fig. 1.3. Paulo's drawing with all the partial answers

A lively discussion ensues as Mr. Tafero and his students talk about why Shauna's and Paulo's methods are different. Shauna and many other students begin to realize that Paulo's method makes a lot of sense. His picture shows all the numbers that need to be multiplied by one another. They can see the partial answers that they forgot to include! They decide that they have to think differently when multiplying versus adding two-digit numbers—they cannot just multiply the tens by the tens and the ones by the ones. By the end of the discussion, Mr. Tafero and his students decide to solve other multiplication problems to see if Paulo's method really works.

✳ DO YOU KNOW What the Rectangular Section Method for Multiplication Is?

Using rectangles to picture the multiplication process is a way to show all the steps for multiplying two 2-digit numbers. Notice that the *factors* 23 and 18 are *decomposed* as 20 and 3 and 10 and 8. There are other ways to break apart these numbers. For instance, 23 could be decomposed as 21 and 2 or 15 and 8, but breaking apart 23 and 18 as 20 and 3 and 10 and 8 makes it easier to work with the tens and ones. After the two-digit numbers are decomposed, each number is multiplied by the two parts of the other factor exactly once (20 × 10 and 20 × 8; 3 × 10 and 3 × 8). The answer for each individual multiplication problem is written inside the corresponding rectangle. Teachers and children use this approach to keep track of all the numbers that are multiplied. The answer is the sum of the products from all the individual multiplication problems.

Is this classroom discussion like or unlike the ones you recall from your own school experiences? How did your math teacher handle wrong answers? Mr. Tafero accepted Shauna's answer and planned to use it with other students' work to explore multiplication. If you could relive your school experiences, would you return to the math classes you attended or would you opt to learn math in Mr. Tafero's classroom? Regardless of your choice, why do you think you chose it? More important, in which classroom do you think your child would have a better chance to perform at his or her best and really learn the ins and outs of mathematics without fear and anxiety?

Maybe you think your child should learn math the way you did—in a traditional classroom with prescribed methods for problem solving and lots of drills in the basics. You learned what you had to and have done well. You might also question whether your child would actually learn and remember any math unless it is taught in the usual way.

Or maybe you think that you would have done better in math if you had had a teacher like Mr. Tafero. At the very least, math class would have been more inviting. Now you feel that your child might be more successful in a classroom like Mr. Tafero's, although you can't explain exactly why. If this is your viewpoint, many educators and mathematicians share it. They maintain that Mr. Tafero's classroom typifies effective mathematics instruction. In fact, numerous research studies show that this kind of classroom atmosphere helps students better understand the mathematics they are learning. Classrooms like Mr. Tafero's are places where teachers and their students work together to explore, investigate, ask questions, and so on. For example, Deborah Ball and Maggie Lampert's work in similar third- and fifth-grade classrooms illustrated how students can defend and even prove important concepts as they explore ideas about numbers. What makes Mr. Tafero's mathematics instruction more productive as well as different? We answer this and other questions in the following sections.

Classrooms as Communities of Mathematical Learners

Education research often refers to the classroom setting as a *microculture*, one in which the teacher and students establish norms, or rules, for how they engage in their daily work together. This idea is not a new one in education. Often researchers describe what classroom life is like using terms such as *norms* and *rules* (Jackson 1990). Researchers have also provided convincing evidence that students and their teachers create these rules together, some that are unspoken and others that are explicitly discussed. For instance, how is it that students know from grade to grade that classroom desks are usually organized in rows? Or why do students know that it is okay to take risks and give wrong answers? Or how do they know that in one teacher's classroom it is okay to ask questions and share ideas, whereas they know it is not okay to do the same in another teacher's classroom? Each classroom's rules and ways of conducting business are unique to it and can be described as its *culture*. For example, a teacher may have certain expectations for how students should participate during class discussions, how they explain their ideas, or what counts as an acceptable way of communicating one's ideas. But students play a part in developing these rules as well. How they respond to the teacher's expectations helps them and their teachers understand how to work together.

Over the last two decades researchers such as Paul Cobb, Erna Yackel, and others have made the case that, as with any culture, there are outside influences that contribute to what rules are established in the mathematics classroom. For instance, although teachers and their students work together to develop *sociomathematical norms* (norms particular to math settings), teachers will also consider school district and state-level expectations about their students' performance, such as on annual standardized tests. These factors may influence the content that the teacher chooses to cover as well as how it is taught. Children bring their individual backgrounds to bear on the classroom setting as well. They will have had different experiences in the neighborhoods in which they live, and they will have encountered cultural practices that also shape them, some of which may be shared with other students and others that are quite unique to the child. So classrooms are very diverse places. And yet as the teachers and students work together day in and day out, they establish a *community* with a set of rules and practices for how they will work together during the school year.

This notion of classrooms as *communities of mathematical learners* is important because it helps us describe the learning experiences that children do or can have. The teacher can draw on the students' backgrounds and experiences to provide appropriate and meaningful activities as well as manage discussions that involve all the students. The students come to believe that their ideas are relevant and valued by the teacher and their classmates. And together they create an environment in which students can exchange and build on ideas and have opportunities to learn new concepts. Returning to the example at the beginning of the chapter, Mr. Tafero and his students have established a classroom culture where it is safe for children to share and examine classmates' mathematical ideas. It is okay to make mistakes. As students discuss correct and incorrect procedures, spontaneous openings to examine math concepts present themselves, and together, Mr. Tafero and his students explore ideas, explain their thinking, and reach consensus.

The classroom settings in which your children work may look remarkably like the classrooms in which you learned mathematics or they may look markedly different. You may be happy, distressed, or confused by either situation. Perhaps you hoped that teaching and learning mathematics had changed since you sat in a desk, and you are surprised and disappointed that your children are learning math in a similar fashion. On the other hand, you may be relieved to see the familiar layout of your children's classrooms. Rather than compare and contrast various settings, we highlight some common features that effective mathematics classrooms share when it comes to teaching and learning mathematics and the types of curriculum materials used.

 TAKING A CLOSER LOOK at Sociomathematical Norms

Just as all cultures have rules or norms that are unique, there are also norms that are particular to the math classroom. They are referred to as *sociomathematical norms*. What is considered as a mathematical explanation, a *different* mathematical explanation, and a *sophisticated* mathematical solution method are three examples of sociomathematical norms. Let's look more closely at what counts as a different mathematical explanation.

Because students may not be able to tell which methods are mathematically different, the teacher's role during a discussion is to help students learn to recognize them. Suppose one student says he counted by ones to solve 8 + 5, first by counting 8 and then counting 5 more. And for each count, he kept track by using his fingers. Another student explains she used counters to count a group of 8 and then a group of 5 to arrive at her answer of 13. From the teacher's point of view, these two methods draw on related mathematical ideas about counting, so the teacher would indicate that the second student solved the problem with a similar technique, but used counters instead of fingers. The teacher is helping the class understand that the two methods are *not* mathematically different. Both students counted out the parts. The next student explains that he first broke apart 5 into 2 and 3 so he could make 10 by adding 8 + 2, and then added the 3 to make 13. In this case, the student has offered an approach that is mathematically different. Typically, the teacher would restate this method, and then ask students if they understand it. By restating the student's method, the teacher indicates that his strategy does count as a mathematically different approach. The teacher shapes discussions to help students understand what counts as suitable mathematical explanations or more efficient explanations and to help them recognize and compare the different methods.

You may wonder why teachers take the time to make these distinctions between solution strategies. After all, everyone got the right answer. However, by doing so, the teacher provides students more opportunities to see and think about the different mathematical ideas that underpin like versus unlike methods. The conversation might even lead some students to develop new and sometimes better, more efficient approaches for solving problems. In other words, pointing out different solution methods gives students another chance to learn new ideas, such as decomposing numbers, as in the example above. In time, sharing ideas and explanations becomes routine, and the result is a community of learners in which there are agreed-upon ways of talking about and doing mathematics.

Teaching Mathematics

Teaching in today's classrooms is likely to be much more complex than when you were in elementary school. The teacher has a range of strategies and lesson formats that she can use to implement lessons. One of the more common structures, one that you may remember, is the lecture format. When a teacher uses this format, she lectures or uses demonstrations to present information that the students are responsible for learning. Teachers may use this technique to deliver part of or the entire lesson. Education researchers sometimes refer to this type of instruction as *direct instruction*. The teacher often directly explains the information that students are to learn; the students are held accountable for understanding that information. Once the teacher has presented the information, students typically are assigned problems to solve so they can practice the procedures or methods that the teacher has demonstrated during the lecture. Students may also have additional practice problems to complete for homework.

Teachers may also use a *problem-solving approach* rather than a lecture to help students learn the content. When using this method, the teacher may introduce a problem or tell a story to set the stage before assigning students a set of problems. He may choose to have students work independently or to pair or group classmates to solve the assigned problems. Once students have completed the problems, they may either hand in their work, or if time permits, they may share their solutions or the strategies they used during a follow-up discussion. If the students explain how they solved a problem on the whiteboard, for instance, the teacher may use the students' work to engage the whole class in a conversation in which they compare and contrast classmates' methods, discuss different ideas, or, perhaps, investigate a claim that a student has made. These follow-up or whole-class discussions are an important part of the lesson. Students have opportunities to think about different ideas or to possibly clear up any confusion they are experiencing. The teacher's role during these whole-class discussions is also important. He may ask students questions that help them explore ideas, check to see if they understand the content, and so on. When a teacher chooses to use a problem-solving approach, he actually has more options in how to deliver instruction.

What makes the teacher's work even more complex is determining how to lead the discussions in such a way that all the students participate in these whole-class conversations. Directing successful discussions is hard work. Teachers need to know when to step in, when to move the dialogue along, when to stop and help students explore related ideas, and so on. And of course, the teacher must also have good classroom management skills that help him make sure that students are engaging in the activity, listening to one another, being courteous and respectful, and, generally, staying on task.

In addition to direct instruction and problem-solving approaches, there are also other formats that a teacher can employ. For instance, some teachers use *collaborative learning*. This technique usually involves students working with one to three classmates to complete the assigned problems. If you entered a classroom in which students are working in collaborative groups, you might wonder how anyone could learn anything because the classroom would be noisy with students talking to classmates and the teacher talking to different student groups, and all the while, students would be sitting in different locations in the classroom (including the floor). These types of situations are a far cry from students sitting quietly at their desks while the teacher lectures. You may be surprised to know there is abundant research that suggests that collaborative learning approaches are more beneficial for students. Amy Nebesniak and Ruth Heaton, for instance, have found that when students work collaboratively, they remember the material better and build confidence about themselves as learners.

We have shared a few of these teaching styles to give you an idea of how teaching has changed over the last two decades. Each of these formats is advantageous. And a teacher may use one or more of these formats from day to day, or he or she may use one format almost exclusively. For instance, some teachers may choose to have students work independently to complete assignments whereas others may only use collaborative learning. And still other teachers may use a combination of these methods as well as other techniques to instruct mathematics. Regardless of the approaches teachers use, the goal is that children benefit from these different learning experiences. Teachers who effectively use various formats can serve children's academic needs quite well.

DO YOU KNOW What Collaborative Learning Is?

Collaborative learning is one of the newer instruction approaches that teachers use to implement lessons. Some educators also refer to this approach as *cooperative learning* or *small-group learning*. Although there are slight variations in how collaborative learning is carried out during instruction, researchers agree that the teacher plays a crucial role in making this an effective learning tool. The teacher must monitor the students' discussions, ask questions, and help students work together productively. For instance, what happens when a teacher discovers that one student seems to do all the work for her group? In this situation, the teacher must guide students toward learning how to share the workload with partners—where each partner is equally responsible for completing activities and explaining his or her work to others. Researchers also agree that students benefit a great deal from working together. They learn more, are more motivated, have more opportunities to communicate ideas, and learn how to ask effective questions, to name just a few of the advantages. And by collaborating with classmates, students create a safe, nonthreatening working environment. There are also more general benefits to working collaboratively. Students learn communication and leadership skills that can serve them well in the workplace. Being a team member and working well with others are important life skills that help individuals operate effectively in many fields.

We have already talked about some noticeable changes in the classroom teacher's work. We list a few of the more striking differences in the chart below.

Teachers Then	Teachers Now
Assign 20–50 practice problems during the lesson.	Assign fewer than 5 problems during the lesson.
Introduce an assignment by illustrating how to solve different types of problems.	Introduce an assignment and have students work on the problem(s) without showing the solution procedure, or the class talks together about the assignment and possible solution strategies.
Typically show students how to solve problems.	Regularly ask students to show how they solve problems.
Require students to solve problems precisely as illustrated.	Encourage students to solve problems using methods that makes sense.
Plan and complete lessons that cover new content each day.	Plan lessons that take more than one day to complete.

Teachers Then	Teachers Now
Rarely deviate from the planned lesson; if students need more time to complete assignments, they are asked to complete them as part of their homework assignment.	Extend a lesson unexpectedly because students need additional time to complete assignments.
Rarely redirect a lesson so that students can investigate a new problem that surfaces during the discussion.	Occasionally redirect the lesson so students can investigate a new problem that surfaces during the discussion.

Another prominent aspect of the teacher's work is conducting whole-group discussions. The basic structure of these discussions is a series of questions and answers; however, in the masterful hands of the teacher, questions are posed that mold the answers and follow-up questions into an open forum to discuss students' work and ideas. A teacher may use some or all of the following strategies during a lesson:

- Asking students to explain how they solved a problem

- Asking students to justify or prove their points

- Restating students' explanations after they have shared their ideas

- Asking students if they understand their classmate's explanation

- Asking students to explain a classmate's method or strategy

- Asking students to compare and contrast students' methods, pictures, or models

- Asking students if they agree or disagree with their classmates' ideas

- Asking students to determine which answers are more reasonable instead of immediately correcting students who provide a wrong answer

As the teacher guides the discussion, he or she also juggles other tasks, such as managing the classroom, deciding how to proceed, pointing out mathematical ideas, and figuring out if and when to move along the discussion or to shift to the next activity. The teacher manages these various parts of the lesson while also making sure that the conversation is in line with state standards and that key mathematical ideas are explored. The discussion also shows the teacher what students do and do not understand, making for better decisions about helping them move forward in their mathematical learning.

Assessment

Assessment is the formal term educators use to describe the process of determining what your child knows and understands in any school subject, including math. Just as when you went to school, test scores are used as a tool to evaluate a child's work. But testing isn't the only tool, although you might think so judging from the amount of attention it receives. Teachers also assign homework and independent projects that are taken into account to track a child's mathematical understanding. Additionally, children write about their answers or explain figures or draw pictures to show how they solved different problems. They may even have a math journal that they write in several times a week. So there are many indicators a teacher uses to judge a student's math learning. One difference with this process since you were in school is the teacher not only considers if the answer is correct, but also assesses the methods, procedures, and explanations students provide. *Both the answer and the process are important.* By engaging in these assessment practices, the teacher can decide what course of action to take next.

As parents, you also have opportunities to assess your children's understanding of the math they are learning in school. Perhaps your child casually mentions that she is having trouble with a particular concept. Or you notice that your child is having difficulty with a homework assignment or is struggling to come up with a strategy while playing a math game. Maybe he keeps getting the wrong answer when solving certain types of problems. In such cases, you have a perfect opening to talk with your child about mathematics. In fact, you can find out some very interesting information by simply asking questions such as "Can you explain how you solved this problem?" To address their confusion, you might ask, "What part of this problem don't you understand?" By listening to your child's explanation, you may find out why she is confused. Perhaps you and your child can work on some problems together to see if you can figure out where your child gets stumped. Or you can talk with your child's teacher about your concerns or observations. He or she may have some suggestions for how you can help your child, or may encourage you not to be too concerned—the mistakes that your child is making are common ones that children make. Together you and your child's teacher can find ways to support your child when he or she encounters obstacles to understanding. (For more information about assessing and working with your child, see chapter 7.)

 TAKING A CLOSER LOOK at Leading Classroom Discussions

What do these types of discussions sound like during a math lesson? Taking an example from Whitenack et al. 2001, a first-grade teacher talks with students about the strategies that they used when playing "Tens Go Fish." This game is similar to "Go Fish," but instead of asking for a card to make matching pairs, students ask their partner for cards to make sums of ten.

This student's solution method is discussed because it is one of the first instances in which a child is heard using a *counting-on* strategy. Notice how the teacher helps George talk about his strategy and how she helps the other first graders talk about George's work. Some of the key points of the discussion are italicized for easy reference.

Teacher: I want to quickly tell you a couple of things because we have to get our homework and head home. First, I need to talk about some great thinking that I saw going on with George and Timothy [as they played "Tens Go Fish"]. George has a strategy; can I share your strategy with them? (George nods.) OK. He had three cards on his tray. He was looking at ...

George:	A 3, 9, and a 10.
Teacher:	*George, could you tell them what you did?* (Teacher places the 3, 9, and 10 cards on the blackboard chalk tray.)
George:	I was looking for 7, a 1, and a 0.
Teacher:	*He figured out the cards that he needed to make tens.*
George:	I put up three fingers to figure out that I needed a 7 to make 10.
Teacher:	How did you use your fingers to figure out that you needed a 7?
George:	Because I have 3 fingers up and then I counted the rest of the fingers, "1, 2, 3, 4, 5, 6, 7." So I have to have a 7 (to go with the 3 to make 10).
Teacher:	(Addresses all the students.) *Do you see how he used his fingers?* George, see if I do it right. He knew he had a 3 so he held up three fingers on his hand. Then he knew that he had to have all of his fingers up to make a 10. *Amy, does it make sense to you? It was kind of confusing to me at first too. Timothy, does it makes sense to you? Can you explain what George did to find 7?*
Timothy:	Because he's showing how much he needs to make 10. It makes sense to me.
Teacher:	So really he is counting the fingers that are down?
Timothy:	Yes.
Teacher:	OK, he is just counting them as he puts them up.
Timothy:	He is just working his way up to 10.

The discussion may be different from those you have observed in a first-grade classroom. This teacher encouraged her students to share their ideas. She also asked them to think about and try to explain how George figured out he needed a 7 to make a pair that added up to 10. She worked hard during this part of the conversation to help her students and George discuss his strategy. It was an important discussion, too. George was the first student to share a strategy in which he counted on starting from three, not one, to figure out his answer. Many of the students did not use this strategy, so the teacher was helping them make sense of George's approach so, they might begin to use a similar technique.

Learning Mathematics

Children are still expected to participate in classroom discussions, do homework, and keep up with the material covered just as you were. But how might these tasks be accomplished in today's classroom?

Working in Small Groups. Two of the more noticeable shifts from your school career is that children regularly talk with classmates as they complete assignments and desks are arranged in such a way as to make this easy and natural. Why is it important for students to collaborate on assignments? When working with others, students learn how to listen to and talk about mathematical ideas. Children might also learn new ways to solve problems as they try to make sense of each other's work.

Participating during Whole-Group Discussions. Rather than focusing on a single "right" way to solve a problem and getting the correct answer, teachers help students talk about their work and what they were thinking during whole-group discussions. Children may report on their individual problem solving, or their small group may discuss the group's solution. As they talk about their work, students not only explain their answers but also why they solved problems in particular ways or used a certain drawing, specific materials, and so on. Eventually, they can agree on the correct answer(s). In this type of discussion, children actively participate in new ways of learning. They contribute ideas and insights during these conversations that can be helpful to their classmates. And by talking about and clarifying ideas during math class, children may naturally extend these skills outside the classroom.

Taking Risks. It is important for children to work in a supportive environment so that they can take risks without fear of being criticized for giving a wrong answer or expressing a new idea. Children should be comfortable asking questions or contributing to the discussion no matter the circumstances, whether it is because they don't understand a problem, they want something to be explained again, or they want to share a solution or strategy that is different from the solutions of others. Ideally, the teacher and her students have created a classroom community in which disagreements, errors, and divergent thinking are appreciated, so children have opportunities to learn with and from classmates. If the teacher does not value these types of norms, it is less likely that students will have these types of supportive learning experiences.

Making Sense of Mathematics. The focus of math studies has moved away from solely memorizing what procedures to use to systematically solve problems (sometimes called using *standard algorithms*) to one in which children are encouraged to use methods that help them make sense of the concept and the numbers and how they work together. One child may draw a picture to solve a problem; another may write number sentences (equations); and another may count out objects such as pennies or blocks (manipulatives). The solution to 2 + 2 is always 4, but children may arrive at the answer using different methods—ones that make sense to them. Eventually, they will develop more advanced methods to solve problems. And as children's understanding develops, the teacher will build on that to guide them to more efficient ways to solve problems using the standard algorithms.

But making sense of mathematics does not only mean being able to solve problems sensibly or efficiently with a standard algorithm. Part of sense making in mathematics includes being able to use a range of different ways to think about and solve problems whether using pictures, numbers, or words—not unlike what all mathematicians do.

Assignments and Activities

It's likely that your teacher considered your assignments to be acceptable if your answers were correct *and* you mimicked the steps that the teacher had demonstrated. You probably solved numerous problems of the same type. Textbook computational problems might have been listed on a single page at the end of each section and word problems listed at the end of a unit or chapter. Or perhaps the only time you saw word problems was on a chapter test. One of the more noticeable changes in your children's math studies is that word problems (also called *story problems*) are an everyday feature of class. In fact, story problems may even appear *first*, not last, and well before any computational procedure is discussed.

The types of word problems children encounter have changed as well. Word problems may not have *key words* that provide hints (e.g., *altogether* means to add, or *left* means to subtract) to the student as to which operation is to be performed. Or key words such as *altogether* might be used, but to solve the problem, addition is not needed. Furthermore, students are expected to represent their ideas using pictures, numbers, and words as well as use different strategies to solve problems in ways that make sense to them. Other changes to activities and assignments include the following:

- ◆ Examples may not direct the student to solve the problem using a particular method.

- ◆ Problems may have more than one correct answer. For example, "In the garden, Tyler counted 15 flowers. Some were pink, some were white, and some were yellow. How many of each color might he have seen?"

- ◆ Each activity may only have three to five problems per page.

Because of the changes in how math is taught, teachers can address children's different academic and social needs more readily during instruction. In the past, teachers may have taught the same topic, the same way to all of their students. When students play a more active role during lessons, the teacher is in a better position to individualize activities. Although children may play the same game during the lesson, the teacher can adjust the game for individual students so they can be more successful. For instance, he can adjust the numbers so they are larger or smaller and children are appropriately challenged. Similarly, the teacher can carefully manage whole-class discussions so several students' various methods are highlighted and addressed, ranging from the less to the more sophisticated during a lesson. By guiding the conversation along these lines, the teacher makes it possible for each student to engage with the mathematics in a way that is accessible to him or her while putting forward ideas that challenge the student to develop new insights. Thus, students who are still learning a concept will have a chance to begin to master it, while students who are further along in grasping the idea will have opportunities to strengthen the connections among the concepts. (When a teacher makes these types of adjustments during the lesson, he differentiates instruction. For this reason, education researchers sometimes refer to these types of teaching strategies as *differentiated instruction*.)

Curriculum Materials

Teachers typically use a range of instructional materials to plan lessons, from textbooks supplied by school districts and generally used for several years to Internet resources that offer a constant supply of new products. Some teachers use the teacher manuals that accompany a particular textbook series (or *program*) as a key resource while others do not. Furthermore, two different math programs may be vastly different in their look and approach, even if they are teaching similar content. One might give teachers examples of student strategies they are likely to hear during a lesson while another may emphasize teaching students a single standard procedure. The student workbook in one program may have very few problems on a page while a workbook in another program may have many problems. Some programs might have textbooks and workbooks that resemble those you had as an elementary student, and others may look markedly different— perhaps with more "white space" for your child to write or draw a solution. And of course, some teachers rarely use manuals and workbooks. Instead, they might develop lessons and activities while co-planning with colleagues, or use some ideas they got from a professional development session or an education magazine. Teachers might draw from several other resources, too, to develop lessons, including the following:

- ◆ School district websites
- ◆ State department of education websites
- ◆ Supplemental materials from educational materials developers
- ◆ Materials from a program different from their district's official program
- ◆ Professional organization websites such as the National Council of Teachers of Mathematics

In addition to using these types of materials, it is not uncommon for teachers to create new lessons or adapt materials when planning for instruction. As they carefully listen to their students and work with them, teachers become aware of their students' work and interests, and then generate new activities that are an extension of those. For example,

Mrs. Cochran, a fourth-grade teacher, overheard her students talking about building a scale model of the Great Wall of China out of 1-inch cubes. She used this idea to develop a new math lesson for them. She challenged her students to build a scale model of the wall. There was one catch. They had a limited number of cubes to make their models. Students had to use ideas about scaling to figure out how many miles of wall each 1-inch cube would represent. During the lesson, they discussed the different models they employed, and discovered that to build the wall to scale, each 1-inch cube had to represent about 6.5 miles of "wall." Students explored ideas about estimating, working with decimals, and ratios—all of Mrs. Cochran's objectives for the lesson!

 DO YOU KNOW How School Districts Adopt New Math Textbooks?

Every six to seven years, school districts may purchase, or *adopt*, new math textbooks. To adopt new books, a textbook committee is formed, including teachers and administrators, and it begins the process of reviewing math textbooks that might be appropriate. The committee contacts various publishers, who send materials for members to review. The committee then decides which textbook best matches the district's math program and aligns with state and national standards for learning math. In some states, textbooks cannot be adopted if they do not appear on a textbook adoption list. However, this does not mean that a teacher may not use another textbook as a planning resource.

Things to Remember

◆ A classroom is a *community of learners* with rules and ways of conducting business that can be described as its *culture*. Both teachers and students contribute to a class's culture.

◆ The focus of teaching mathematics may have shifted from your school days. Teachers instruct mathematics using methods that will help children *make sense of mathematics*, not only to get the right answer.

◆ Teaching may also look different from what you remember; for instance, a teacher may not always lecture from the front of the room (called *direct instruction)*. Teachers also employ other methods of instruction like *problem-solving approaches* and *collaborative learning*.

◆ *Whole-class discussions* can be applied with any teaching method. During these conversations, students are asked to share their solutions and explain their methods. The teacher monitors and guides the discussion to help children explore, investigate, and make sense of the mathematical ideas under consideration.

◆ Whether students are problem solving individually, in pairs, or in small groups, teachers monitor and assess children's work.

◆ Every student is responsible for solving problems regardless of the teaching style used in the classroom.

◆ Students are expected to develop and use strategies and methods that make sense to them. These may include using manipulatives (e.g., blocks, coins), drawings, and words. Eventually these methods and strategies become more advanced and children start to apply standard algorithms to problems.

◆ When children work collaboratively in the mathematics classroom, they not only learn more math but also learn how to communicate about ideas and how to effectively work with others, and they gain life skills regarding teamwork and leadership.

Things to Do

You'll get a good idea of the teaching methods and math program at your children's schools by doing a few of the following:

◆ Attend parent/teacher sessions to meet your children's teachers, ask questions, and see the classroom setups.

◆ If your child's school holds parents' days, do go. If you are allowed to sit in on a class, see if some of the teaching methods we've talked about are used.

◆ Check the schoolwork your children bring home to see how they solve problems and explain their thinking; note any teacher comments.

◆ Make an appointment to talk to your child's teacher or principal or the math coach or math specialist to get a better idea of the math program at the school and find out what you can do at home to help your child.

Resources

We have tried to address many key ideas in this chapter, but we can only touch upon the topics. Resources you may find helpful and informative are listed below.

For Adults

Boaler, Jo. *What's Math Got to Do with It? How Teachers and Parents can Transform Mathematics Learning and Inspire Success.* New York: Penguin Books, 2015.

Council of the Great City Schools. "Parent Roadmaps to the Common Core Standards-Mathematics." Council of the Great City Schools. June 2012. http://www.cgcs.org/Page/244

Fuglei, Monica. "Number Sense: Helping Parents Understand Today's Math Education." Concordia Online Education. April 2014. http://education.cu-portland.edu/blog/news/number-sense-helping-parents-understand-todays-math-education/

Figure This! "Family Corner." National Council of Teachers of Mathematics. May 2015. http://figurethis.nctm.org/fc/family_corner.htm

National Education Association. "Helping Your Child with Today's Math." National Education Association. May 2015. http://www.nea.org/home/59862.htm

National PTA. "Parent's Guides to Student Success." National PTA. May 2015. http://www.pta.org/parents/content.cfm?ItemNumber=2583&navItemNumber=3363

Ross, Meghan. "20 Questions to Ask During a Parent-Teacher Conference." Care.com. September 2013. https://www.care.com/a/20-questions-to-ask-during-a-parent-teacher-conference-1309201640

More4U Online Resources

You can find a listing of additional helpful resources with links, including recommended games, by entering the access code on this book's title page at NCTM's More4U page (nctm.org/more4u).

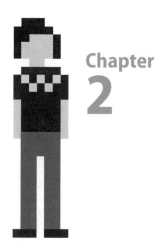

Mathematical Processes and Skills

Ms. Wynn's Classroom

Ms. Wynn's second graders are working on subtraction. She begins the day's lesson by writing the following problem on the board:

$$\begin{array}{r} 34 \\ -19 \\ \hline \end{array}$$

She then asks the students what the first step might be in finding a solution. A student responds that the teacher should "cross out the 3, make it a 2, then put a 1 next to the 4 to make it 14." Another student picks up where his classmate left off, "14 minus 9 is 5," he says. The teacher writes a 5 in the ones place. "Then 2 minus 1 is 1. So 34 minus 19 is 15."

This scene may bring to mind your own elementary math experience. Your teacher probably taught you this very procedure for two-digit subtraction. Like most young students, you did your best to practice and apply the procedure. But how would you have solved it if you had not been taught this procedure?

Mr. Allen's Classroom

Mr. Allen's class of second graders is trying to reach a class reading goal of 34 books. So far, the students have collectively read 19 books. Mr. Allen asks, "How many more books do we need to read until we reach our goal?" He does not demonstrate a specific procedure for subtraction. One student raises her hand and says, "I added my way up from 19 because 19 books is what we've already read: 19 plus 1 is 20; 20 plus 10 is 30; 30 plus 4 is 34. So I need to add all those bits together—1 plus 10 plus 4 is 15."

Both scenarios feature students solving a subtraction problem, yet the problem is presented and solved in very different ways. What exactly are the benefits of children sharing strategies like those in Mr. Allen's or Ms. Wynn's classes? The answer lies in the processes and skills that children must have to be successful with mathematics.

What do mathematics teachers mean by *processes* and *skills*? Processes are *how you think about and solve mathematical problems.* You use number relationships with which you are familiar to answer mathematical questions. You may use different math ideas to make these connections as well. Skills are *processes that have become automatic or routine.* In the examples above, all three children explain the steps they used to solve the problem. The first two children described how they used the standard algorithm to solve the problem. The third child used an *adding-up* approach, one that students sometimes invent to solve subtraction problems. Notice that she first added 1 to get to a *friendly number*, 20, and then continued adding up—10, and then 4 more—until she reached 34 (see "Do You Know What Adding Up Is?" below). The students correctly solved the same subtraction problem but used different information about numbers and different strategies to arrive at the answer. None of the children explained the mathematics behind the steps nor the procedures they used; they performed these steps routinely. To explain the processes behind the steps, they would have to provide information about why the steps make sense. In the second example, for instance, the student would need to show why it makes sense to break 34 into two parts, 19 and the missing part. To find the unknown part, she added 1, 10, and 4 to get to 34, making 15 the solution to the problem.

Assume that the approaches the children used were routine ways to solve problems at that point in the school year—they did not need to explain why the steps make sense. Of course, either child could have mimicked the steps without understanding why they worked. Students can learn how to solve a problem and yet not understand why those steps make mathematical sense. Perhaps this is what you experienced, learning how to solve certain types of problems but not understanding why those procedures made sense.

The distinction between understanding the mathematics to apply a procedure and automatically following "rules" to use a procedure is crucial. If children do not develop understanding of mathematical concepts and processes, eventually they reach a roadblock; mathematics may no longer make sense. Children may even come to believe that mathematics is not supposed to make sense. An immediate consequence of this situation is that students may have no way to figure out what to do if an answer is incorrect because they do not understand why the steps make sense in the first place.

 DO YOU KNOW What Adding Up Is?

As you've seen above, not all children solve subtraction problems the same way. Some children solve subtraction problems using addition. The strategy is called *adding up.* Whether a child solves 34 – 19 by *taking away* 19 from 34 or *adds up* from 19 to make 34, the answer is 15. How a child arrives at an answer is just as important as getting the correct answer. The process a child uses can reveal how he or she thinks about relationships between numbers. For instance, children who subtract 19 are taking away part of the amount that makes the total of 34. Children who add up are filling the "gap" between 19 and 34. Adding up also helps children think about how the operations of addition and subtraction are connected to each other. They can consider the two operations as opposite ways of thinking how numbers are related.

In figure 2.1 we illustrate how the adding-up strategy can be represented with a number line. All the numbers that Mr. Allen's student mentioned when explaining her approach are represented. The three "jumps" she made are the quantities she added to find the *difference* between 34 and 19. (The line in the diagram is called an *open number line* because it does not indicate every whole number from 19 to 34, but the landing spots (20, 30, and 34) are placed on the line in relative proximity to each other.) The student also uses the number line to keep track of the jumps as she records her thinking to solve the problem. Of course, a student could choose to make the hops in different ways, for example, a jump of 10 to make 29, a second of 1 to make 30, and a jump of 4 to make 34. A student could make jumps of any amounts as well, for example, a jump of 7 to make 26 and a jump of 8 to make 34. But using what this student knows about 20 to add on 10 and 4 is a more efficient approach, one in which the student uses mathematical ideas that make sense to her and that take advantage of using groups of tens and ones.

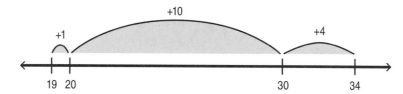

Fig. 2.1. Mr. Allen's student's approach to solving the problem

Process: Solving Problems

A child makes sense of a problem when he or she figures out a way to think about and solve that problem. Making sense of a problem involves figuring out what exactly is being asked, what each number represents, and what methods to use—addition, subtraction, multiplication, division, or a combination—to come up with an answer. Learning to make sense of problems requires children to think about how they can use what they already know about mathematics to work out a new situation, and that can take time.

To grasp mathematical concepts, students need to solve problems in ways that make sense to them, so they will often draw pictures to represent the information in a problem.

Whether it's a sports coach drawing plays on a board or a child sketching goldfish in fishbowls, pictures help people make information visible and concrete. Some children may use only number sentences (equations) or words to justify their answers while others may use a combination of number sentences, words, and pictures. In classrooms where teachers encourage their students to use methods that make the most sense to them, it is quite possible that your child will develop a range of ways to think about and solve problems using pictures, numbers, and words.

The solution strategy pictured in figure 2.2 is a slightly different approach used by another student for 34 – 19. Here the student uses number sentences instead of jumps on a number line to keep track of his thinking. It may appear confusing, but it's helpful to know that the student first wrote 19 + 1 = 20, and then wrote 20 + 14 above it. Rather than taking three small jumps as in the open number line example, he takes a larger second jump of 14 instead of adding 10 and 4 separately. Regardless of the size of the jumps, he is recording his thinking as he solves the problem. When asked why he wrote his second step above his first step, he said, "Because in my strategy, I'm adding up. It just sort of matches better." Every stage of his thinking is documented, and all symbols, including the "loop" and arrow, are meaningful. Even the way the equations appear on the page (from bottom to top) is significant.

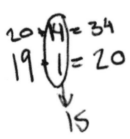

Fig. 2.2. A second student's solution to 34 – 19

When a student solves a problem, she must also determine if the solution is reasonable. Does the answer make sense? For instance, if a student is considering whether 15 is a reasonable solution for the problem of 34 – 19, she might explain that 34 minus 20 is 14, so it makes sense that 34 minus 19 is one more than that.

Would it surprise you to know that many students come up with 25 as the answer to this problem? It's interesting to note that when the numbers are stacked, it is not uncommon for some children to treat the subtraction in the ones place as 9 – 4 instead of 4 – 9. In this case, the student is focusing only on the digits in the ones place (here, 4 and 9); he does not understand that 4 is part of 34. The child might explain, "I have to subtract the smaller number from the bigger number," because he is trying to match an isolated step (subtracting a digit from another digit) to what he knows about subtraction (you subtract a smaller number from a bigger number). This process is quite different from the standard algorithm for two-digit subtraction that the students in Ms. Wynn's classroom used to solve the problem.

If the student does not check to see if his answer makes sense, he may not realize that 25 could not possibly be the correct solution. Fortunately, the teacher (or his classmates) can and will challenge the reasonableness of a solution like 25 by making comments such as, "But that would mean 19 + 25 is 34. And 19 + 20 is 39, and that's already too high." So making sense of a problem does not stop when the student finds a solution; the solution also needs to be logical.

Increasingly, teachers at all grade levels use problem solving to teach mathematics. When children make sense of problems, they not only provide answers but also know how they arrived at those answers, and they can supply reasons why their solutions make sense.

 TAKING A CLOSER LOOK at Two Types of Knowledge

Both procedural and conceptual knowledge are built when students make sense of problems, and both are necessary to be a successful math learner. A student uses *procedural knowledge* when he applies a particular method (often memorized or *routinized*) to solve a problem, for instance, the standard procedure for two-digit subtraction depicted in Ms. Wynn's class. The same student uses *conceptual knowledge* when he explains why the procedure works, or justifies why his answer is mathematically reasonable.

Process: Explaining and Justifying Solutions

Although explaining and justifying solutions might sound like an intimidating expectation for young children, all it means is that children tell their teacher and classmates in their own words how they got their answers and why their solution works or makes sense. Sometimes the teacher will help the student along with leading questions or by restating the child's explanation. Even kindergarten children learn how to explain and justify their methods when they are asked questions about why, for instance, they counted everyone in a group just once to determine how many children are present.

Our example of Mr. Allen's second-grade class shows just one simple way students might explain their thinking during a classroom discussion. As the student describes her thinking, she or Mr. Allen can record her ideas. Her classmates and the teacher might ask questions or make comments such as, "Why did you start with 19? Shouldn't you start with 34?" "We've already read 19. We need to know how many more to read until we get to 34. We need to find the space between 19 and 34," and so on.

To address others' questions, sometimes the student must do more than explain her thinking; she will need to *justify*, or prove, her solution. Usually a student will need to justify an idea or a step, for instance, when another student does not agree with her method. To justify her answer then, the student would need to re-explain the procedures she used, provide some additional information that shows why her approach makes sense, or perhaps draw a picture to address the classmate's question or challenge.

After watching teachers and classmates explain and justify their answers, and doing so themselves, students accept it as just another part of learning mathematics. They also realize that when teachers and classmates ask questions, it does not necessarily mean that an answer is wrong. In the ideal mathematics classroom, teachers and students ask questions regardless of the "correctness" of answers: They are all invested in understanding and comparing strategies to reach the answer. When students exchange mathematical ideas and solution strategies, they learn that their contributions are as meaningful as their final answer. As a kindergarten teacher describes her role in this type of classroom discussion, "It is not so much that we are standing in front of the children but *behind* them."

Often, when justifying and defending solutions, students will notice errors in their own reasoning. This doesn't at all detract from the value of justifying solutions. In fact, when students spot their own mistakes and discover why a solution is incorrect, it can be just as thrilling and informative as arriving at a correct solution or making an insightful contribution during the class discussion.

Learning procedures or developing methods that eventually become procedures that are routinely performed are among the significant goals of teaching and learning mathematics. Justifying solutions helps children understand the procedures they use, whether standard or self-created. And the procedures that children use must also make *mathematical sense*. To make mathematical sense, children must understand how to use procedures *and* be able to justify why those procedures work. They also learn that they can use mathematical concepts such as the connections between division and multiplication and why the "invert and multiply" method makes sense when dividing fractions to explain or justify the procedures they use. How does this all work in the classroom? And just what does it all mean? We explore the procedure for dividing fractions to show you.

 DO YOU KNOW Why We Multiply to Divide Fractions?

Most of us recall the phrase "invert and multiply" to remind us of the procedure used to divide by a fraction, but why does it work? Teachers want their fifth and sixth graders to understand why "invert and multiply" works and why it makes sense. To do that one needs to understand the meaning of division and how it and multiplication are related. Teachers often use a story problem as a starting point (Michigan State University 2006):

Sally has $2\frac{2}{3}$ feet of ribbon and she wants to cut the ribbon into $\frac{1}{2}$-foot pieces to make bows. How many bows can she make?

First think about what the problem is asking: How many $1/2$-foot pieces of ribbon are in $2\,2/3$ feet of ribbon? Because you want to know how many times $1/2$ "goes into" $2\,2/3$, to answer the question, you need to solve the division problem $2\,2/3 \div 1/2$.

Figure 2.3 shows how someone might solve this division problem without using the "invert and multiply" procedure. When you count the number of $1/2$-foot pieces in $2\,2/3$ feet of ribbon, you have $2 + 2 + 1 + 1/3 = 5\,1/3$.

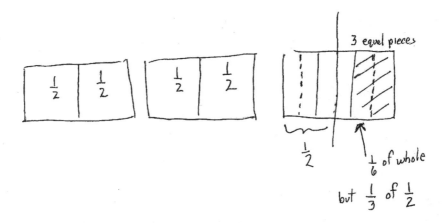

Fig. 2.3. A solution for solving $2\,2/3 \div 1/2$

However, drawing pictures to divide fractions isn't efficient. So what happens when you "invert and multiply" to solve this division situation? The problem is rewritten as $2\,2/3 \times 2$, but what do the numbers in this multiplication mean? The quantity of ribbon remains the same, $2\,2/3$ feet; the *factor* 2 represents the number of ½-foot pieces in each foot of ribbon ($1/2 + 1/2 = 1$). When the factors are multiplied, the answer $5\,1/3$ is the number of ½-foot pieces in $2\,2/3$ feet of ribbon. Remarkably, the answer to the division and multiplication problems is the same. So $2\,2/3 \div 1/2 = 2\,2/3 \times 2$.

Look at figure 2.3 again. Does the "invert and multiply" answer of $5\,1/3$ ($1/2$-foot pieces) make sense to you? What makes the Ribbon problem interesting is although the correct calculation is $5\,1/3$, it is not the correct answer for this word problem, which is asking you to find the number of *whole* $1/2$-foot ribbons. Therefore, the answer to the story problem is actually 5 whole $1/2$-foot ribbons.

Students in fifth or sixth grade should be able to grapple with this type of problem, and if they invert and multiply, then they should understand why the multiplication operation makes sense. Students would also be expected to explain why the answer makes sense. As they do so, they can uncover important relationships between the multiplication and division of fractions; for example, when a student is dividing fractions by inverting the *divisor* (the number by which another number is divided) and multiplying, he is finding out how many of the divisor units are in the *dividend* (the number being divided). In the example above, you found how many of the divisor units ($^1/_2$ foot) of ribbon are in $2^2/_3$ feet of ribbon by multiplying the inverse of $^1/_2$ (i.e., 2) by the number of feet of ribbon.

As our example illustrates, understanding the mathematical ideas behind common procedures helps everyone—teachers, parents, and students—realize that mathematics can and does makes sense. Even the most routine processes contain important mathematics. To be successful math learners, students must be able to explain the procedures they use, whether those procedures are self-created or standard algorithms. If you also have a better grasp of how math makes sense, you are in a better position to help your children.

Process: Using Models

What do you do to solve a math problem? Some people like to go right to an equation and solve from there. Others like to draw a diagram or sketch a graph to help them visualize the problem. People have been using and inventing different ways to support their mathematical thinking for thousands of years. However people represent their thinking, they are modeling their ideas (using a model) to think about the problem. Sometimes, they even use these models to communicate to others how they thought about and solved a problem. In a pinch, a good stick and a patch of sand will do! Models used to solve mathematical problems are referred to, not surprisingly, as *models for mathematics*.

The types of models children use include acting out a problem, employing physical materials, drawing pictures or diagrams, and so on. In today's math classroom, students also have exposure to many commercial models, such as number lines and hundredths grids. Figure 2.4 shows how Alisha used a hundredths grid to represent the number 0.23 (twenty-three hundredths). She used the larger square to represent one whole (or 1) and then colored 23 squares, each of which was $^1/_{100}$ of the whole (or 0.01). Her classmate, Bryn, also represented 0.23 (fig. 2.5), but traced around a base-ten *flat* (a plastic model in the form of a 10-by-10 square), drew the vertical and horizontal lines, and then colored 23 small squares. When asked why she made her own grid rather than use a preprinted one, Bryn replied, "Because this way I *know* mine is correct."

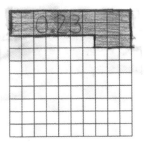

Fig. 2.4. Alisha uses a premade grid to show 0.23.

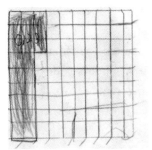

Fig. 2.5. Bryn uses her own picture of a grid to show 0.23.

 TAKING A CLOSER LOOK at Why a Picture Is Worth a Thousand Words

Figure 2.6 shows an example of a student modeling a story problem using a picture and numbers to show his solution (TERC 2008):

Fig. 2.6. How one student solved the four children and two dogs problem

The child's picture is easy to follow. In this case, he created a model for the problem by drawing pictures of the characters. It appears that the child counted by twos to figure out the number of legs. The child even counted four legs as two groups of two, a concept he uses to solve the problem.

Bryn used a model that made sense to her by tracing her own grid, but students sometimes create or use other physical objects to think about and solve problems. In Ms. Green's fourth-grade classroom, for example, students were debating whether there was more than one answer for $13 \div 2$. To explain why the solution was $6\frac{1}{2}$, one student made 13 paper cookies and shared them equally between two classmates, cutting the last cookie in half so that it could also be shared evenly between the two children. To solve a slightly different problem, another student started with 13 classmates and separated them into two groups of unequal size to make two teams. He explained, "I can't have half a person, so the size of one team is 6 and the other is 7." In both of these situations, students were representing ideas about division to solve the problem sensibly, but the answers are different because they are answering different questions.

Acting out problems (either with materials or people) is by no means restricted to the elementary years. In Mr. Burke's middle school classroom, students were trying to figure out the number of handshakes exchanged among six members of a team if everyone shook every other team member's hand once. To solve this problem, many students first thought that the answer would be 5 x 6, or 30 handshakes, because each team member would need to shake hands with five other people. But when they acted it out, they realized that they had overcounted the handshakes—there were only 15 handshakes. Many of them quickly realized this fact when they heard, "I already shook your hand!" As they acted out the problem, they gathered new information about it that prompted the students to adjust their thinking.

 READER'S CHALLENGE

What models might help you think about the Handshake problem with six people? One child drew a circle with six different points to represent the people.

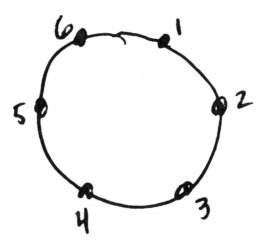

Fig. 2.7. One way to picture the Handshake problem

How might you use this diagram to solve the problem? As one approach, you could draw a line between the numbered points—each line representing one handshake between two people. You might start with Person 1 and draw in all the handshakes possible, then continue to Persons 2, 3, 4, 5, and 6. When you are finished, you might notice that when counting the handshakes with each new person, there are fewer and fewer handshakes. So what's the answer?

Other people find it helpful to play with the numbers. They might start with a simpler problem. For two people, there would be only one handshake; if you add a person (three people), there are two more handshakes. Each time a person is added, each of the previous people must shake hands with the newcomer. Continue exploring the Handshake problem using this pattern to determine the total number of handshakes. By solving the problem, is it now clear why the number of handshakes is half as many as the students in Mr. Burke's class originally thought? You can find an explanation for the solution in Appendix A (page 193).

Children also model and reason about problems using technology such as calculators, software, or online activities. For example, the National Library of Virtual Manipulatives (http://nlvm.usu.edu/en/nav/vlibrary.html) provides electronic versions of physical materials that students frequently use in the classroom. One of the more common types of materials, base blocks, is often used to reason about numbers in our base-ten number system. An online base-blocks program (applet) lets children freely choose how to represent numbers. And they can use this applet either in class or at home. As another example, children can use the "Sieve of Eratosthenes" applet to explore the different multiplication factors for numbers. This applet can also be used to encourage children to investigate their own mathematical questions about factors. Even casual browsing reveals there are many computer-based programs and applets available to children that they can use to model, explore, practice, and just have mathematical fun. We highlight some of our favorites later in chapter 7.

 TAKING A CLOSER LOOK at Calculators

Parents often worry that calculators inhibit mathematics learning, but thoughtful and appropriate use of calculators can actually enrich children's exploration of numbers and operations. For instance, key in 2 × 2 = on your calculator to display the product 4. Then press EQUALS (=; or ENTER) three or four more times. What happens on the calculator's screen? You should have seen an 8, then 16, and then 32. This happens because most calculators will perform the last operation on the previous answer each time you hit the equals or enter key. The calculator should have continued to multiply each new answer by 2. By repeatedly multiplying by 2, you can quickly make a list of numbers that grow exponentially. Can you imagine how children might benefit from tinkering in the same way?

Then try it again, but this time select the add (+) operation key. Start with 2 + 2 = to get 4. Hit EQUALS (=) several times. How are the displays different from those before? In what ways are they the same? This time, you should have generated a list of numbers that grow additively, or linearly, because the difference between any two successive numbers is always 2. You probably noticed how much more rapidly the numbers increased when you multiplied rather than added. Calculators can provide new opportunities for students to analyze patterns, examine numbers, and in the later grades, even explore *functions*.

As mentioned earlier in this chapter, skills are processes that have become automatic or routine. Next, we look at two crucial skills that children develop to be successful math learners and the role of practice in developing skills. For most children, these skills naturally develop over time as they participate in problem solving and whole-group discussions in the classroom.

Skill: Basic Fact Fluency

No doubt you have a story to tell about taking timed math tests in elementary school. Your teachers administered these tests to determine if you could recall the basic facts quickly and accurately. Basic addition facts are problems for which the addends (or factors if you are multiplying) are less than 10, for example, 3 + 4, 4 + 5, 6 + 7, 8 + 7, 9 + 9, and so on. Basic subtraction and division facts are related to facts for addition and multiplication, for example, 15 – 8 = 7 because 7 + 8 = 15 and 81 ÷ 9 = 9 because 9 x 9 = 81. When children can recall the answers to these basic facts automatically (in three to four seconds), they have achieved *basic fact fluency*. While students progress toward basic fact mastery at different rates and achieve it at different times, it is helpful for students to achieve basic fact mastery before entering middle school. Without this skill, students may have a difficult time studying and mastering more advanced mathematics, such as patterns and functions in middle and high school algebra.

Whether or not students should learn basic addition and multiplication facts through memorization or through building number relationships has been a topic of controversy since the early part of the twentieth century. As in other situations where people argue for one of two extremes, a balanced approach is often best. Students can benefit greatly from developing skills by making connections among different number combinations as they solve problems. Once they make these connections, they can master the skills through drill and practice. The research of Thomas Carpenter, Catherine Fosnot, Constance Kamii, and James Hiebert, for instance, overwhelmingly supports this approach. They all agree that developing students' understanding of mathematics is most crucial to students' future success in mathematics, and that focusing on children's comprehension will enable them to master the skills needed for advanced study.

An example might help here. Counting by ones is inefficient if a child can solve 6 + 7 using other methods. However, if a child uses what he knows about 6 + 6 to solve 6 + 7, he is using his understanding about numbers to learn basic facts. We can make a similar case about skip counting. Skip counting by threes (3, 6, 9, 12, …) to solve 3 x 9 is an acceptable approach, but it is a less efficient method as compared to starting with 3 x 10 and then subtracting one group of 3 from the answer. This is a more efficient strategy and good mathematics too! When children use what they know about numbers to develop basic fact fluency, they can build on these types of relationships and make new connections among numbers. And when they do not remember a basic fact, they will have another way of finding the answer for that fact. But if children only know the facts by memorizing them, they have no other strategies for finding the answer if they forget the fact.

However, even efficient strategies for learning basic math facts take more than three or four seconds to accomplish—the standard for basic fact fluency. This is when drills become a tool for honing a skill a child has already ably demonstrated. If students have created sensible strategies for basic facts, drills can help them increase their speed and accuracy in recalling the facts. (See the section on practice beginning on the next page for more information on when the use of drills is appropriate.)

Skill: Computational Fluency

The ability to efficiently and accurately solve addition, subtraction, multiplication, and division problems is called *computational fluency*. Some parents worry that it is falling by the wayside in today's mathematics classroom. Be assured that computational fluency is still a critical part of the elementary curriculum. It is also necessary for students to develop *the ability to choose an appropriate strategy "as the numbers and the context change"* (Van de Walle et al. 2010). So students need to develop efficient and accurate strategies to solve problems as well as choose the methods that work best. Returning to our example at the beginning of the chapter, adding up from 19 to 34 and subtracting 19 from 34 to solve 34 – 19 are equally valued approaches. Both methods are sensible and efficient.

Here is a different problem:

A class has collected $34 for supplies and pays $16 for art pencils. How much money remains?

Look at the student work in figure 2.8 on page 40 to see how she used computational fluency to solve the problem. First, she broke 16 into 10 and 6; then she subtracted 10 from 34, getting 24. Finally, she subtracted 6 from 24. How does she know 24 – 6 = 18? Maybe she used a related fact such as 14 – 6, or mentally broke 6 into 4 and 2. If so, she knew that 24 – 4 = 20 and 20 – 2 = 18. Even though she did not "borrow and carry," her method is appropriate and demonstrates computational fluency. Note that she may have used several different number relationships, 10 + 6 = 16, 4 + 2 = 6, and 34 – 10 = 24, to solve the problem.

$$34 - 16 = 18$$
$$34 - 16 = 24$$
$$24 - 6 = 18$$

Fig. 2.8. A student's solution for $34 – $16

What does it mean for a child to use *efficient* strategies? When a child uses an efficient strategy, he makes decisions about the best possible way to solve a problem. For instance, to solve 34 – 19, a child can accurately solve the problem by making 34 tally marks, erasing 19, and then counting the remaining tallies to find the difference. This counting-by-ones method works, but it isn't the most efficient strategy. And this strategy is also prone to errors: The child may draw the wrong number of marks or erase the wrong number of tallies or miscount the end result, to name a few. Ideally, efficient strategies capitalize on what the child knows about number relationships to help him solve the problem. So what is an efficient strategy that a student might use to solve 34 – 19? One possibility is using what she knows about the relationship between 19 and 20, that is, 19 + 1 = 20 (fig. 2.9). So she subtracts 20 from 34 to get 14, and then adds one more to her answer of 14 because she subtracted one too many—she only needed to subtract 19, not 20. Choosing to subtract 20 rather than 19 is an efficient strategy.

$$34 - 19 = \underline{\qquad}$$

$$34 - 20 = 14$$
$$14 + 1 = 15$$

Fig. 2.9. A student's method for efficiently solving 34 – 19

As children continue to practice solving problems, making connections, and exploring mathematical relationships, their strategies usually become more efficient.

The Role of Practice

Practice has a special place in school mathematics. You probably remember practicing procedures in class or in homework assignments. At the time you may have thought all that repeated practice was a waste of time, but the goal was to enable you to use those procedures easily and quickly. This is still largely true today. The ability to recall procedures or facts automatically is helpful to students when they need to expend mental effort on more complex features of a problem. For example, multiplying 60 x 70 is much easier for a student who can recall with speed and accuracy the basic multiplication fact 6 x 7 than for one who can't. In fact, students may have more success learning more advanced mathematics in middle and high school if they have basic fact fluency and computational fluency.

Practicing procedures by solving worksheets of similar problems or by drilling have their places in the modern curriculum, but practice that is built into other mathematical activities, such as games, problem-solving activities, and extended projects, is also a very effective way to bolster children's ongoing learning. Students are given many opportunities through a variety of methods to achieve automatic recall, or what mathematics educators call *automaticity*.

Increasingly, teachers are incorporating games into mathematics instruction to provide just such opportunities. Games are not only one of the best ways for children to practice and improve their mathematical skills but also an activity in which students are eager to participate, so they can get lots of practice that is also engaging and fun. And because they are invested in winning a game, children are motivated to refine their strategies as they play—and this may happen quite rapidly. Later on in the book we talk more about the crucial role games can play in children's learning and mastery of mathematical concepts and procedures.

 DO YOU KNOW When and How Much to Drill?

When is the right time to use speed drills? If a student is counting by ones to solve 6 + 7, then a speed drill is *not* appropriate. He may count faster, but the drill will not help him build basic fact relationships. When used too early in the learning process, drills can hinder a child's view of himself as a mathematical learner—he may begin to see himself as someone who cannot be successful in mathematics.

Yet you may wonder just how much or how little practice is enough. In 2001, the U.S. National Research Council, organized in 1916 under a congressional charter, published *Adding It Up: Helping Children Learn Mathematics* (Kilpatrick, Swafford, and Findell). One of the interesting findings reported in this document was that children's computational performance was not negatively affected if teachers did not spend a great deal of time developing these skills through traditional practice and drills. When students were in classrooms in which making sense of and solving problems were the priorities, they had occasions to practice computational skills and make connections among new concepts as part of the learning process. Children gained experience with breaking up numbers in different ways and experimenting with number combinations and relationships, just to name two of the skills they practiced in their classrooms.

In the chart below, we summarize some of the changes in today's mathematics classrooms. As you can see, educators' thinking about basic fact fluency, drill, practice, computational fluency, problem solving, and using models has changed markedly over the last thirty or so years in the mathematics classroom.

Then	Now
Basic fact fluency is the ability to recall facts within three to four seconds. Fluency is achieved mainly through memorization, drills, and repeatedly practicing solving similar problems.	Basic fact fluency is the ability to recall facts within three to four seconds. Fluency is achieved by making sense of problems and making connections among numbers.
Drills are used to build basic fact fluency.	Drills are only used as a form of practice *after* a child has demonstrated the beginnings of fact fluency.
Computational fluency is applying a single procedure accurately.	Computational fluency is using a sensible strategy to compute efficiently and accurately.
Making sense of problems is recalling the correct procedure for the type of problem.	Making sense of problems is devising and implementing a strategy that will generate a reasonable solution.
Problem solving is introduced as extension problems that students solve once they have mastered skills and procedures.	Problem solving is integral to the ways students build, practice, and master skills.
Models, such as pictures and other manipulatives, are occasionally used by students to think about and solve problems.	Models, including pictures, applets, calculators, diagrams, and self-created or premade manipulatives, are used regularly to represent, learn about, and communicate mathematical concepts.

Things to Remember

- To be successful math learners, children need to engage in mathematical processes and develop specific mathematical skills.

- Processes are how you think about and solve mathematical problems.

- Skills are processes that have become automatic or routine.

- Math makes sense. Children (and adults) may make sense of it with pictures, diagrams, premade and self-created materials, numbers, words, and other approaches.

◆ Basic fact fluency and computational fluency are best learned when grounded in making sense of problems and understanding relationships among numbers.

◆ Practice is still necessary to learn mathematics, but using drills *before* a child is ready to handle them does not develop skill and, in fact, can adversely affect her view of herself as a math learner.

◆ Understanding why procedures work is as important for children as learning the procedures. Doing so gives the child the tools to reconstruct a procedure if he does not remember how to perform it.

◆ Explaining and justifying solution methods helps children clarify and understand their own thinking about mathematical concepts and methods. As part of whole-class discussions, children learn about and use a variety of problem-solving strategies.

◆ Basic fact fluency and computational fluency are important skills for students to develop. These skills can be very helpful when they study more advanced mathematics in middle and high school.

Things to Do

◆ Read the full explanation of the solution to the "Handshake" problem on page 193 in Appendix A.

◆ Learn about the "plus" side of calculators in the classroom by reading "Taking a Closer Look at Calculators" on page 37, and discover fun and educational "tricks" a calculator can perform.

◆ Ask your child's teacher what math games would be appropriate for your child.

◆ If you want to jump ahead to find out more about the role of games in teaching children mathematics and some of our favorites, read "Games" in chapter 7.

◆ Read the entries in the Glossary for the math terms used in this chapter. You'll have a better sense of the vocabulary your child hears in his or her math class.

Resources

We have tried to address many key ideas in this chapter, but we can only touch upon the topics. Additional resources you may find helpful and informative are listed below.

For Adults

Kilpatrick, Jeremy, Jane Swafford, and Bradford Findell, eds. *Adding It Up: Helping Children Learn Mathematics.* D.C.: National Academy Press, 2001.

Seeley, Cathy L. *Faster isn't Smarter: Messages about Math, Teaching, and Learning in the 21st Century: A Resource for Teachers, Leaders, Policy Makers, and Families.* Sausalito, Calif.: Math Solutions, 2009.

For Children

Scieszka, Jon, and Lane Smith. *Math Curse.* New York, NY: Viking, 1995.

More4U Online Resources

You can find a listing of additional helpful resources with links, including recommended games, by entering the access code on this book's title page at NCTM's More4U page (nctm.org/more4u).

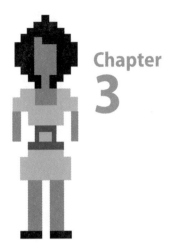

Number Sense

In a preschool class, the children were asked how many stairs they had to climb to get to their classroom. One of the three-year-olds drew the picture in figure 3.1 to show the number of stairs to the second floor. Can you figure out how many steps the child drew? What could the vertical and horizontal lines in this child's picture mean?

Fig. 3.1. A three-year-old child's drawing of the number of stairs

The number of stairs is *four*. When his teacher asked him about his picture, the little boy said that he knew three lines "came out" of the number three, so "four lines must come out of four." His picture is instructive in several ways. First the child is making marks to denote the number of stairs. While the picture could, in part, illustrate the stairs, the child clearly explains that his drawing is a *symbol* for four—the number of stairs that lead to the classroom. This is a profound mental leap—thinking of numerals as symbols used to represent numbers.

Fig. 3.2. A digital rendition of the numeral 3

This child saw the numeral three as three horizontal segments with a vertical line. This notion of the numeral three is similar to the display of three on a digital alarm clock (fig. 3.2) where straight-line segments replace the usual curved lines. In fact, it is not hard to imagine how this child's invented numeral for four may be related to how numerals have been created by humans throughout history.

As the example shows, children can and do make sense of numbers in many different ways. So what is *number sense*? And what does it mean for children to have it? How do they develop number sense, and are there predictable stages of its development?

Number sense is understanding how numbers are related, including the ability to make connections among the different sets of numbers and to use these number relationships to solve problems. Children begin to build an understanding about numbers as early as kindergarten and first grade. At this stage, they begin to represent numbers and to learn what the numbers mean. They can even solve simple problems. Eventually, children start to see how numerals and numbers are related. For instance, they can use the numerals 0, 1, 2, 3, … 9 to represent very large or very small numbers. And they make connections regarding how numbers are "a part of" one another. You can think of the number 10, for instance, as 10 ones (1 + 1 + 1 + 1 + 1 + 1 + 1 + 1 + 1 + 1) or as different combinations of two or more numbers, such as 8 + 2, 6 + 4, 6 + 3 + 1, 5 + 5 + 0, and so on. All of these ideas are part of developing number sense. As children progress in school, they discover other relationships between numbers, such as how they can be represented multiplicatively. The number 6 can be represented as 3 + 3, but it can also be specified as 2×3 or $^3/_2 \times 4$, for instance. In middle school, students learn about other types of numbers such as π and $\sqrt{2}$ and begin to understand ideas about different number systems. High school students continue to develop a deeper understanding of different number systems and routinely perform calculations using rational numbers (fractions, repeating and terminating decimals) and irrational numbers (nonrepeating, nonterminating decimals) to solve problems using calculus, geometry, and trigonometry.

In summary, number sense is a way of thinking about numbers that includes understanding how numbers are related, making connections among different sets of numbers, and using these number relationships to solve problems.

Beginning in kindergarten, children start making connections and organizing their ideas about numbers and how they are structured.

Early Number Strategies

When asked to solve 3 + 3, one kindergartener gave an answer of six almost immediately. When asked how he solved the problem, he explained, "I went one, two, three, cut, and four, five, six." What does this child mean? He was so confident and clear about his thinking (Whitenack et al. 2000).

Another child, when asked to show seven using her fingers, first raised six fingers and then another finger. When I asked how she knew that she had seven fingers showing, she explained that today was her birthday. She was seven years old. So I asked her to show me nine fingers. She quickly said that she could not do so. When I asked her to tell me more, she explained that she could not show nine because "nine is way out there" (Whitenack 1995).

Young children's understanding of and thoughts about numbers can be very different at various ages. Notice that the kindergartener kept track of six by counting three and then three more. It was as if he counted in his head, "One, two, three" and "One, two, three," but verbalized the second group as "Four, five, six." The last number he counted, six, was his answer. The first grader, by way of contrast, was not able to use her fingers to show nine. For her, the number nine was less familiar, or perhaps it did not exist in her world of numbers.

Children's number sense becomes more sophisticated as they develop new techniques for counting and more strategies for making connections between numbers and their relationships to each other. For instance, as they continue to explore the number 6, children begin to understand that it can be thought of in many ways, such as 2 + 4, 6 + 0, 2 + 1 + 3, and so on. And they relate 6 to numbers that are larger and those that are smaller as well as by how much larger or smaller. These are just a few of the ideas with which each young child begins to build his or her own world of numbers.

Even preschoolers have intuitive ideas about numbers up to five (or sometimes higher) and those thoughts develop and become more sophisticated over time, both in and out of school.

Intuitive Ideas about Number

Children come to preschool and kindergarten with an intuitive understanding of numbers. They may be able to say and even write numbers. Some can count correctly up to more than one hundred or one thousand, and others may already have developed efficient counting methods to solve simple addition or subtraction problems.

> You meet a friend and her young daughter at the grocery store. When you ask the little girl how old she is, she says she is three years old, holding up one hand with three fingers raised. She then says again, with great confidence, that she is three years old.

What does this little girl understand about numbers? Most likely, with some help from others, she has learned to raise three fingers when she tells people her age. However, if you were to ask her how many fingers she is holding up, she may not remember, or she may not be able to count each finger to tell you that she has three fingers raised. Similarly, five-year-olds may be able to count up to ten or more objects correctly, but for them to tell you "how many" they have counted, they usually need to recount all the objects. For instance, to correctly count the crayons in a box of ten, the child can only do so by stating each number in the correct order while picking up a crayon: The blue crayon is one, the red crayon is two, the brown is three, and so on. Children who skip over numbers as they count are still learning to say numbers in the correct order. To actually count "how many" successfully, children must have a good command of reciting numbers in sequence and assigning one number to each object they count. As they develop these skills, children will be able to accurately determine how many objects are in a collection.

Counting to Find "How Many"

There are various ways children can count to determine how many are in one collection or several collections. We mentioned earlier that children might need to count each item—*count all*—in a group in order to tell you how many they have counted. If so, children are developing the beginnings of a basic understanding of *cardinality*, or "how many" objects are in a collection.

As early as kindergarten, children develop more efficient methods to count collections. The most notable change they make is the use of *counting-on* strategies. For example, when asked to solve 6 + 5, a child says, "six," and then uses his fingers to count five more on one hand. He may raise each finger as he says each number from seven through eleven. Once he has raised all five fingers, he knows that he has counted five more. When a child switches from counting all to counting on, he has made a significant shift in how he finds how many objects are in a collection. Figure 3.3 illustrates two ways children might count a collection of pips (dots).

One child counts all: "One, two, three, four, five, six, seven, eight, nine."

A second child counts on: "Six. Seven, eight, nine."

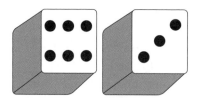

Fig. 3.3. How students might count nine pips

The second child readily sees the two groups of three pips on the first die as six. He uses this information to count on three more.

Children in kindergarten or first grade will later develop techniques for *counting back*. To count back, a child needs a way to keep track of her counting. For instance, a child solving 11 – 6 might count down from 11 and keep track with her fingers for each of the 6 objects she must remove. She might be thinking, "If I take away 1 there are 10 crayons left; if I take away 2, there are 9 crayons left; 3 is 8; 4 is 7; 5 is 6; and 6 is 5." The child knows she has removed 6 because she has counted back 6; she may even hold up an additional finger each time she counts back.

Whether a child is counting on or counting back, she appears to be *double counting*. For instance, she is keeping track of the number of objects she has taken away as well as the number of objects that remain—and of course, she must also know when to stop counting. While adults take it for granted, this method of counting is truly remarkable and represents a significant shift in a child's world of numbers. She can see both parts of 11: the part that she counts to take away 6 (11, 10, 9, 8, 7, 6) and the part that remains—5.

There are many nuances and distinctions about children's counting strategies and methods that for the sake of brevity we have not touched upon here. There is a wealth of information about these topics, and if you would like to read more about them, we list some additional resources at the end of this chapter.

Using More Advanced Strategies

Once children have developed routine ways to count, their next step is to develop strategies for which they no longer need to count all, count on, or count back to solve problems. Researchers, in fact, suggest that moving beyond counting is a crucial step in a child's understanding of numbers.

Let's look at a second grader's strategy for solving $8 + 5$ (fig. 3.4). She explained that she "broke up" (decomposed) 5 into 3 and 2, and then added 8 and 2 to make 10. She then added the remaining 3 to the 10 to arrive at her answer of 13.

$$8 + 2 = 10$$
$$10 + 3 = 13$$
I got the 2 3
3 from 5

Fig. 3.4. Second grader's strategy for solving $8 + 5$

Figure 3.4 illustrates a *chunking strategy*; it is one type of strategy that children use as they begin to develop non-counting methods to solve problems. This student's method is an example of a special kind of chunking strategy—a *make-ten strategy*. When using a make-ten strategy, the student decomposes one or more of the numbers, and then uses her knowledge of number facts for ten to solve the problem. Other types of strategies, like *doubles facts*, can also be used to solve the problem. A student could decompose the 8 into 5 and 3, and then add 5 and 5 to make 10. Then he would add the 3 to the 10 to make 13. Or, solving $9 + 8$, another child might remember that $8 + 8 = 16$, and because 9 is one more, he need only add one more to his answer of 16. This strategy is called *doubles ±1*.

 TAKING A CLOSER LOOK at Doubles ±1

Can you solve $8 + 7$ using a doubles ±1 strategy? Can you find more than one way to solve the problem using this strategy?

Either $8 + 8$ or $7 + 7$ works. Let's assume a student uses what he knows about $8 + 8 = 16$ to figure out a solution. He decomposes one of the eights into $7 + 1$, and then realizes if he subtracts one from his answer for $8 + 8$, the answer is 15.

Younger children at the beginning of first grade use this strategy too. A child might use 3 + 3 = 6 to find the sum of 4 and 3. Because 4 = 3 + 1, she might realize that 4 + 3 is one more than 3 + 3 and conclude the answer is 7.

Children in first and second grade begin using a variety of strategies to solve other types of problems too. For instance, a student might use what she knows about 11 + 11 to employ a doubles strategy to solve 11 + 15. She first decomposes 15 using the fact 15 = 11 + 4, and then explains that 11 + 11 = 22 and 22 + 4 = 26 to solve the problem. Or, approaching the problem from a different starting point, she might use the doubles fact 15 + 15 = 30. In this case, she would subtract 4 instead of adding 4 to arrive at the correct answer of 26. As you can see, once a student begins to use various chunking strategies, she can also develop more flexible ways to reason about numbers.

Children usually master the various counting techniques before they can move on to developing strategies such as chunking and doubles ±1, and some may need to count all or count on for some time before they're ready for the more efficient methods of problem solving. Interestingly, some children will develop these strategies on their own. It is actually very natural for children to find and use more efficient methods for reasoning with and about numbers. (In fact, some children will covertly use these strategies if they are not encouraged to develop diverse ways to solve problems in their classroom.) Others may need additional help with exploring numbers before they can step up to more advanced methods. As long as students have opportunities to think about and investigate number ideas, these efficient strategies and methods will unfold for them as they become ready to develop them.

 TAKING A CLOSER LOOK at Early Number Strategies

Children can do some pretty remarkable work involving number sense. Let's consider the efforts of two students who are at different stages in their development of number sense.

Student 1, a four-year-old, was given a box of seashells and asked how many were in the box. He drew a picture (fig. 3.5) of each of the shells and then counted each shell. We can see that the student is still learning how to write his numbers correctly, but the ideas that he is writing about are foundational to developing number sense. Notice that he draws each object to be counted, and then writes the numbers alongside the shells in order to know how many shells there are. Each shell is assigned one number, the numbers are in a stable order (going up by one each time), and they are, in fact, in the correct sequence.

Fig. 3.5. Prekindergarten student counts seashells

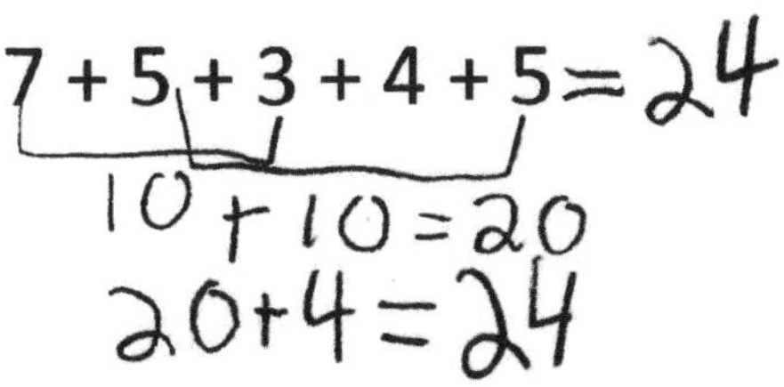

$$7 + 5 + 3 + 4 + 5 = 24$$
$$10 + 10 = 20$$
$$20 + 4 = 24$$

Fig. 3.6. Solution strategy for $7 + 5 + 3 + 4 + 5 = \square$

Early in the school year, Student 2, a second grader, was given the addition problem in figure 3.6 and asked to determine the sum. Rather than draw a representation for each number and counting (e.g., 7 dots, 5 dots, and so on), she decided to group, or chunk, numbers to solve the problem by making tens. She made two groups of 10 (7 + 3 and 5 + 5), and then added them to get 20. She then added the 4 to arrive at her answer of 24. So by early second grade, a student might determine "how many" not by drawing and counting but by using number facts that she knows. Each number stands for a quantity that she may rearrange to make adding them easier. So, both children are putting their current ideas about numbers to use when solving problems, whether it is matching numbers to pictures or finding combinations that make ten.

Numbers: What's the Math?

In mathematics, a collection of objects is typically referred to as a *set*. (This concept is not only fundamental to developing number sense but also comes into play when studying more advanced mathematics topics such as algebra and geometry.) When children refer to collections of toy cars or candy, they can also call these collections a set of toy cars or a set of candy. And when children use numbers to describe how many they count in a collection, they are actually referring to the cardinality of the set.

 DO YOU KNOW How Children Learn Correct Math Terms?

To instruct mathematics, teachers need to introduce vocabulary for math ideas from time to time. As children talk about and explain their thinking, the teacher can use their words to connect to terms that are often used by mathematicians. For instance, a child might say that he counted all the things in the box on his paper. The teacher can use his words, "counted all the things in the box," to explain that mathematicians have a word for "things in the box"; they use the word "set." All these things are part of a set! Teachers regularly use children's everyday language to help them learn math vocabulary. And children have a better chance of understanding the meaning of the new terms if they are described using familiar words that children know.

Sets can also be made up of collections of geometric shapes with common characteristics, such as the measure of their interior angles or the number of sides; the number of students who are wearing striped shirts; or collections of numbers that have common characteristics, such as all the even numbers between 10 and 20. In fact, young students use set concepts to describe three different types of numbers introduced in the K–5 curriculum: *natural numbers, whole numbers,* and *integers.*

Natural Numbers. The *natural numbers* are numbers that, quite literally, occur naturally. Believe it or not, they are familiar to other animals besides humans. There is actual evidence that crows and dogs can count! In fact, the natural numbers are sometimes referred to as the "set of counting numbers" because we use them to count things like the number of chairs in a classroom. The smallest natural number in the set is 1. All other numbers in the set can be generated by repeatedly adding the number 1 ($2 = 1 + 1, 3 = 1 + 1 + 1, \ldots 8 = 1 + 1 + 1 + 1 + 1 + 1 + 1 + 1$, and so on). Each natural number is exactly one away from the previous or the next natural number. In other words, consecutive natural numbers differ by one.

A *natural number* is any number that can be generated by repeatedly adding 1, starting at 1. Specifically, the natural numbers are the numbers 1, 2, 3, 4, and so on.

Whole Numbers. Interestingly, there are some textbook authors (and mathematicians) who include the number 0 in the set of natural numbers. Others define a new set that includes zero along with the natural numbers as the set of *whole numbers.*

A *whole number* is any number that can be generated by repeatedly adding 1, starting at 0. Specifically, the whole numbers are the numbers 0, 1, 2, 3, 4, and so on.

A number line is often used to illustrate how numbers are related (fig. 3.7). Marks on a number line are used to indicate the distance a number is away from zero. The number line in the figure below is marked to illustrate the whole numbers from zero to ten. Note, however, that the distance between zero and one is not any particular measurement, per se. That is because there is a certain degree of freedom when a number line is created. The location of 1 could have been marked farther away or closer to 0. What is important is that the distance between any two consecutive whole numbers is the same because consecutive whole numbers differ by 1.

Fig. 3.7. Whole numbers on a number line

The number line is also used to illustrate how particular numbers are ordered from least to greatest. It is usual practice to mark smaller numbers to the left of larger numbers along the line. So, looking at the number line above, we can conclude that 7 is less than 10 (or 7 < 10) and that 7 is greater than 2 (or 7 > 2). We will use number lines to introduce other sets of numbers too.

Integers. The set of *integers* not only includes the set of whole numbers but also negative numbers. Negative numbers are numbers that are less than zero. To include these numbers on a number line, the line is extended and the negative numbers are written to the left of zero. *Negative integers* can be generated by repeatedly subtracting (instead of adding) 1 from 0. So 0 − 1 = −1 and 0 − 1 − 1 = −2. The number −1 is exactly 1 less than 0, and −2 is exactly 2 less than 0, and so on. As you can see, these numbers are produced in a consistent manner—by adding or subtracting 1—to generate the set of whole numbers or integers.

An *integer* is any number that can be generated by either repeatedly adding 1 or repeatedly subtracting 1, starting at 0. The set of integers are the numbers … −3, −2, −1, 0, 1, 2, 3, …

Integers extend infinitely in two directions—positive to the right of zero and negative to the left; recall that the number line reflects this idea, with arrows marked at both ends of the line.

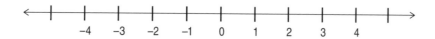

Fig. 3.8. Integers on a number line

Notice in figure 3.8 the symmetry of positive and negative integers on either side of zero. Each number has a corresponding "opposite" number. This observation leads to other interesting mathematical results. In general terms, the numbers *a* and *–a* are exactly *a* units from zero, so *a* and *–a* are *opposites*; for example, 3 and –3 are opposites. Thus, 3 is the opposite of –3, and –3 is the opposite of 3. Further, we define the *absolute value* of the number *a* to be the positive distance that number is away from zero. So the absolute value of 3 is 3 and the absolute value of –3 is also 3 because both numbers are exactly three units from zero.

Place Value and the Base-Ten System

You may have heard people refer to *Hindu-Arabic numerals* in reference to the system of numeration that we use every day. This system was popularized by Arabic culture around the ninth century C.E. The numerals 1 through 9 were in use in Hindu culture around the third century B.C.E. Zero was introduced some seven hundred years later, around the fifth century C.E., in what is now modern-day India. Although other ancient cultures also used concepts of zero and place-value systems, the Hindu-Arabic system is now the most widely used across the globe.

To develop a deep sense of numbers—what they mean and their relationships to each other—children must wrestle with several ideas regarding the Hindu-Arabic number system, starting with the importance of the position of a digit when representing a number. Because the system is a positional one, each position (or place) of a numeral is associated with a particular value.

How might children understand these ideas? What does it mean for children to comprehend our numeration system? In the elementary school curriculum, this question is often rephrased: How do children understand our base-ten system? Let's start by exploring how children learn to write numbers.

Writing Numbers

The symbols we use to represent numbers have an elegant simplicity about them. But the words we use to talk about numbers can be a bit confusing for children. For instance, in English the numbers eleven, twelve, thirteen, fourteen, fifteen, sixteen, seventeen, eighteen, and nineteen are difficult for younger children to learn. The names of numbers do not always highlight the importance of the number ten in our numeration system.

Languages like Chinese and Japanese have number names that emphasize the tens structure of numbers more clearly. For example, in Japanese, the word for "eleven" is "ten-one," whereas in English, the word "eleven" actually means "one left." In Chinese, ninety-seven is "nine-ten-seven" or 9 tens plus seven, but in French, ninety-seven is "quatre-vingt-dix-sept," which literally translates in English to "four twenty ten seven," meaning 4 twenties (or eighty) plus ten and seven (or seventeen). The names of numbers in some languages are clearly more attuned to base ten in structure than in others, which can influence how quickly and easily children learn to say and write numbers. Think about the English word "sixteen." When asked to write it using numerals, many children write 61 instead of 16 because they hear the word "six" first.

Writing larger numbers can be challenging for young children too. Take a look at the number written by a seven-year-old in figure 3.9. What number was he trying to represent?

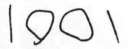

Fig. 3.9. A number written by a seven-year-old

To you, it looks like one thousand one. Actually, he had been writing numbers sequentially on a long strip of paper, and this number immediately followed the number 100. He read the number out loud as "a hundred and one." What does his written work reveal about what he does and does not understand about writing numbers correctly using the base-ten number system?

Manipulatives such as base-ten blocks are widely used in classrooms to help children "see" numbers and operations. Let's look at how another student might model the number 101 using base-ten blocks (fig. 3.10).

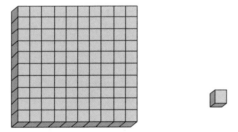

Fig. 3.10. Base-ten blocks: one flat of 100 small cubes and 1 small cube

She explains that each of the *small cubes* is one unit and that the 10-by-10 square (called a *flat*) is 100 small cubes (or 100 ones). She states that these two blocks, together, show 101 small cubes. She also explains that when she writes the number of small cubes, the numeral 1 that she places in the hundreds position represents the one flat of 100 small cubes. The numeral 1 in the ones position represents one small cube. The zero in the tens place means that there are no *longs*, or separate groups of ten. (One of the ideas that students grapple with is why the zero in the tens position makes sense for this problem.) Another student might explain why it is important to have zero tens: "If I write the number 110, the 1 in the tens position does not show 101 small cubes. I would have to use a different block—a long—to show 10 small cubes" (fig. 3.11).

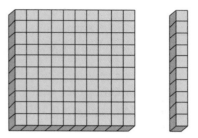

Fig. 3.11. Base-ten blocks: one flat and one long

One of the important connections that children need to develop is how the blocks and the numerals in the number relate to each other. As you may have observed, the long is ten *times* a small cube, and the flat is ten *times* a long. The action of multiplying by ten for the next place value undergirds the meaning of our number system. What would happen if you had ten of the hundreds flats? You would have 1000 of the small cubes, and you would have a new place value: the thousands place. Because the position of each digit in a number is crucial to its meaning, textbooks commonly describe our number system as a *place-value number system*—it is a positional number system. The position of each digit in a number is key to its meaning and value in the number.

One way to understand our place-value system is to observe the pattern that emerges as you count. Let's look at the numbers 8 through 21 below:

8
9
10
11
12
13
14
15
16
17
18
19
20
21

Notice the numbers 9 and 19. What happens after each count? After the number 9, the ones place changes to 0 and there is a 1 in the tens place. That means there is 1 group of ten and 0 ones. What would this look like using base-ten blocks? If you had 9 single cubes and you wanted to add one more, you could trade in all the single cubes for one long. (Children sometimes call it a "ten stick.") So you would have one long, or 1 ten, and 0 ones. You could continue to add single cubes until you had one long and nine single cubes. What happens when you add one more single cube? You could trade in the single cubes for another long. Two longs and 0 ones mean you have 20. Notice how the digit 2 in the number 20 is in the *tens place.* So the number is not "two" but "twenty."

What happens as you count from 97 to 102? Let's look below to see how the pattern continues:

$$97$$
$$98$$
$$99$$
$$100$$
$$101$$
$$102$$

Notice how the number 99 means "9 tens" and "9 ones." So what would happen if you added just one more single cube? You could trade in the single cubes for another long, and you would have ten longs. When you have ten of any particular type of base-ten block, that's your cue to trade them in. You could trade in those ten longs for a flat, or 1 hundred. Indeed, you would have 1 flat, 0 longs (because you traded them), and 0 single cubes (because you traded them). Your number is written as 100.

Understanding Place Value

What does it mean to understand our place-value system? Let's consider the number 362. Adults can see that each digit represents a different place (ones, tens, hundreds) and can even appreciate how the digits are related proportionally. But to a young child, understanding that *10 ones are the same as 1 ten* or that the 6 in 362 is not 6 ones, but 6 tens is by no means automatic. It takes time and experience for children to understand that 2 tens are the same as 20 ones, 3 tens are the same as 30 ones, and so on. Eventually, children count groups of ten as quickly and naturally as they count groups of one.

Let's look again at the first grader's way of writing the number 101 (fig. 3.9). He seems to understand the additive nature of writing numbers, that is, the number is one hundred *and* one, but he does not yet see that one hundred is denoted by writing the single digit 1 in the *hundreds place.* Base-ten ideas can be as difficult for young children as, for instance, base-five ideas might be for adults. (We examine this point more specifically later in this chapter.) Developmentally, how this first grader wrote the number 101 is quite appropriate. He needs time and more experience to connect his ideas about place value with correctly writing larger numbers.

 TAKING A CLOSER LOOK at Place-Value Ideas

In Mr. Foster's second-grade classroom, students are playing "Place Value Dice Roll," a game available on the Internet (teacherspayteachers.com). A die is rolled four times and students try to arrange three of the four numbers to make the largest possible three-digit number; the unused number is discarded. On his first roll of the die, the number 3 comes up for Salim. He says, "Three's not the biggest and not the smallest, so I'm going to put it in the tens." The next number rolled is 1. He laughs and immediately writes a 1 in the trash can—he even draws a frowning face next to it. Salim then rolls a 2, and he writes a 2 in the ones place. On the final roll of the die a 5 comes up. Salim cheers and writes a 5 in the hundreds place (fig. 3.12). "I got 532." Other players get different results, but as they continue to play, the students are learning that the position of the digits matters greatly when trying to make the largest number possible.

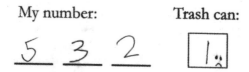

Fig. 3.12. Salim's number after four rolls of the die

In a fourth-grade classroom, students are playing a game of "Close to 1,000." Students draw a total of eight "digit cards" (cards printed with a digit, 0 through 9), select six of them, and then create two three-digit numbers with the cards. The goal is to create two numbers that when added together result in a sum as close to one thousand as possible. Thom drew 9, 8, 7, 2, 2, 1, 0, and 0, and discarded 1 and 0. He explained his strategy to his partner: "I picked 0 and 9 to put in the hundreds places so I would have 900. Then I put 7 and 2 for the tens places because it's really 70 and 20, which is 90. So I have 990 and I need ten more to get 1,000. That's why I have 8 and 2 here in the ones (fig.3.13)." His partner, Grant, was confused by the placement of the zero in the hundreds place in Thom's first number and asked, "Can you *do* that?" Thom asserted, "Sure. It just means you don't have any hundreds. It's 78."

$$\underline{0\ \ 7\ \ 8} + \underline{9\ \ 2\ \ 2} = \underline{1000}$$

Fig. 3.13. Thom adds 78 and 922.

Thom not only starts with the highest place value when adding but also uses the zero digit to his advantage. This game improves addition skills as well as deepens understanding about place value.

Place Value: What's the Math?

The examples above illustrate how students begin to associate the position of a digit and the numerical value that it represents. As an adult, working with numbers in base ten is automatic to you, so it can be difficult to relate to the challenges young learners have with place value. But the base-ten system is only one of many number systems that can be used to represent numerical values. For example, computers store information using a binary system (base two) while Roman numerals are still used in many ways, from identifying the modern Olympiads to indicating copyright dates for movies, to name just two. We consider some alternative approaches to representing numerical values as we take a closer look at some of the formal mathematical ideas involved in understanding place value.

Working with Roman Numerals. The ancient Romans assigned symbols for units of 1, 5, 10, 50, 100, 500, and 1,000. It is called an *additive system* because the digits must be added to determine the size of the number, and digits can only repeat up to three times before it becomes necessary to select a different unit. To appreciate the efficiency of our modern numeration system, think about writing 362 using Roman numerals. How would you represent 362? Because C = 100, L = 50, X = 10 and I = 1, 362 = 100 + 100 + 100 + 50 + 10 + 1 + 1 or CCCLXII. Notice that three hundred is represented by C + C + C, not because the symbol C appears in any particular position. So the Roman numeral system is essentially a nonpositional system.

Very large numbers can take a long time to write in Roman numerals, and computation is so cumbersome that even the ancient Romans used a completely different method, using an instrument much like an abacus.

Position *does* play a role in the ancient Roman system, but not in the same way it does in our base-ten system. If the symbol I means 1 and the symbol X represents 10, why does IX denote 9 and not 11? When a symbol of lesser value precedes a symbol of greater value, subtraction is implied, so XL represents 50 – 10, or 40.

Base Ten. Where, then, do we see three hundred in 362? For figure 3.14, we created columns and wrote 362 so each column is filled with exactly one digit.

Fig. 3.14. Positional representation of three hundred sixty-two

For a whole number like 362, the rightmost column tells you how many ones, the next column to the left tells you how many tens, and the next column to the left (third from the right) tells you how many hundreds. The digit 3 is in the third column from the right; its position means "3 groups of 100."

In mathematics, "three groups of hundred" may also be expressed using multiplication, 3 x 100. Similarly, six groups of ten is 6 x 10, and two groups of one is 2 x 1. When these components are put together, you can see both multiplication and addition at work: 362 = (3 x 100) + (6 x 10) + (2 x 1).

We have already discussed base-ten blocks of a single unit, longs, and flats. Continuing to the next construction, ten flats form a cube of 1,000 (fig. 3.15).

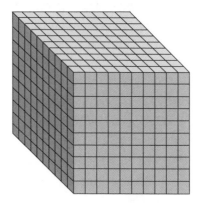

Fig. 3.15. Large base-ten cube is equivalent to 1,000 small cubes.

Each time a digit is added to the next column to the left, the digit is being multiplied by ten: ten groups of one, ten groups of ten, ten groups of one hundred, and so on. Therefore you can rewrite the equation above to show how many times ten is a factor in each column: $362 = (3 \times 10 \times 10) + (6 \times 10) + (2 \times 1)$. The names of our place values (tens, hundreds, thousands, etc.) are related to powers of ten. A power is simply the number of times a number is repeated as a factor; for example 2^3 is the same as $2 \times 2 \times 2$. We can simplify the expression above using exponents: $362 = (3 \times 10^2) + (6 \times 10^1) + (2 \times 10^0)$. Note that 10^0 is equal to 1, not 0.

 DO YOU KNOW Why $10^0 = 1$?

Take a look below at the list of powers of 10:

$10^1 = 10$

$10^2 = 10 \times 10 = 100$

$10^3 = 10 \times 10 \times 10 = 1000$

Already, you can probably see the pattern in the number of zeros associated with the power of 10; 10^1 is a 1 with one zero, 10^2 is a 1 with two zeros, 10^3 is a 1 with three zeros, and so on. By the pattern, you would likely guess that $10^8 = 100,000,000$ (a 1 with eight zeros.) What happens when we go in the other direction? Each time we decrease the power by one, we drop a zero. In mathematics, we need these types of patterns to continue so that operations are consistent. Thus, 10^0 is a 1 with no zeros. In fact, any nonzero number raised to the zero power is 1.

When you untangle the meaning behind written numbers, you can appreciate how our system is simultaneously efficient and complicated. Among its hidden features are addition, multiplication, exponentiation, position, and the critical role of the number ten.

READER'S CHALLENGE: Base Five

Like the base-ten system, the base-five system is a positional system that represents numerical values using digits; in this case, the digits 0, 1, 2, 3, 4 are used. And instead of using powers of ten to determine the value of a digit, the powers of five are used. You can think of this system of numeration in terms of counting fingers (ones) and hands (groups of five fingers or five ones). Counting in base five starts with 0, 1, 2, 3, 4.

The next base-five number is 10. You can think of this as 1 hand and 0 fingers (or 1 group of five and 0 groups of one). The counting continues as 10_5, 11_5, 12_5, 13_5, 14_5. Once you have 14_5 (1 hand and 4 fingers) you are only one away from having two hands (or 2 groups of five). So, the next number is 20_5. The next "big" jump occurs when the count has reached 44_5 (4 hands and 4 fingers), which is only one away from the next power of five (or $5 \times 5 = 5^2$ [25] in base ten). And the next number in the base-five count is written 100_5. What does it mean? Literally, 100 in base five is $(1 \times 5^2) + (0 \times 5^1) + (0 \times 5^0)$. (Base-five numbers are written using 5 as a subscript.)

To experience some of the puzzlement that young students go through while learning how to work with numbers written in base ten, challenge yourself to think in base five as much as possible as you try one or two of the following problems.

◆ What number comes after 4444_5?

◆ What is $13_5 + 24_5$?

◆ What is $32_5 - 14_5$?

Because these problems are in base five, you do not have a single numeral for five. This is similar to what happens in base ten, which has single symbols representing the counting numbers from zero to nine. Once a count of ten is reached, the numerals 1 and 0 are combined to represent that amount. Here, once you get to five, you would combine numerals 1 and 0 to represent five. This jump happens every time a new place value (or power of five) is reached. So, the number after 4444_5 is 10000_5. As with counting, when larger numbers are added, you need to add the amounts in each place. So $13_5 + 24_5$ initially results in 3 fives and 7 ones. The answer is 4 fives and 2 ones or 42_5. To determine $32_5 - 14_5$ you must figure out how to take away 1 five and 4 ones from 3 fives and 2 ones. Some regrouping is necessary. The 3 fives and 2 ones are the same as 2 fives and 7 ones (traded 1 group of five for 5 ones). Take away 1 five and 4 ones, and you are left with 1 five and 3 ones, or 13_5.

Early Algebraic Thinking

It may seem odd that we have included a section on algebraic thinking in a chapter on number sense. However, algebraic thinking is simply an extension of number sense. It occurs as children begin making and justifying their observations about number operations. Whether a child is developing her number sense or algebraic thinking, the critical components of that development include making connections, solving problems, and justifying her thinking (fig. 3.16).

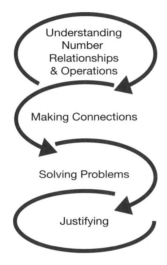

Fig. 3.16. The critical components of developing number sense and algebraic thinking

Consider the problem in figure 3.17:

> I have 8 toys.
> Some are blocks. Some are marbles.
> How many of each could I have?
> How many blocks? How many marbles?
>
> Find as many combinations as you can.

Fig. 3.17. The Blocks and Marbles problem (TERC 2008)

Oliver, a first grader, made the table shown in figure 3.18 when working on this problem. Notice how he organized his list of possible combinations. In the marbles column, Oliver listed the numbers 1 through 7 in increasing order while in the blocks column he listed the same numbers in decreasing order.

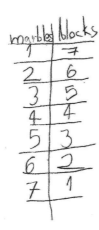

Fig. 3.18. Oliver's solution to the Blocks and Marbles problem

Another classmate, Selena, organized her list differently. She wrote pairs of numbers, keeping track of when she reversed the pair of numbers along the way (fig. 3.19). For instance, she made sure that she wrote both 2 marbles and 6 blocks and 6 marbles and 2 blocks.

Marbles	Blocks
1	7
7	1
2	6
6	2
3	5
5	3
4	4

Fig. 3.19. Selena's list of numbers

Both children are reasoning in sophisticated ways and both made sure they had accounted for all possible combinations of blocks and marbles. Oliver listed all the numbers from 1 through 7 while Selena "swapped" the number of marbles and blocks for each different pair.

This type of problem is a typical one that a teacher might use in a classroom discussion to encourage students to think about how they know whether or not they have found all possible combinations. This opens the conversation so students can investigate the idea of combinations in more general terms. Oliver could use his table to prove that he has found all the different combinations. By ordering all the possible numbers in each column, he has exhausted the different ways he could make combinations of eight, knowing that he had to have some of each toy. Selena might make her case for all the pairs by stating that because she had listed 2 marbles and 6 blocks and then 6 marbles and 2 blocks, she could not use these numbers again. When students can prove they have all the different combinations of blocks and marbles, they are moving beyond performing basic arithmetic to giving general explanations that can be applied to similar problems, an important process that is an indicator of algebraic thinking.

You may be surprised that the students' strategies for exhausting all possible combinations are significant, albeit intuitive, algebra ideas. And, remarkably, students may happen upon many such concepts that pave the way for algebraic thinking while they are solving mathematical problems. In fact, several fundamental concepts of algebra are addressed in the elementary school curriculum, although they are not described as "algebra." First, let's look at how algebra can be viewed as *generalized arithmetic*, emerging naturally from students' work with numbers.

 DO YOU KNOW What Generalized Arithmetic Is?

> *Generalized arithmetic* is a phrase that mathematics educators use to describe how algebra can be thought of as an extension of our work with numbers. General equations can be used to illustrate different properties for the operations (addition, subtraction, multiplication, and division) and to represent relationships among numbers. For instance, we know that you can change the order of the factors in multiplication and the product remains the same. That generalization is called the commutative property of multiplication, and we can write an equation to represent that, $a \times b = b \times a$.

Algebra as Generalized Arithmetic

Whether you realized it or not, the typical algebra course you probably took in middle school or high school was a more formalized study of numbers and the ideas that you first learned in elementary school. For instance, a typical problem in second grade might have been, "What number x makes the equation $8 = x + 2$ true?" Even then, you may have been able to solve the problem by simply using your number sense. The answer is 6. But suppose that the equation is $8 = x + y$. Assuming that x and y are natural numbers, then our problem could represent the different combinations for eight that Oliver and Selena explored in our earlier example. So the notion that algebra can be thought of as generalized arithmetic begins to make a lot more sense. Algebra merely gives us a way to express relationships that may be true for a range of numbers.

As students gain experience with the operations, they begin to notice patterns that can be generalized as properties for a particular operation. For example, students like Selena notice early on that it does not matter in which order they add two numbers ($6 + 2 = 8$ and $2 + 6 = 8$). This is a basic property in the study of algebra, but as you can see, it is used as early as first grade. It is referred to as the *commutative property of addition*. Likewise, third-grade students notice that the order in which they multiply two numbers does not matter; for example, 5 x 3 = 15 and 3 x 5 = 15. Younger children might discover this property as they work with groups of objects; five groups of three toys is the same number of toys as three groups of five toys. It does not matter in which order we multiply the numbers; the *commutative property of multiplication* holds true.

Children's use of the commutative property usually surfaces when they solve addition problems. For instance, a child may solve 6 + 10 + 4 by adding 6 and 4 to make 10, and then adding the 2 tens to make 20. In order to add in this way, the child may reason that 10 + 4 is the same as 4 + 10. Basically, he solves the problem 6 + 4 + 10. Moving from left to right, he simply adds the 6 and 4 first; then adds 10 and 10 to arrive at his answer of 20. So students use the commutative property early on to make problems easier to solve. Later, when working with more complex expressions, the commutative property is necessary to employ to solve problems and justify solutions. Interestingly, there is another property involved in this example. Not only has the child reordered the numbers involved in the calculation, he has also grouped them a particular way. The equation below summarizes his work.

$$6 + 10 + 4 = 6 + 4 + 10 = (6 + 4) + 10 = 10 + 10$$

Notice that parentheses are included to group 6 + 4 to show that the student added these two numbers first. In theory, it doesn't matter which pair of numbers are added together. After reordering 6 + 10 + 4 to 6 + 4 + 10, he could have added 6 to the sum of 4 and 10, that is, 6 + (4 + 10). Instead, he chose to add 10 to the sum of 6 and 4, that is, (6 + 4) + 10. This freedom to choose which pair of numbers to add together is called the *associative property of addition*. So when children use different strategies, they may apply these two properties, perhaps intuitively, to solve problems.

As you might suspect, there is an associative property of multiplication too. When applying this property, a child can choose which pairs of numbers she will multiply first. For example, if multiplying $3 \times 2 \times 5$, she might decide to multiply 3 and 2, and then multiply the product (6) by 5. This approach can be represented symbolically as $3 \times 2 \times 5 = (3 \times 2) \times 5 = 6 \times 5 = 30$. Alternatively, the student might choose to multiply 2 and 5 first, and then multiply that product (10) by 3. Symbolically that is $3 \times 2 \times 5 = 3 \times (2 \times 5) = 3 \times 10 = 30$. Either way, the child reaches the same result. Working through both of these options, the child may realize that $(3 \times 2) \times 5 = 3 \times (2 \times 5)$. The teacher will likely need to help with writing or recording these ideas. He may even choose to break apart the two steps, multiplying $3 \times 2 = 6$ and $6 \times 5 = 30$, to help students keep track of which numbers they are working with first. For older students, the teacher can challenge them to record these ideas.

> We use letters as *variables* in the definitions below to describe the properties in a general manner:
>
> *Commutative Property of Addition:* $a + b = b + a$ for any numbers a and b.
>
> *Commutative Property of Multiplication:* $a \times b = b \times a$ for any numbers a and b.
>
> *Associative Property of Addition:* $(a + b) + c = a + (b + c)$ for any numbers a, b, and c.

You may be wondering about the operations of subtraction and division. Is there a commutative property of subtraction? What about division? Does it matter in which order numbers are subtracted or divided? And what about an associative property of subtraction or division? Does it matter how numbers are grouped together for subtraction or division?

 ## READER'S CHALLENGE

◆ Solve the following subtractions to find out whether or not number order matters when subtracting or dividing:

4 – 5

5 – 4

6 ÷ 2

2 ÷ 6

◆ Do the same to the following to find out if grouping matters when subtracting or dividing:

(10 – 5) – 4

10 – (5 – 4)

(24 ÷ 4) ÷ 2

24 ÷ (4 ÷ 2)

As the examples illustrate, if you reverse the order of the numbers when subtracting or dividing, the result is not always the same ($4 - 5 = -1$ and $5 - 4 = 1$; $6 \div 2 = 3$ but $2 \div 6 = \frac{1}{3}$). So this indispensable algebra concept, the commutative property, does not hold for all four whole number operations; it only applies to addition and multiplication. Even so, you might have noticed some patterns in the subtraction examples (table 3.1).

Table 3.1. Switching the order of the numbers in subtraction

4 – 5 = –1	5 – 4 = 1
8 – 10 = –2	10 – 8 = 2
6 – 9 = –3	9 – 6 = 3
7 – 12 = –5	12 – 7 = 5
10 – 18 = –8	18 – 10 = 8

When examining the chart, a sixth-grade student might comment that the results are opposites (1 and –1; 2 and –2, etc.), so, even though subtraction is not commutative, there is still interesting mathematics associated with switching the order of numbers in a subtraction problem.

As children continue to work with numbers, they begin to realize that they can decompose numbers, using multiplication and addition, into equivalent expressions that are easier to handle. This is the distributive property of multiplication over addition. It is a particularly useful skill when solving multiplication problems mentally. For example, a fourth-grade student might determine 4×21 by first decomposing 21 into $20 + 1$, and then thinking, "Four times twenty is eighty and four times one is four, so four times twenty-one is eighty plus four and equals eighty-four." She has noticed that $4 \times 21 = 4 \times (20 + 1) = 4 \times 20 + 4 \times 1$, and has literally distributed multiplication over addition. Multiplication can also be distributed over subtraction. To solve 5×99, think of 99 as $100 - 1$; the product is five times one hundred minus five times one. Symbolically, it is represented as $5 \times 99 = 5 \times (100 - 1) = 5 \times 100 - 5 \times 1$.

Although young children solve multiplication problems using this strategy, they usually do not know they are using a primary property of mathematics. To them, it may simply be an obvious way of making sense of a problem. They may, for example, explain that they are finding the number of objects in all the groups. With the first example, a student might explain that twenty-one groups of four are the same as twenty groups of four plus one more group. Or they may use a diagram, such as an area model for multiplication (page 70), to justify their thinking.

The distributive property is a critical component in understanding multidigit multiplication as well as area diagrams to represent multiplication in the elementary years. Starting in the middle grades, the distributive property is a regular part of students' mathematical work, especially as it pertains to rewriting math expressions that involve multiplication. The importance of understanding these mathematical properties cannot be overstated.

> *Distributive Property of Multiplication over Addition:* $a \times (b + c) = (a \times b) + (a \times c)$
>
> *Distributive Property of Multiplication over Subtraction:* $a \times (b - c) = (a \times b) - (a \times c)$

Children also grapple with other broad concepts about number operations. One of these ideas relates to the *identity property*; for instance, second-grade children understand that $0 + 3 = 3$ and $3 + 0 = 3$. They notice that when adding a number and zero, the number is unchanged. By the fourth grade, this idea is widely accepted by children, and they apply this property when working with different sets of numbers (natural, whole, and integers).

Zero is called the additive identity because when 0 is added to a number, the sum is simply the number. The number 1 has a similar role for multiplication. Students come to realize that when multiplying any number by 1, the product is the number, for example $4 \times 1 = 4$ and $1 \times 4 = 4$. We can use symbolic representations to express these different relationships succinctly; it is easier to read (and write) than trying to express these relationships in words. That is part of the power of algebra!

> *Additive Identity:* $a + 0 = 0 + a = a$ *for any number* a
>
> *Multiplicative Identity:* $a \times 1 = 1 \times a = a$ *for any number* a

As you can see, general properties of arithmetic surface early on, and then become accepted as students move through the elementary grades. Teachers not only address these concepts throughout the mathematics curriculum but their most important role may be to help students recognize the properties they are using to solve problems. Students are then in a better position to identify other problem situations in which a particular property applies. The next big idea that we address is that of equality.

The Equals Sign

In the previous section, we talked about several properties of numbers that emerge as you notice relationships among numbers when doing arithmetic. Each property describes equivalent ways to operate with numbers. The idea that there are perhaps many ways to express the same number is at the heart of the mathematical idea of *equivalence*. The equals sign is the symbol we use to indicate such equivalences. Consider how you would expect a second grader to solve the problem in figure 3.20. How about a sixth grader?

What number goes in the box?

$$8 + 4 = \Box + 5$$

Fig. 3.20. Number in the box problem

Children respond differently when working with the equals sign. For instance, many children, at various grade levels, initially decide that the number 12 should go in the box. Students might only pay attention to $8 + 4 = \Box$ and read the problem as "8 plus 4 equals blank." They think the equals sign means "to do something" with the numbers. So they do the computations to the left of the equals sign and write the result on the right. Some students might carry the computation further by adding the 5 to 12, that is, $8 + 4 + 5$, and then writing 17 to the right of the given equation. Children who solve the problem correctly recognize that the total on the left of the equals sign must be the same as the total on the right for the equation to be true. Thus, the number in the box should be 7.

Children may be confused or have incomplete notions about the equals sign for different reasons. They often solve problems and place their answers to the right of the equals sign, so young students come to view the equals sign as a signal to compute an answer. To avoid this misunderstanding, it is important that problems are not always presented with the equals sign to the right of the numbers. Most teachers are aware of this issue and take steps to promote a correct idea of the meaning of the equals sign. Varying the words and phrases used when reading and writing equations easily does this; for instance, instead of writing $9 + 7 = 16$, the teacher writes $16 = 9 + 7$. Students then come to realize that the equals sign is used to represent equivalent amounts (16 is the same amount as $9 + 7$). They begin to reason that the amounts on each side of the equals sign need to be the same for the equation to be true.

Looking again at figure 3.20, a child's incomplete ideas about the equals sign could be addressed another way by asking if $8 + 4 = 12 + 5$ is true. Most children will realize that $8 + 4$ is not the same amount as $12 + 5$ because $8 + 4$ is 12. If a student writes 12 in the box, the teacher wants them to realize that equation is false. To make the equation true, the student needs to find the number that when added to 5 is the same as $8 + 4$.

As students begin using symbols to represent the operations (typically as early as first grade), teachers have countless openings to emphasize that the equals sign actually means "the same amount as." Understanding the equals sign is an important development in algebraic thinking that can be nurtured in the earliest grades as children begin representing their ideas about numbers. Indeed, students must develop the ability to read and write equations. This skill is essential to communicating mathematical ideas.

Variables

What are variables? They are symbols, letters, or words used to represent one or more numbers, and are used in equations, formulas, inequalities, and in other instances for which a number is either known, unknown, or for which there are a range of values.

We have used variables to express relationships that are true for many, if not all, numbers. Using variables is a handy way to make general claims about numbers and operations, such as defining the commutative property of addition. Variables are also used to express relationships that exist for solutions to a given problem, such as the blocks and marbles problem Oliver and Selena solved. If b represents the number of blocks and m represents the number of marbles, then $b + m = 8$ for each possible combination of blocks and marbles. This equation states a relationship that is true for particular natural numbers b and m between 1 and 7, inclusive. If we know the number of blocks (b), we can automatically determine the number of marbles (m). Representing general mathematical ideas with variables is a major developmental step for students that typically occurs by fourth grade.

Children begin to use variables when they start describing general concepts with words or letters; for instance, a child may say, "Any number times 1 is that any number" to talk about 1 as the identity element for multiplication. Some children may even begin to use letters or symbols to describe this idea as $\square \times 1 = 1$. Even younger children use letters to represent ideas; for instance, one first grader used the letters p and n to write different combinations of pennies and nickels to show 11 cents as $2n + 1p$, $1n + 6p$, and $0n + 11p$.

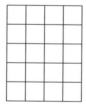

Fig. 3.21. A 4 × 5 rectangle with 20 unit squares

Older children use words to describe more complicated number relationships; for instance, a fourth grader might explain that the area of a rectangle with 20 unit squares, that is, 4 x 5, is the number of unit squares on the bottom row times the number of unit squares in one of the columns (fig. 3.21). Another student may simply explain the area as the length of the short side multiplied by the length of the long side. As students present these types of general concepts, they see how useful it can be to use variables to describe ideas more succinctly.

Variables: What's the Math?

Can you describe the meaning of each statement?

    i. $a(b + c) = ab + ac$

    ii. Area = length × height

    iii. $1 \leq b \leq 7$

In the first equation, variables are used to represent the distributive property of multiplication over addition, which is true for all numbers a, b, and c. In this case, the numbers a, b, and c can be any number. (In algebra, to avoid confusion with the variable x, the multiplication symbol is not used. Variables are placed next to each other to indicate multiplication.) In the second equation, words are used to define the formula for the area of a parallelogram. For any parallelogram, the area can be determined by multiplying its length by its height, so in this case, the values for the variables are limited to positive numbers given the context. This formula (or equation) is specific to parallelograms; it is not true when the lengths and heights are associated with another type of figure, such as a triangle. And in the third equation, the inequality is true only if b is a number between and including 1 and 7.

Things to Remember

- ◆ Children develop rudimentary ideas about numbers before prekindergarten.

- ◆ *Cardinality* is the number of items that can be counted in a group or *set*.

- ◆ The first strategies that children use to figure "how many" objects are in a set are *counting all, counting on,* and *counting back.*

- ◆ Number sense is the foundation of learning mathematics. It entails understanding how numbers are related, making connections among different sets of numbers, and using these number relationships to solve problems. We continue to build number sense throughout our lives.

- ◆ Understanding place value does not come "naturally." It is a challenging concept for children to learn.

- ◆ In the course of learning about numbers and operations, children encounter several mathematical properties of numbers, including the commutative property (of either addition or multiplication), the associative property (of either addition or multiplication), and the distributive property of multiplication over addition (or subtraction).

- ◆ The properties addressed in this chapter are fundamental to the later study of algebra.

Things to Do

- If you have very young children, look for chances to count objects, for example, the number of red cars while driving to the supermarket, the number of cupcakes in a package, and so on.

- Play "Close to 1,000" (page 58), adjusting the game as needed (e.g., "Close to 20" or "Close to 100"), or other place-value games with your children.

- If you didn't have time to solve the base-five problems on page 61, go back and try one or two. The practice will give you a better idea of what your child is mentally experiencing as he or she is learning about place value.

Resources

We have tried to address many key ideas in this chapter, but we can only touch upon the topics. Resources you may find helpful and informative are listed below.

For Adults

Guedj, Denis, and Lory Frankel. *Numbers: The Universal Language.* New York: Thames & Hudson, 1998.

For Children

Anno, Mitsumasa. *Anno's Counting Book.* New York: Crowell, 1977.

Clement, Rod. *Counting on Frank.* Milwaukee: Gareth Stevens Publishing, 1999.

Crews, Donald. *Ten Black Dots.* New York: Greenwillow Books, 1986.

Schwartz, David M., and Steven Kellogg. *How Much is a Million?* New York: Lothrop, Lee & Shepard Books, 1985.

More4U Online Resources

You can find a listing of additional helpful resources with links, including recommended games, by entering the access code on this book's title page at NCTM's More4U page (nctm.org/more4u).

Chapter
4

Working with Whole Number Operations

Children use number sense to solve addition, subtraction, multiplication, and division problems. Young children will use their understanding about numbers to perform one of these four operations on problems like 2 + 3, 15 – 5, 10 × 25, 30 ÷ 6. Addition, subtraction, multiplication, and division are the four fundamental operations. Helping students understand and reason sensibly with these operations is the crucial goal of the elementary school curriculum. How do children make sense of each operation? As we explore each one, you may recognize some methods and strategies that will be familiar, while others will be something that you never thought to consider. And you'll notice that many of the ideas that we have already addressed will continue to surface as we talk about how children make sense of the four operations.

Addition

Let's look at a fifth grader's method for adding 5,295 and 6,438 (fig. 4.1). At first glance, this student's work might seem inefficient or incorrect because he did not use the standard formula that you remember from school. However, if you look more carefully at his work, you will notice that the student first changed the problem to 5,300 + 6,433—that is, he took 5 from 6,438 and added it to 5,295 to change it to 5,300. Once he did that, he added like digits—the thousands, hundreds, tens, and ones. He drew on his understanding of addition and place value to correctly solve the problem.

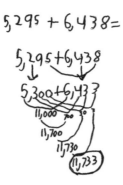

Fig. 4.1. A fifth grader's method for adding 5,295 + 6,438

Why does this strategy work? He made one of the numbers easier to work with by subtracting 5 from one number and adding it to the other, making 5,295 a multiple of 100 (5,300). Because he added to one number the 5 that he subtracted from the other, the answer is correct and no different than if he had used the standard formula.

How do children develop these types of strategies? When do they begin to use these clever and creative ways to add numbers? Some young children can count a small collection of objects accurately before they enter school; others can count large numbers by rote in correct order. To find the total number of objects in two collections—to add— six-year-olds usually need to count all the objects. When they find the total number of objects, they are beginning to explore the various facets of addition.

Adding Numbers Up to Twenty

Markus has 8 pieces of gum and Josiah gives him 5 more pieces of gum. How many pieces of gum does Markus have now?

As an adult, you don't need to calculate the answer, but for children who are just beginning to develop number sense, they might imagine Josiah giving Markus five more pieces of gum. To find the total pieces of gum, the child needs to count all of the pieces— the pieces that Markus has with the pieces that Josiah gave him. Somehow the child determines a way to add more to Markus's original amount.

The question above is an example of the most common type of addition situation that your children will encounter—*combining* (or *joining*). When children solve this type of problem, they determine the total number of objects in a "new" collection— the amount of the original collection together with the amount put into the original collection. To solve combining situations, a child must imagine an action such as giving or getting more objects and adding them to the original collection. For instance, "My friend has some objects and I am going to give him more objects," or "I have some objects and I am going to get some more objects."

To figure out the total, your child might physically add more pieces of gum to the original collection and then count all the pieces to come up with the new total in

Markus's collection. Alternatively, some students might count the pieces of gum in the original collection (8), count those to be added (5), and then count all the pieces, or others might start with the total number in the original collection (8) and count on (9, 10, … 13). In all these scenarios, children are trying to determine the new total amount in Markus's enlarged collection.

 DO YOU KNOW How to Talk about Addition?

"If I give you my peas, how many peas do you have now?" "How many pieces of candy do you have if I give you mine too?" When you ask these types of questions, you are asking your child to combine two collections in order to find the total of a new collection. Notice that these two questions are different from "How many peas are on your plate?" where a child only has to count the peas to find the number in one collection. By asking questions that require your child to combine two different collections, you are giving him or her the chance to explore addition ideas in familiar situations.

In chapter 3 we talked about how children build their understanding of numbers by exploring different combinations (or decompositions), for example, $5 = 2 + 3 = 4 + 1 = 0 + 5 = 3 + 2 = 1 + 4 = 5 + 0$. Combining and decomposing numbers are also natural ways for children to learn about addition.

Look again at Oliver's work (fig. 4.2) for the Blocks and Marbles problem first presented in chapter 3. Oliver, a first grader, wrote the various combinations of the two collections, each row showing different groups of marbles and blocks, resulting in a total of eight objects. To solve this problem, Oliver needed to stretch his thinking about addition to imagine a new collection made from two existing collections, adding the combinations of marbles and blocks to create a new group of eight toys. The smaller sets are composed of different types of objects, so the new set represents a more general collection of objects (toys). This type of addition problem is called a *part-whole situation*.

marbles	blocks
1	7
2	6
3	5
4	4
5	3
6	2
7	1

Fig. 4.2. Oliver makes different combinations of 8 using marbles and blocks.

If David has 5 red crayons and 4 blue crayons, how many crayons does David have that are either red or blue?

Again, to solve this problem, a child forms a new collection (red *and* blue crayons) by adding two different collections (the group of red crayons and the group of blue crayons) to find the total number of red and blue crayons in the new set. Just what are the differences between combining and part-whole addition situations? We summarize some of the differences in the chart below (fig. 4.3).

Combining Addition Situation	Part-Whole Addition Situation
Objects from one collection are put into another collection to make a new collection.	Objects from two different types of collections are put together to make a new collection.
The new collection has the same type of objects. The sum is the total of objects in the new collection. For example, more pieces of candy are added to a collection of candy pieces.	The new collection is a more general set of objects. The sum is the total of objects in the new collection. For example, a group of apples added to a group of oranges creates a collection of fruit.

Fig. 4.3. Combining and part-whole addition situations

The main differences between the two situations is that in combining problems, the collection to be added *into* the original involves some type of action (e.g., giving or getting more pieces of candy), and the total is made up of *like* objects. For part-whole situations, you do not perform an action to the original collection to find the total. You simply determine how many objects are in a new collection—a more general type of collection.

Adding Two- and Three-Digit Numbers

Building on those processes and skills they acquired adding numbers to twenty, children continue developing their number sense to solve two- and three-digit problems. Finding the total (also called the *sum*) can be difficult if a child does not progress to noncounting strategies for working with numbers up to twenty and beyond. Not surprisingly, addition and subtraction of two- and three-digit numbers are particularly challenging for children because as they are exploring the operations with these larger numbers, they are also wrestling with our place-value system. Using pictures or base-ten blocks can help children make sense of the numbers as they work to solve these types of problems.

Do you remember how you learned to add two-digit numbers? Did you follow a series of procedures that included "carrying"? But are there other ways that children might solve these problems? What would be the benefit of solving problems using different methods? We addressed these questions in the previous chapters, but as you think about the challenges that second and third graders experience when solving addition problems for two- and three-digit numbers, you begin to realize why it is so important for children to develop different approaches that make sense.

Let's take a look at a few examples of how children solved some two-digit problems using pictures of base-ten blocks.

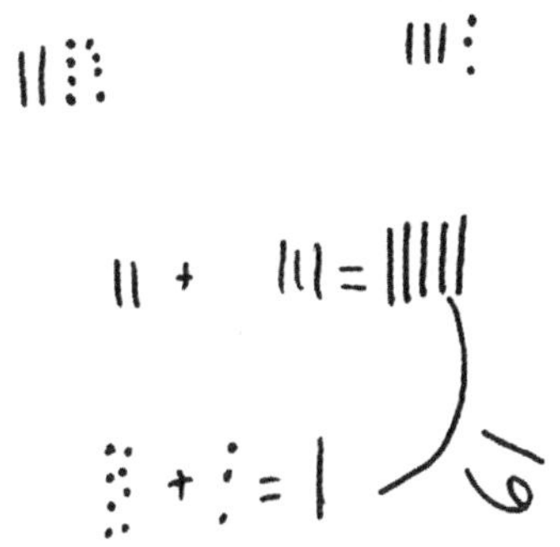

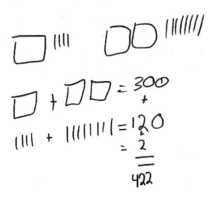

Fig. 4.4. Jamel's solution for 28 + 33 using pictures of base-ten blocks

In figure 4.4, Jamel drew pictures to represent 28 candies and 33 candies. He figured out how many tens (longs) and then how many ones (units) he had. He then added (regrouped) 10 ones to make another ten. Once he had regrouped his tens and ones, he added them to arrive at 61 for his answer. We can assume that it made more sense to him to first add the tens, then the ones, and then determine the total by adding the partial answers. Jamel seems to have a good understanding about how to add two-digit numbers using place-value ideas.

Jamel used a similar approach to solve 142 + 280 (fig. 4.5). He added the hundreds first (flats) and then the tens. He added these two partial answers and the two ones to arrive at his answer. Once again he started by adding from left to right instead of right to left when using the standard algorithm. Whether he counted all twelve longs by tens or mentally made another hundred (flat), he somehow determined he needed to add 120 to the 300 to have 420. Then he simply needed to add the 2 ones to get his answer. As his work on both problems illustrates, he drew on a self-invented method for adding ones, tens, and hundreds to determine his answers. His understanding about place value seems to have aided him in solving these addition problems.

Fig. 4.5. Jamel's solution for 142 + 280

DO YOU KNOW What the Standard Algorithm for Addition Is?

The standard algorithm for addition is as an important topic in today's classrooms as it was in yours. What is different is that it is only introduced *after* children have had ample time to develop an understanding of two- and three-digit number addition using their ideas about place value. Teachers introduce the algorithm as one of the efficient ways for children to keep track of their work. Let's look at the standard algorithm for 280 + 142 (fig. 4.6).

$$\begin{array}{r} {}^{1}280 \\ +\ 142 \\ \hline 422 \end{array}$$

Fig. 4.6. Finding the sum of 280 + 142 using the standard algorithm

Using the standard algorithm, the ones are added first, then the tens, and, last, the hundreds. You add 0 + 2 for a total of 2 ones, then 8 + 4 for a total of 12 tens. Because 10 tens is the same as 1 hundred, you *carry* a 1 into the hundreds column. Then adding the hundreds, you have 1 + 2 + 1 for a total of 4 hundreds. Recall this is the sum that Jamel computed with base-ten blocks (fig. 4.5). Notice that each part of the standard algorithm is represented in his drawing—he just computed the necessary sums in a slightly different order.

Older children also use different strategies and methods to solve more challenging addition situations. The fifth grader's work at the beginning of this section is an informative example of one way older children might solve an addition problem. Problem stories become more complex, but the types of addition situations remain the same. For instance, older children might encounter something similar to the following problem:

Smithton Elementary School has collected $5,295 for the school fundraiser. Several local companies donated $6,438. Did Smithton Elementary School meet its goal of $10,500?

The problem is slightly different from this section's opening one, but it is still a combining situation. Let's look at another student's solution method for adding 5,295 and 6,438 (fig. 4.7). See if you can figure out how this student's approach differs from the fifth grader's solution on page 74.

$$5{,}295 + 6{,}438 = \underline{11{,}733}$$

$$5{,}300 + 6{,}438 = 11{,}738$$

$$11{,}738 - 5 = 11{,}733$$

Fig. 4.7. Another student's solution for 5,295 + 6,438

You might have noticed that this student added 5 to 5,295 to work with 5,300 like the fifth grader, but unlike the first student, he then added the numbers to get a total of 11,738. Only at that point did he subtract the 5 he had added to 5,295. Recall that the first student also added 5 to 5,295 but immediately subtracted 5 from 6,438; then he added the thousands, hundreds, tens, and one separately to solve the problem. So students can and do develop different but equally skillful ways to solve problems.

 TAKING A CLOSER LOOK at Three-Digit Addition Methods

Three students add 839 + 472 (figs. 4.8, 4.9, and 4.10). They all use their knowledge of place value, adding the like digits separately, and then adding each of the partial answers (sums) to find the total. Although they don't use pictures of base-ten blocks, they use similar ideas to solve the problem.

$$8\,39 + 472 = 1{,}311$$

$$800 + 400 = 1{,}200$$
$$30 + 70 = 100 \quad \Big> 1{,}300$$
$$9 + 2 = 11 \quad \Big> 1{,}311$$

Fig. 4.8. Student 1's method for 839 + 472

$$839 + 472 = \underline{1{,}311}$$
$$800 + 400 = 12{,}00$$
$$30 + 70 = 1{,}00$$
$$9 + 2 = 11$$
$$1200 + 100 + 11 = 1{,}311$$

Fig. 4.9. Student 2's method for 839 + 472

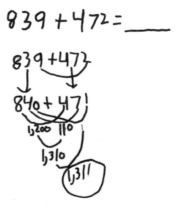

Fig. 4.10. Student 3's method for 839 + 472

Students 1 and 2 worked the problem in essentially the same way, but they recorded their ideas differently. Student 3 used a similar strategy but first altered the problem by subtracting 1 from 472 and adding 1 to 839; in this way, he made the numbers easier to work with (or "friendlier"). He also added the hundreds, tens, and ones separately to solve the problem, using lines to connect like values.

 As you can see, the methods and strategies that children develop when solving small-number addition problems can easily be applied and refined when they later work with larger numbers. This idea of connecting what is known to figure out new situations is fundamental to a child's progress in math.

Teachers foster this practice of connecting the known to the unknown in classrooms every day. By simply asking students to use ideas they already understand to solve problems, teachers help children tackle problems for which they may have no ready way to solve. Parents can reinforce this habit by asking the same kind of questions at home. You might ask, "Does it matter which numbers (ones, tens, or hundreds) we add first?" When asked these types of questions, children are prompted to consider options and choose methods that use number relationships they already know.

Addition: What's the Math?

Addition is the building block of the three other fundamental mathematical operations, subtraction, multiplication, and division. (You may wonder how this can be. As we examine the other operations, this relationship will become evident, but for the moment, an easy concept to consider is how repeated addition [adding the same number several times] forms the basis for multiplication, for example, 2 + 2 + 2 = 3 × 2.) It is the operation for which even prekindergarten children have an intuitive sense; they understand what it is to add "more" of something to something else (a set).

Whether you are solving combining or part-whole problems, you are finding the total number of objects in two sets that together form a new set (what mathematicians call the *union* of two sets). Students use this idea even when working on addition problems that are not associated with a "story" situation. Let's look at the very simple addition problem 5 + 8. The student work below illustrates how a child might think about this problem as the union of a set of 5 circles with a set of 8 squares, that is, as a part-whole situation (fig. 4.11).

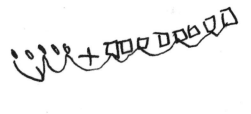

Fig. 4.11. A student's method for solving 5 + 8 as a part-whole situation

The student pictured the first set as 5 circles and the second set as 8 squares, and then determined the total number of objects (shapes) in the new set as 13.

When adding in part-whole situations, it is important that the two sets to be added together do not have any common elements, that is, the sets should be *disjoint*. To see why this matters, consider this scenario:

Two half-brothers, Sam and John, are each working on their individual family trees, but there are some family members that are on both trees. Sam has five people on his tree and John has eight.

First notice that this is a more complex part-whole situation. To determine the total number of family members on both trees, you cannot simply add five and eight. If you added the number of family members from the two trees, you would double count the people who appear on both trees. These two sets of family members are *not* disjoint. For this reason, the formal definition of addition requires the two sets involved be disjoint.

> **The operation of addition can be thought of as the number of objects obtained by forming the union of two disjoint sets. The total number of objects is the sum.**

This definition makes sense whether you are working with combining or part-whole situations. It can also be used to make sense of special circumstances, such as adding zero. You can think about 5 + 0, for example, as a group of five toys with zero toys added to it, resulting in five toys. For this reason, zero is called the *additive identity*. Adding zero objects does not change the number of objects in the collection.

The operation of addition can also be shown as moving along a number line. Natural numbers (page 52), the numbers we count with, are defined as any number that can be generated by repeatedly adding 1, starting with the number 1. So, when adding 1 on a number line, you move 1 unit to the right. To add 8, you move 8 units to the right. And to solve 5 + 8 using a number line, you first move 5 units (0 to 5), then move 8 units to the right of 5. You land on 13, the sum (fig. 4.12).

Fig. 4.12. Solving 5 + 8 using a number line

In fourth and fifth grades, children build on these ideas about addition using number lines when they work with decimals. Let's consider how you can use a number line to solve 0.2 + 0.5 (fig. 4.13). Here you are adding tenths of one unit instead of units of one. You first move from 0 to 0.2, which is exactly two tenths of one unit to the right of 0. Then you move five tenths to the right of 0.2.

Fig. 4.13. Solving 0.2 + 0.5 using a number line

Notice that this number line is marked every tenth of a unit, which allows you to easily move any number of tenths. In fact, because the addends are written in terms of the same decimal unit (tenths), the addition process is similar to the addition of natural numbers. This is a key point in the addition of fractions and decimals as well as other types of numbers. (We explore working with fractions and decimals in the next chapter.)

We mentioned earlier that addition is the building block of the other three operations, including subtraction. How can that be?

Subtraction

Sheneka's fourth-grade class was asked to solve the subtraction 2,703 – 1,476. When Sheneka's teacher, Ms. Harper, was grading her work, her first thought was to mark Sheneka's method as incorrect even though she had arrived at the correct answer. Ms. Harper then realized that not only was Sheneka's method correct, but it was also very logical. Take a look at figure 4.14 and see if you can figure out Sheneka's strategy for the problem.

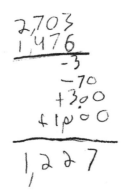

Fig. 4.14. Sheneka's strategy

Sheneka found the solution by first subtracting the ones, 6 from 3, and writing –3 on the first line underneath the problem. She then subtracted the tens, and wrote –70 on the second line; then 400 from 700 and 1,000 from 2,000, writing her partial answers as +300 and +1,000, respectively. She added all these partial answers to arrive at her result of 1,227.

Sheneka's strategy is fairly common among students who have a thorough understanding of numbers and place value and can think flexibly and logically to solve problems. Yet it is oftentimes not taught nor particularly valued by teachers or other adults. Sheneka was fortunate because her teacher recognized the perceptive thinking that she demonstrated in her work.

So how do students figure out these insightful and creative methods to solve subtraction problems? To answer this question, we must first look more closely at the different ways young children reason about subtraction.

Subtracting Numbers Up to Twenty

Prior to entering kindergarten, most children can tell the difference between *more* and *less* if two piles are obviously unequal in size, such as ten candies versus five pieces or eight candies compared to two candies, but if the piles are close in size, such as eight versus six candies, they are unable to point out the pile with more or less. The concept of subtraction is even more abstract for children. When they enter elementary school, most children have a more intuitive understanding about what it means to add than what it means to subtract. While very young children might be able to tell you which pile has more pieces of candy (assuming the candies are relatively the same size), most would find it difficult, if not impossible, to determine the difference between the number of candies in the two piles. By the end of kindergarten or during first grade, once children are comfortable adding one or two more to a given amount, they are ready to find the difference between two piles.

The most common type of subtraction situation that children encounter is *take away*. In take-away situations, objects are removed from the original number of objects (or *start number*). The part that is not removed, the number of objects that remain, is the *difference*. Children can and do act out these types of situations. They count out the original number of objects, remove the required number of those objects, and count the remaining objects to find the difference.

(As an aside, there are other types of subtraction [and addition] problems for which either the start numbers or the amount taken away [or added] may not be given in the problem. We do not address these different problem types here. For more information on this topic, see Carpenter and his colleagues' book, *Children's Mathematics: Cognitively Guided Instruction* [2nd ed.] in References at the back of the book.)

 DO YOU KNOW How to Talk about Subtraction?

Parents can help their children build an understanding of take-away subtraction by asking questions about daily situations that give them the chance to explore subtraction ideas in ways that make sense to them. For instance, you can ask your child, "What if you give me one of the pieces of candy in your pile? How many candies would you have left? How do you know?" "What if you give me two pieces of candy? Now how many pieces would you have?"

A different type of subtraction situation can be created if the context is changed slightly. For instance, what happens when two children compare their piles of candy? They match each candy from one pile with a piece from the second pile. If there are "leftover" pieces in one pile, the children can count them to determine the difference between the two piles of candy. They might talk about how many more or how many fewer pieces of candy one child has than the other. This situation is referred to as a *comparison subtraction situation*.

How are take-away and comparison subtraction situations different? In the take-away situation, the child removed pieces of candy from the original pile. In the second example, two children compared their piles of candy. They did not remove any pieces from their piles; instead, they matched pieces and then determined how many were left over. The two situations are quite different when you think about the children's actions in each. In the take-away situation, the child removed part of one set of objects; in the second, the two children compared two different sets of objects. Figure 4.15 summarizes these differences.

Take-Away Situation	Comparison Subtraction Situation
Objects from the original collection are removed to make a new collection. For example, I have some pieces of candy. I give some to you. How many pieces do I have now?	Objects in one collection are matched with the objects in another collection to determine which collection has more (or less). For example, I have some pieces of candy and you have some pieces of candy. How many more pieces of candy do you have than I have?
The *difference* is the amount that remains after a certain amount is removed.	The *difference* is the amount more or less one collection has than another.

Fig. 4.15. Take-away and comparison subtraction situations

Your friend Robert is going to give you 15 pieces of candy. If he has already given you 6 pieces of candy, how many more pieces of candy does he still need to give you?

This problem is neither a take-away situation (no candy is removed) nor is it a comparison subtraction situation (nothing is compared). It illustrates a third type of situation—missing-addend subtraction. The question calls for finding the difference between the amount needed and the amount already in hand. To find the difference, you subtract the two quantities. You can also find the difference by *adding* nine more pieces of candy. You may recall that in the example from chapter 2 (page 27), Mr. Allen's student actually used addition to solve the subtraction problem. Thinking about subtraction problems as missing-addend situations is one of the meaningful ways children begin to make connections between addition and subtraction.

These situations illustrate the various types of subtraction contexts that children encounter in their worlds. For children to adequately explore whole number subtraction, they must become competent in solving all three of these subtraction situations. As they do so, they also begin to make connections between addition and subtraction. For instance, as they study missing-addend situations, they can discover ways in which these two operations work hand in hand.

 TAKING A CLOSER LOOK at Early Elementary Children's Subtraction Methods

We begin our exploration with two simple take-away problems posed to first graders, the Balloon problem (TERC 2008) and the Blocks problem.

Sally has 15 balloons; she shares 7 with her friend. How many balloons does Sally have now?

Student 1 drew Sally and her friend and then pictured the 15 balloons by first drawing the 7 balloons that Sally gave to her friend, then drawing and counting the number of balloons she had left. She wrote numbers inside each balloon to count how many Sally had left (fig. 4.16).

Fig. 4.16. Student 1's method for 15 – 7

Sally has 11 blocks. She gives 4 of them to a friend. How many does she have left?

Sally has 7.

Fig. 4.17. Student 2's method for 11 – 4

Student 2 solved his problem using a different method than Student 1. He drew all 11 blocks first, and then crossed out 4 blocks to show the part that Sally gave to her friend. Then he circled the part that remained and wrote how many Sally had left underneath his drawing (fig. 4.17). Unlike Student 1, he did not write numbers for each cube to show how many were left.

By the third grade, students are solving more complicated comparison subtraction problems like the Trading Cards situation below (figs. 4.18 and 4.19).

Jack has collected 63 trading cards. He has 15 more cards than Marta. How many trading cards does Marta have?

$$63-10=53 \quad \boxed{63-15=48}$$
$$53-3=50$$
$$50-2=48$$

$$63-15=\boxed{48}$$
$$\overline{63-10=53}$$
$$53-5=\boxed{48}$$
$$\boxed{48 \text{ trading cards}}$$

| **Fig. 4.18. Student 3's method** | **Fig. 4.19. Student 4's method** |

How are the students' methods different? How are they similar? Student 3 used the fact that 15 = 10 + 3 + 2. By decomposing 15 in this way, she could easily subtract 10 from 63. She then subtracted 3 from 53, presumably because subtracting 3 would provide her with the friendly number 50 (a multiple of 10). She could then easily subtract 2 more from 50 to arrive at her answer of 48. Student 4 used a different fact: 15 = 10 + 5. He, too, first subtracted 10 from 63, but then subtracted 5 from 53 to arrive at his answer of 48. Both of these methods highlight how children can draw on their understanding of numbers (number sense) and decompose them to efficiently solve two-digit number problems.

None of these students used the standard method for subtraction, yet all arrived at the correct answer for their problems.

Subtracting Two- and Three-Digit Numbers

Children extend their ideas for take-away, comparison subtraction, and missing-addend situations when they work with larger numbers—numbers over 100; 1,000; 1,000,000; and so on. Here is a typical take-away situation posed to second-grade classes:

Rosa had a package of 100 balloons. She gave 30 balloons to her sister so that her sister could have a birthday party. How many balloons does Rosa have now?

To solve this problem, the student must somehow keep track of subtracting 30 from the collection of 100 balloons. She may decide to remove 10 balloons at a time by subtracting three groups of 10 from 100: 100 – 10 = 90, 90 – 10 = 80, and 80 – 10 = 70.

Another student might use connections to addition to solve the problem. He could explain that because he knows 30 + 70 = 100, then 100 – 30 must be 70. A third student might take a different addition approach. She could state that she knows that 50 + 50 = 100, and then explain that 50 – 30 = 20 and the remaining parts, 20 and 50, equal 70, so the answer is 70. Of course, students might also use the standard algorithm to solve the problem. To subtract 30 from 100, the student would need to rename 100 as 10 tens before taking away 3 tens. If the problem were 100 – 33, the student would also need to rename 1 ten as 10 ones before subtracting. Usually, if the student uses the standard algorithm, after renaming groups of tens and ones, she would likely move right to left, subtracting ones from ones, tens from tens, hundreds from hundreds, and so on.

Each of these methods for solving a take-away situation has its own merits. As a student develops new connections between the operations of addition and subtraction, his or her reasoning about take-away situations also expands and new solution methods are tried.

DO YOU KNOW What the Standard Algorithm for Subtraction Is?

Understanding the standard algorithm for subtraction can be quite challenging for young students. In fact, teachers see it as one of the major hurdles for their second graders. You may recall that when solving a problem like 58 – 29, you began from the right, realized that you did not have enough ones, and so you needed to "borrow" or what, nowadays, teachers refer to as *rename* one of your tens as 10 ones. These 10 ones are then added to the 8 ones to make 18. Now that you have 18 ones, you can easily subtract 9 from 18 to arrive at your partial answer of 9. Instead of subtracting 20 from 50, you will subtract 20 from 40 because you renamed one of your original tens as 10 ones. We write this set of procedures as follows (fig. 4.20):

$$\begin{array}{r} {}^{4}\!\!\not{5}\,{}^{1}\!\not{8} \\ -\,2\,9 \\ \hline 2\,9 \end{array}$$

Fig. 4.20. Finding the difference for 58 – 29 using the standard algorithm

Perhaps this is the only approach you were taught. You have seen in this discussion that children may decide to work from left to right to solve such a problem. Their methods are quite different, but they arrive at the same answer. So there are different approaches for working out this problem: some that require explicit use of place-value concepts and others that may only require children to use number relationships that they know (e.g., 58 – 30 = 28 and 28 + 1 = 29; "I needed to add one because I subtracted one too many").

If students are encouraged to think about a variety of methods, they can build a more robust view of subtraction as they connect related concepts between it and addition. Comparison subtraction and missing-addend situations also contribute to fostering these connections. As students solve these distinct types of subtraction problems, they can more fully develop their understanding of the operation and become more flexible when reasoning about subtraction situations.

TAKING A CLOSER LOOK at Fifth Graders' Subtraction Methods

The Wilson family is taking a road trip from Richmond, Virginia, to Lansing, Michigan. Lansing is 686 miles from Richmond. After the first day of travel, the Wilsons stopped in Pittsburgh, Pennsylvania, which is 349 miles from Richmond. How much farther do they need to travel to reach Lansing?

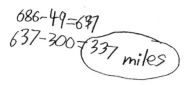

Fig. 4.21. Student 1's work

Student 1 used subtraction to solve the problem. She decomposed 349 (to make it easier to work with) into 300 and 49, and then subtracted 49 from 686 and 300 from 637 to arrive at her answer of 337 miles still to travel (fig. 4.21).

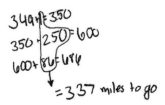

Fig. 4.22. Student 2's work

Student 2 used an adding-up strategy (page 28). He added 1 to 349 to make 350; then added 250, the amount needed to make 600. Next he added 86 to get 686 (total miles to be traveled). His answer is 1 + 250 + 86 = 337 miles to go (fig. 4.22).

2. 349 + 337 = 686

337 miles

Fig. 4.23. Student 3's work

Student 3 also used an adding-up strategy but took a slightly different approach than Student 2. She added 51 to 349 (miles traveled) to make 400 before adding what she needed to make 600 and then 686 (total miles to be traveled), respectively. Unlike the other students, she also used an open number line to keep track of the jumps, summing them up to the right of the number line (fig. 4.23).

Subtraction: What's the Math?

Subtraction reverses the process of addition. For example, if you add 5 to 11, the answer is 16. If you then subtract 5 from 16, the answer is 11. By adding and then subtracting the same number, the final answer is the number with which you started. For this reason, subtraction is referred to as the *inverse* of addition. On a number line, to add 5 to 11, first move from 0 to 11 to show "11" and then move 5 units to the right to show "plus 5," stopping at 16, the sum (fig. 4.24). To subtract 5 from 16, first move from 0 to 16 to show "16," and then move 5 units to the left; the result is 11 (fig. 4.25).

Fig. 4.24. Showing 11 + 5 = 16 on a number line

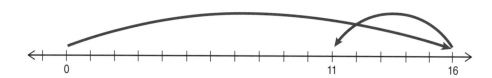

Fig. 4.25. Showing 16 – 5 = 11 on a number line

Does this reversing process work with other types of numbers? Yes, it does. It works for integers too. If you add 5 to –2, moving 5 units to the right of –2, you get 3 (fig. 4.26); subtracting 5 from 3 results in –2 (fig. 4.27).

Fig. 4.26. Showing –2 + 5 = 3 on a number line

Fig. 4.27. Showing 3 – 5 = –2 on a number line

The number line examples in figures 4.25 and 4.27 illustrate subtraction as "take away." In each case, an amount is removed from another amount by moving to the left. What does a comparison subtraction problem look like on the number line? Let's look at 16 – 5 again. To compare a collection of 16 objects with a collection of 5 objects on the number line, start by showing "16" and "5." The difference is represented by the distance between 16 and 5 on the number line (fig. 4.28).

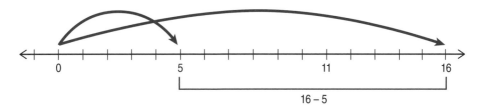

Fig. 4.28. Comparing 16 and 5 on a number line

In other words, the difference is the amount you add to 5 to get 16. So with either type of subtraction situation, you can think of subtraction as the inverse of addition.

> The operation of subtraction can be defined as follows: When *a* is subtracted from *b*, the result is the number *c*, only when *a* added to *c* is *b*. It is represented symbolically as *b* – *a* = *c* only when *c* + *a* = *b*. The result of subtraction is called the difference.

Notice that subtraction is defined *in terms of addition*. You can also prove that you have subtracted correctly when you have considered the corresponding addition problem; that is, there is always a corresponding addition statement that must be true in order for a subtraction statement to be true.

A special case arises when a number is subtracted from itself; the answer is always zero, for example, 3 – 3 = 0 and 8 – 8 = 0. Further, a number added to the opposite of that number is zero, that is, 3 + –3 = 0 and 8 + –8 = 0. We say that 3 and –3 (as well as 8 and –8) are *additive inverses* because when added, the result is zero.

Multiplication is typically the next operation that students learn about. How is that related to addition?

Multiplication

> Rachel, a third grader, remembers the moment she first discovered multiplication:
>
> "I was really little, like four years old, and I was standing near our fireplace at home. I was looking at my hands and holding two fingers out on each hand. You know, like the peace sign. I noticed that made four fingers altogether. So then I made four fingers on each hand, and that made a total of eight. I think I was too little to call it multiplication, but that's what it was. I was timesing by two."

Rachel's story illuminates early notions about multiplication, including the role of counting, addition, equal groups, and doubling—all very important as children explore multiplication. By holding up two fingers on each hand and then four, Rachel was connecting some facts about numbers: 2 + 2 = 4, 4 + 4 = 8, and so on.

In elementary school, many young students are excited about learning multiplication, a concept that to them seems reserved for "big kids." Children's first encounters with the idea of multiplication are usually repeated addition situations. These types of problems present an opening for children to connect familiar addition concepts with the idea of multiplication. When students begin to make sense of multiplication, it can be exhilarating and motivating for them. Often children will say, "It's so much faster."

Early Ideas about Multiplication

Kendra, a first grader, is solving the Pennies problem (TERC 2008):

There are four children sitting at the table. Each child has five pennies. How many pennies do they have together?

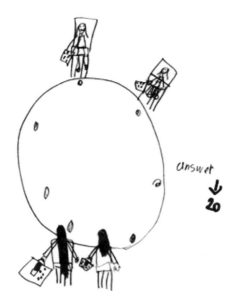

Fig. 4.29. Kendra's drawing for 4 × 5

She solves the problem by drawing a picture of the children sitting at the table; there are five coins next to each child (fig. 4.29). She then skip-counts by fives to arrive at her answer of 20 pennies, basically counting 4 fives, doing what is referred to as *repeated addition,* to determine the total number of pennies.

Jay also uses repeated addition to solve the problem, but he illustrates the situation differently (fig. 4.30):

20

Fig. 4.30. Jay's drawing for 4 × 5

He has drawn four groups with five pennies in each—*four groups of five.* He might have started with the leftmost group and counted individual pennies, or he might have added the 4 fives, 5 + 5 + 5 + 5.

Both of these illustrations reveal that students often use addition to solve basic multiplication problems. Notice they are not solving just any addition problem; they are repeatedly adding equal-size collections. Whether they count by ones, add up the collections, or recall the fact 4 × 5 by rote, the total number of pennies is 20, which is the product (answer) of 4 × 5. In this sense, children's early experiences with multiplication are related to special types of addition problems.

While students in elementary grades usually ask about writing 4 × 5 or 5 × 4 to match this type of problem, the crucial matter is that the child's representation relates to the numbers (factors) in the multiplication problem. Look again at figure 4.30. Where do you see four? Where do you see five? If the child can explain that the four is associated with the number of collections (people, in this case) and the five is associated with the number of items in each collection, it doesn't matter if he writes the statement as 4 × 5 or as 5 × 4.

 DO YOU KNOW How to Talk about Multiplication?

Daily life presents many repeated addition situations. Use them to help your children build an understanding of multiplication by asking questions about these situations; for example, grocery shopping for a child's favorite cereal might suggest a conversation like this: "When I was in the grocery store the other day I saw that the cereal you like cost $3 a box. How much would 4 boxes cost? How do you know?" "What if one box of cereal costs $3.50? How much would four cost?"

Let's consider a multiplication situation that is not repeated addition.

Luis has a red shirt, a yellow shirt, and a green shirt. He also has blue jeans and khaki pants. If Luis wants to make an outfit with a shirt and a pair of pants, how many different combinations are there?

How could students solve this problem? In this situation, the student must consider all the possible pairings between the objects in the two collections—pants and shirts. To do this, a child might start by making "copies" of the items, as second grader Selena did (fig. 4.31).

Fig. 4.31. Selena's method for combinations of three shirts and two pants

Notice that Selena draws the jeans three times and the khakis three times because there are three shirts. She counts a total of six possible combinations, the jeans with each of the three shirts and the khakis with each of the shirts. Each pairing (each outfit) is unique in some way.

By comparison, look at second grader Maria's solution for the same problem (fig. 4.32):

Fig. 4.32. Maria's solution for combinations of three shirts and two pants

The pairings are not represented by copies of the clothing as in Selena's solution, but by connecting lines. Maria connected each pair of pants to each of the shirts and labeled the lines "1st Day, 2nd Day," and so on. Maria also understands that each pair of pants must connect to each of the shirts. In fact, her strategy resembles a *tree diagram* (fig. 4.33).

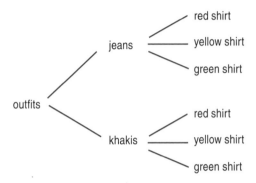

Fig. 4.33. Tree diagram for combinations of three shirts and two pants

Selena's and Maria's work represent a type of multiplication situation that uses the fundamental counting principle, which provides a way to count all the different combinations to determine the total number of choices. In our example, there are two choices for pants and three choices for shirts, so there are 2 x 3 unique combinations of pants and shirts. Interestingly, another way to organize the pairings of shirts and pants is to use a chart (fig. 4.34).

	Red Shirt	**Yellow Shirt**	**Green Shirt**
Jeans	*jeans, red shirt*	*jeans, yellow shirt*	*jeans, green shirt*
Khakis	*khakis, red shirt*	*khakis, yellow shirt*	*khakis, green shirt*

Fig. 4.34. Using a chart to organize the pants-shirt pairings

Making copies, connecting lines, using tree diagrams, or building charts or tables are all ways children across the elementary grades, and even beyond, make sense of problems involving the fundamental counting principle.

The principle also applies to more complex situations in which combinations are formed across three or more collections of objects.

John wants to order a pizza at a place that has 2 types of sauces, 3 crust options, and 10 possible toppings. John likes to have only one topping on his pizza. How many different options does he have?

One approach is to work through the sauce/crust pairings, of which there are 6; then pair the 10 toppings with each sauce/crust pairing to realize there are 60 options. Children might use drawings, charts, or other diagrams to help them find the solution.

In counting-principle situations, it is not necessary for the collections to be the same size, although they can be, but the objects must be linked across the collections. Only one object can be chosen from each collection at a time. This is a very different process from repeated addition.

Children deal with yet another type of multiplication situation as well.

Lily has a rectangular throw rug that is 4 feet wide and 6 feet long. How much floor space does that cover?

The student is being asked to find the area of the rug. She multiplies the dimensions to find it. But why would the student do this?

She might solve this problem by using grid paper to show the dimensions of the rug (fig. 4.35) and then explain that a rug 4 feet wide and 6 feet long is 6 rows of grid squares with 4 squares in each row. She then finds the total of 24 squares, either by counting or by using some other facts that she knows (e.g., $3 \times 4 = 12$, and there are two groups of 3×4). Because each square represents 1 foot × 1 foot, or 1 square foot, she knows that the area of the rug is 24 square feet.

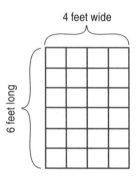

Fig. 4.35. The area model for multiplication

Another way to think about and represent this problem is by using *rectangular arrays*. A rectangular array is an arrangement of a set of objects into rows and columns. It is a tool for solving some multiplication problems. The picture of the rectangular rug in figure 4.35 can be thought of as a rectangular array with four columns and six rows.

Children may solve other multiplication situations using rectangular arrays too. Nick, a first grader, draws a rectangular array to solve the Pennies problem introduced on page 92.

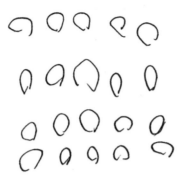

Fig. 4.36. Nick's array with four groups of five pennies

Nick arranges four groups with five pennies in each row (fig. 4.36)—similar to the array for the Rug problem—even though the Pennies problem has nothing to do with area or covering space. Each row represents the five pennies that each person has. The result, twenty pennies, is arranged in a rough rectangle. So arrays can be used to determine the total number of objects in a repeated addition situation, in this case, the number of pennies, by counting equal-size groups.

Rectangular arrays are an extremely useful model that children can use to solve simple or more complex multiplication situations. They can use arrays to easily keep track of the number of equal groups and calculate the total number of objects.

 READER'S CHALLENGE

Mr. White has to arrange 24 chairs in rows for an upcoming performance. Each row must have the same number of chairs. How many different arrangements can he make with the 24 chairs?

How would you go about solving this problem? Are 4 rows with 6 chairs in each the same as 6 rows with 4 chairs in each? How does an arrangement of 2 rows with 12 chairs compare to 4 rows with 6 chairs? How about 1 row with 24 chairs versus 12 rows with 2 chairs in each or 3 rows with 8 chairs in each versus 8 rows with 3 chairs in each? In this problem, you are invited to explore the different arrangements; that is, all possible rectangular arrays with 24 objects (chairs). Notice that you are limited to numbers of rows and chairs that are factors of 24. You should recognize that the reversing the number of rows and chairs (3 rows and 8 chairs in each versus 8 rows and 3 chairs in each) results in different arrangements. So thinking about the possible rectangular arrays invites you to explore factors along with the commutative property of multiplication.

Multiplying with Larger Numbers

How would you go about solving 28 × 12? Compare your method with this solution from fourth grader Natalie (fig. 4.37).

$$28 \times 10 = 280$$
$$28 \times 2 = 56$$
$$280 + 56 = 336$$

Fig. 4.37. Natalie's solution for 28 × 12

Natalie's first step was to decompose the factor 12 as 10 and 2 because those numbers are easier for her to work with. Then she multiplied 28 × 10, which is simple for her. Knowing she still needed two more groups of 28, she multiplied 28 × 2 and then added the partial products for her answer. By multiplying in steps, Natalie made what might have been an intimidating problem into something quite manageable.

Her classmate Alicia decomposed both factors by place value and used partial products to find her solution (fig. 4.38):

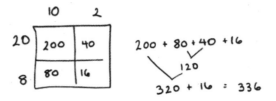

Fig. 4.38. Alicia's method for solving 28 × 12

The numbers 200, 80, 40, and 16 inside the rectangles are called partial products. Notice that this strategy looks a little bit like an area array for a 28 × 12 carpet! Although her picture is not drawn to scale, Alicia's method is efficient and accurate, as is Natalie's.

Multiplication: What's the Math?

Multiplication is frequently thought of as repeated addition, which involves finding the total for several sets with the same number of objects, illustrated earlier in this section and below with the Pennies problem.

Fig. 4.39. Jay's picture of 4 × 5

In Jay's drawing (fig. 4.39), there are four sets, each containing five pennies. Notice how 4 groups of 5 is the same as adding 5 to itself 4 times, 5 + 5 + 5 + 5, or 4 × 5. In a sense, multiplication is a shortcut for addition when one is adding a collection with the same number of objects over and over again. This idea of multiplication as repeated addition is the basis of its formal definition.

> The operation of multiplication involves adding *a* things *b* times. The result is called the product, and the numbers *a* and *b* are factors. The product of *a* and *b* can be written as $a \times b$, $a \cdot b$, $(a)(b)$, or ab.

Mathematically, there are several interesting consequences to this definition. First, when one or both factors is zero, the resulting product is always zero. We can apply the definition to illustrate this fact. Consider a group of zero items added *b* times. We could write this as follows:

$$\underbrace{0 + 0 + 0 + 0 + \ldots + 0}_{b \text{ times}}$$

No matter how many times zero is added to itself, the result will be zero. Similarly, we might imagine adding five to itself exactly zero times. But adding zero of any amount is simply zero. Therefore, *any product that has zero as a factor is zero.*

We also can use this definition for multiplication as repeated addition to demonstrate the fact that every counting number can be represented as a factor of one and the number itself. For example, if a group with one item is added *b* times, the result is the following:

$$\underbrace{1 + 1 + 1 + 1 + \ldots + 1}_{b \text{ times}}$$

This example also illustrates that multiplying $b \times 1$ is the same as counting by ones *b* times. The result is *b*. Likewise, if a group of *b* items is added exactly once, the result is *b*. Thus $b \times 1 = b$ and $1 \times b = b$. Because of this result, the number 1 is called the *multiplicative identity.*

Look at figure 4.40 and determine how many caterpillars are displayed.

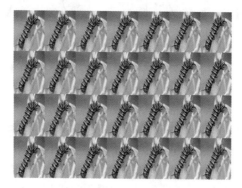

Fig. 4.40. Array of caterpillars

This picture is an array with four rows of seven caterpillars (4 x 7). You probably did not count the caterpillars by ones, but you might have thought about a smaller part of the array. In fact, there are several ways you could focus on smaller portions. For example, you might have noticed that there are fourteen caterpillars in the top two rows, and then another fourteen in the bottom two rows. If you thought about the picture in this way, you applied the *distributive property of multiplication over addition*. Mathematically, you determined that 4 x 7 = (2 + 2) x 7 = 2 x 7 + 2 x 7.

DO YOU KNOW What the Standard Algorithm for Multiplication Is?

The distributive property of multiplication over addition is a fundamental idea behind algorithms for multiplication. Consider the multiplication problem 23 x 18. How would you determine the product? If you are like many adults, you would use the traditional algorithm. Your work might look like figure 4.41:

$$
\begin{array}{r}
\overset{2}{2}3 \\
\times\ 18 \\
\hline
^{1}184 \\
230 \\
\hline
414
\end{array}
$$

Fig. 4.41. Finding the product of 23 x 18 using the standard algorithm

Another way to represent (and think about) the product is to create a rectangular array with 23 columns and 18 rows (fig. 4.42). The product is the total number of unit squares in the rectangle. You probably would not count all the squares to determine the total. It is more efficient to examine smaller portions and then add them together. The traditional algorithm can be justified by using this approach. Look at the portions marked below and then compare them to the calculations involved using the standard method. Look familiar?

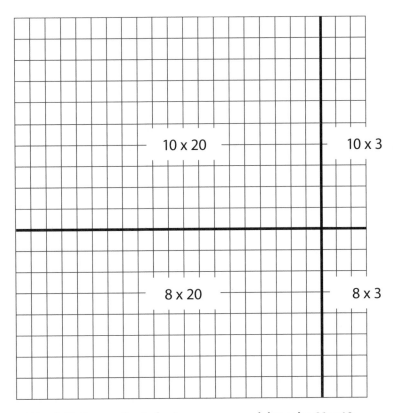

Fig. 4.42. One method of using an array model to solve 23 × 18

In the traditional U.S. algorithm, the 184 is the product of 8 × (20 + 3) or 8 × 20 + 8 × 3. The 230 is the product of 10 × (20 + 3), or 10 × 20 + 10 × 3. So the method you have probably used for years is actually the result of applying the distributive property of multiplication over addition. Notice that your answer, 414, is the result of adding 184 and 230, or 160 + 24 + 200 + 30, all parts of the array.

You may also notice that ideas about place value are behind this approach. The student needs to multiply the value of a digit by the value of each of the other digits. In fact, children using an array model are likely to decompose factors by place value. For example, look again at Alicia's method for solving 28 × 12 (fig. 4.38). She broke up the number 28 into 20 and 8, and then broke up 12 into 10 and 2. She is harnessing her place-value understanding to make easier subproblems: 20 × 2, 8 × 10, and so on. Notice that almost all her partial answers or partial products (the products inside the boxes) have a zero in the ones place.

Only the result of 2 × 8, which is 16, does not end in a zero. Alicia knows that her final step is to add 200, 80, 40, and 16, and for her, those numbers are not too difficult to add. By decomposing the factors by place value, she has turned what might be a difficult problem into a more manageable one. She has done this—at least in part—through making sense of place value.

Division

Children begin to develop understanding of division with whole numbers as they explore two types of division situations, *sharing* and *repeated subtraction*. To solve problems involving these types of situations, children need to find the unknown factor of a multiplication number sentence. Remember that multiplication can be thought of as repeated addition, in which a number of same-size collections (or groups) are added together. The product is the total amount. In sharing division situations, the number of groups is known, but the size of the group is unknown. The opposite is true of repeated-subtraction division situations in which the size of the group is known, but the number of groups is unknown. As with the other operations, children use varying physical actions when solving these types of division situations.

Zoe has a bag of bubble gum that she wants to give away to 3 friends so that each friend receives the same amount of gum. If she has 12 pieces of bubble gum, how many pieces of gum will each friend receive?

Children in second and third grade often solve sharing problems like this by first counting out twelve objects to represent the bubble gum. To distribute the gum, younger children might move blocks one at a time to make three separate piles, representing the amount each of the three friends will receive. This process is much like dealing cards. Older children might solve the problem by distributing larger chunks, two objects (or more), at a time into each pile. In both cases, when there are no objects left to distribute, children determine the solution by counting the number of objects in each pile. In this instance, children determine that each friend gets four pieces of bubble gum. (Notice that we can also refer to the solution as the number of pieces of gum per friend—what we call a *rate*.)

Now let's look at a related problem that is a repeated-subtraction division situation:

Zoe has 12 pieces of bubble gum that she wants to give away to some of her friends. She wants to make sure that each friend gets 4 pieces of gum to last over the weekend. How many friends will receive bubble gum from Zoe?

Here the number of pieces of gum each friend will get is known (four pieces). The student must figure out how many friends will receive bubble gum. The child begins solving this problem the same way as before; he counts out twelve objects. However, in this case he removes four blocks at a time, creating piles of four to represent each friend who will receive gum. When the child cannot make any more piles of four, he then counts the number of piles he has made. In this case, the child determines that three friends will receive gum.

 DO YOU KNOW How to Talk about Division?

Parents can help their children build an understanding of division by asking questions about daily life experiences that are also repeated subtraction situations; for instance, a parent may say, "I bought a package with 36 pieces of candy in it for party favors. How many friends can you invite to your party if you want to give each friend 6 pieces of candy in their goody bags?" "What if you only gave each friend 3 pieces of candy?" "How do you know?" "What if you wanted to give each friend 10 pieces of candy? Is that possible?"

Both situations are related. There are always twelve pieces of gum, but in the sharing division situation, the child determines "four pieces of gum per friend" to solve the problem while in the repeated-subtraction instance, he determines that "three friends" receive gum. One of the two factors is missing in each situation. For this reason, division is often thought of as a method for determining the missing factor in a related multiplication problem.

 TAKING A CLOSER LOOK at Division with Whole Numbers

Mark has 15 trading cards to give away to 3 of his friends. How many cards will each friend receive, assuming that he gives each friend the same number of cards? Use a diagram to support your solution.

Student 1, a fourth grader, solved the problem by distributing cards to each friend (fig. 4.43). She appeared to give each friend one card, one at a time, until all fifteen cards were distributed. Notice the double counting she used to show that each friend receives five cards.

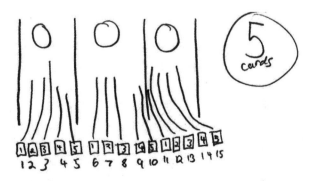

Fig. 4.43. Student 1's solution for 15 ÷ 3

Student 2 appears to have taken a similar approach (fig. 4.44). Although organized differently, his diagram also shows that each friend receives five cards. By giving five cards to each friend, he distributes all fifteen cards.

Fig. 4.44. Student 2's solution for 15 ÷ 5

Student 3's drawing is not as detailed (fig. 4.45). It is less clear how she might have worked through this problem. Perhaps she knew that 15 ÷ 3 = 5 and drew her diagram to illustrate that fact, or counted the number of groups of five once she made each group.

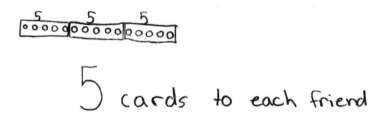

Fig. 4.45. Student 3's solution for 15 ÷ 3

If the numbers in the sharing gum situation are changed slightly, there could be extra pieces of gum left over, or a *remainder*. For example, a child shares thirteen pieces of gum with three friends, but then he has to decide what to do with the extra piece after distributing four pieces to each friend! Younger children may decide to give the extra piece to a parent—a reasonable suggestion. Older children might consider the fractional part that each friend would receive. Of course, some types of problems require children to consider other ways of handling what is left over. Let's look at a different repeated-subtraction situation. How might a student solve this problem? Will the student handle the remainder issue sensibly?

There are 34 people who are taking a field trip in some minibuses. Each minibus holds 8 passengers. How many minibuses will they need?

Ellen, a fourth grader, did deal with the remainder when she solved the problem. She determined that she needed an additional bus to carry the remaining passengers. Figure 4.46 shows Ellen's work. Notice that each time she counted a bus she also appears to be counting groups of eight. Additionally she shows the remainder as part of a bus. Her fifth bus seems to represent part of a group of eight as well as a whole bus, given she decided that five buses are needed.

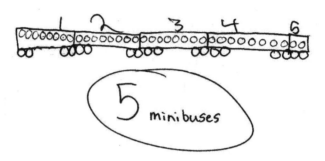

Fig. 4.46. Ellen's work on the minibus problem

 DO YOU KNOW What the Standard Algorithm for Division Is?

Working with division situations is tricky business. Oftentimes children solve division problems using addition, subtraction, or multiplication, requiring them to draw on understandings of all three operations, making division quite complex. The traditional algorithm (or long division) is a case in point. How would you solve $1{,}450 \div 120$? Basically, you need to determine how many groups of 120 are contained in 1,450. Because $12 \times 120 = 1{,}440$, you determine there are 12 groups of 120. You then subtract 1,440 (the product of 12×120) from 1,450 to find there are 10 left over. Because 10 is less than 120, the divisor, you cannot repeat this process again. So the answer, or quotient, is 12 remainder 10 or $12^{10}/_{120}$ (or $12^{1}/_{12}$).

Students in today's classrooms often use a variation of long division (fig. 4.47). The student recognizes that 10 groups of 120 can "fit into" 1,450 because 10×120 is 1,200. After subtracting 1,200 from 1,450 and getting 250, the student realizes 2 more groups of 120 can fit. Because 2×120 is 240, that leaves 10 left over. So the student's answer to the problem is also 12 remainder 10.

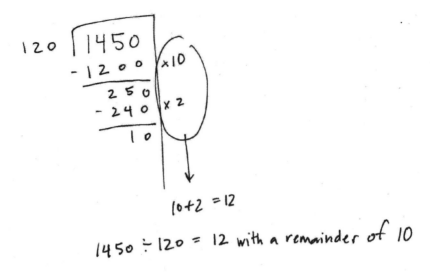

Fig. 4.47. Dividing 1450 ÷ 120 using a variation of the standard algorithm

Division: What's the Math?

In many ways, a division statement is just another way of stating a multiplicative relationship. Whether you are working with a sharing or a repeated subtraction situation, solving a division problem is about finding a missing factor of a multiplication problem. For example, if you want to determine $32 \div 8$, you can simply think about the following question, "What number, when multiplied by 8, results in a product of 32?" You know that $32 \div 8 = 4$ because $8 \times 4 = 32$.

Another way of thinking about the relationship between multiplication and division is that division reverses (or undoes) the process of multiplying. Formally, we refer to division as the *inverse of multiplication*. The definition of division makes this connection clear by building on the idea of finding the missing factor. In this case, the number c is the missing factor.

> The number a divided by the non-zero number b is the number c only when c multiplied by b is a. The definition can be written symbolically as $a \div b = c$ for $b \neq 0$ only when $c \times b = a$.

We say that a is the dividend, b is the divisor, and c is the quotient. For example, we know that $20 \div 4 = 5$ because $5 \times 4 = 20$. Also, because $4 \times 5 = 20$, we know that $20 \div 5 = 4$.

Children use this definition to justify special circumstances that arise in the context of division. For instance, let's see what happens when you try to divide by zero where $a = 1$ and $b = 0$. According to the definition of division, $1 \div 0 = c$ only when $c \times 0 = 1$. (Note that you are temporarily abandoning the requirement that the divisor [*b*] be nonzero so you can understand this part of the definition.) Because you know that any number multiplied by zero is zero, there is no such number *c* that can be multiplied by zero and result in the number 1 (or any other nonzero number for that matter). So there is no number that is the quotient (*c*) of $1 \div 0$. In general, division by zero is *undefined,* and now you see why this is the case. You might try exploring what happens when $a = 0$ and $b = 1$ or when $a = 0$ and $b = 0$. (For the solutions and explanations, see Appendix B, page 195.)

Another special circumstance arises when $a = 1$. In this case we have $1 \div b = c$ and $c \times b = 1$. We say that *c* is the *multiplicative inverse* of *b* and that *b* is the multiplicative inverse of *c*. Multiplicative inverses for multiplication and division are somewhat similar to additive inverses for addition and subtraction. Recall that when additive inverses are added together, the result is zero, which is the additive identity ($+3 + -3 = 0$). Multiplicative inverses are special pairs of numbers that when multiplied one by the other, their product is always one—the *multiplicative identity.* And, because multiplication is *commutative,* you can multiply these numbers in either order and still get one.

Additionally, in order to make full use of this new idea, think of the multiplicative inverse of the whole number *a* as $1/a$, and when the whole number *a* is multiplied by the fraction $1/a$, the resulting product is always the multiplicative identity (1); for example, $2 \times \frac{1}{2} = 1$ and $\frac{1}{2} \times 2 = 1$, so the numbers 2 and $\frac{1}{2}$ are multiplicative inverses. For this reason, concepts about division naturally lead to extending ideas about numbers to include the rational numbers—fractions and decimals (chapter 5).

Things to Remember

- The four fundamental operations are addition, subtraction, multiplication, and division.

- Addition is the building block of subtraction, multiplication, and division.

- Children explore and investigate these operations to figure out how they work and what they mean, so that they can make sense of different methods, including the standard algorithms.

- Children use what they know about math and the operations to figure out solutions to new mathematical situations.

- By solving problems, children discover how the operations are related and how they can be used interchangeably to find solutions to mathematical tasks.

- Children display the ability to use place value in flexible ways to compute.

- A primary goal of the elementary mathematics curriculum is to enable children to develop an understanding of and make connections among the four operations with whole numbers. Children who have a thorough understanding of the operations will more easily build on this knowledge as they explore decimals and fractions.

Things to Do

- Be sure to check out the Do You Know How to Talk About boxes in this chapter for simple ways your child can use the operations in daily situations.

- Impromptu conversations about classwork or homework are your chance to get a better understanding of your child's thinking about the whole number operations.

- Seek out entertaining picture books and storybooks with math themes. *School Library Journal* (http://www.slj.com) has a wealth of material on all types of children's books from prekindergarten through high school levels. Type in "math themed books" for a list of *SLJ* articles and suggestions.

- Throughout the school year, ask your child's teacher about what expectations she or he has for children's learning about addition, subtraction, multiplication, and division.

Resources

We have tried to address many key ideas in this chapter, but we can only touch upon the topics. Additional resources you may find helpful and informative are listed below.

For Children

Carle, Eric. *Rooster's Off to See the World*. Natick, Mass.: Picture Book Studio, 1987.

Hutchins, Pat. *The Doorbell Rang*. New York: Greenwillow Books, 1986.

Long, Lynette. *Domino Addition*. Watertown, Mass.: Charlesbridge, 1996.

Tang, Greg, and Harry Briggs. *The Grapes of Math: Mind Stretching Math Riddles*. New York: Scholastic, 2001.

More4U Online Resources

You can find a listing of additional helpful resources with links, including recommended games, by entering the access code on the title page of this book at NCTM's More4U page (nctm.org/more4u).

Understanding Fractions and Decimals

Elsa, a four-year-old, when asked to explain what one-half means, said that one-half was when you share the pizza so that each person gets half of the pizza. She also drew a diagram to illustrate her thinking (fig. 5.1).

Fig 5.1. Elsa's diagram showing halves of a pizza

Elsa drew a circle to represent the pizza and then made a line to divide the pizza into halves. Although she did not make the two halves the same size, she demonstrates some understanding about the meaning of one-half—the whole is divided into two parts. Her diagram is a nice example of how young children might represent one-half. Elsa's work also illustrates that young children learn about fractions from everyday experiences before they enter school. They may know intuitively what it means to share one-half or one-third of a candy bar or pizza, for instance.

During second and third grades, children begin to develop more formal ideas about fractions using pictures, numbers, and words. As Elsa's solution illustrates, children's experiences of sharing objects, such as food and toys, help make basic ideas associated with fractions more accessible to them. During the elementary school years, students explore these intuitive understandings by drawing pictures to represent a whole amount (like a brownie) that has been divided into a certain number of equal parts. Children also

109

use concrete objects, like a set of blocks, to represent a whole amount and equal parts of that whole. Thus, a big part of early fraction instruction involves representing a fraction as *parts of a whole* with either diagrams or physical materials. And by the upper grades, children solve more challenging problems with fractions.

Fractions are just one area of the rational number landscape, which is quite broad and can be overwhelming for children and adults alike. It includes fractions, decimals, ratios, and rates of change, to name just a few. Children are usually formally introduced to fractions in second or third grade, and continue working with them through the remainder of their mathematics education.

Early Ideas about Fractions: Parts of a Whole

Let's consider how Molly, a fourth grader, used parts-of-a-whole ideas to explain the meaning of one-half.

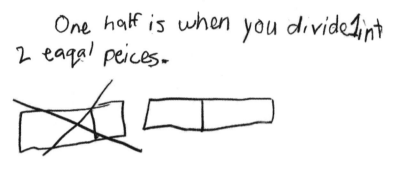

Fig. 5.2. Molly's diagram showing $^1/_2$

In her picture (fig. 5.2), she first drew a rectangle that is an incorrect representation for one-half (left rectangle), and then crossed it out. She had intentionally made two pieces that were not equal. She then drew a second rectangle and divided it into two equal parts ("eaqal peices"). When children like Molly begin to understand the meaning of fractions, they realize that to represent fractions, one must divide the whole into parts so that each part is the same amount. We infer from Molly's explanation that she understood that the whole could be divided into two equal parts and that each of those parts was called one-half. When you compare Molly's drawing with Elsa's on page 109, you notice that Molly has a more complete understanding of one-half; each one-half piece is one of the two equal parts that make up the whole. Elsa is just beginning to develop her parts-of-a-whole understanding about fractions.

Children use other representations to show fractions. Molly, for instance, also showed one-half using a number line (fig. 5.3).

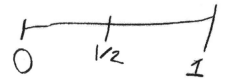

Fig. 5.3. Molly uses a number line to show ¹/₂.

She marked ¹/₂ on the number line about halfway between 0 and 1. Again, she seemed to think about one-half as one of two equal "segments" (parts).

Take a moment and draw a picture for the fraction ²/₃. Did you draw a circle and color in two of three parts? At one time, the typical way to teach fractions was by drawing a circle to represent the whole. In today's classroom, your children are encouraged to use rectangles because they are much easier to subdivide into equal pieces. Picturing fractions this way makes it easier for children to work with and think about their values when they begin exploring these new numbers.

Children also use objects to represent fractions, but this can be more challenging for them. For example, a third grader might have a set of twelve blocks and be asked to show two-thirds of the blocks. To do so, the child first needs to determine how many blocks make up one-third of the set. To show this amount, the student might distribute the blocks, one at a time, into three different groups until all the blocks have been distributed (fig. 5.4).

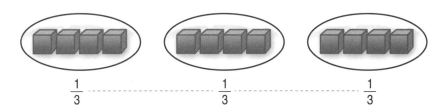

Fig. 5.4. Twelve blocks arranged into groups of one-third

Because the student has three groups, each with the same number of blocks, she knows that each group represents one-third of the set of blocks, and two of those groups represent two-thirds. To show two-thirds of the twelve blocks, she combines two groups to make a group with eight blocks. The group of eight is two-thirds of the set of twelve blocks (fig. 5.5).

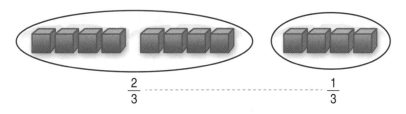

Fig. 5.5. Two-thirds and one-third of twelve blocks

✳ DO YOU KNOW Why Children Use Regions for Fractions?

Because it can be more difficult to represent fractions with sets of objects, teachers encourage children to use *regions,* or rectangles, before working with objects. A child can easily represent two-thirds once she has subdivided a rectangle into three equal parts. To show two-thirds of a number of objects as in our example in figure 5.5, the child needs to distribute the objects to make three equal groups. But when using objects, children can sometimes get confused about what represents the whole. Is the whole each of the individual cubes, or is it the entire collection of cubes? Although these are important ideas for children to grapple with, when they are first learning about fractions in third grade, teachers often encourage them to use rectangles, circles, or some other type of region to make sense of these new types of numbers.

Fig. 5.6. Sarah represents $^2/_3$ of the milk jug.

Sarah's picture of two-thirds is another example of how children use regions to represent fractions (fig. 5.6). In her diagram, Sarah, a fourth grader, illustrates how two-thirds is two of three equal parts of the whole jug of milk; she divided the milk carton into three equal parts and then shaded two of those parts.

Mary, another fourth grader, represented two-thirds using both objects and regions (rectangles; fig. 5.7). Notice that she used collections of three objects ("math cards," circles, and balloons) and she drew regions (the cake and what appears to be a piece of wood to be sawed) and subdivided the regions into three equal parts. What Mary as well as Sarah seem to understand is that two-thirds is two parts of a whole that is made up of three equal parts. They can represent these parts either with a collection of objects (e.g., cards, circles, or balloons) or by using the area of a specific region (e.g., containers, cake, or rectangles).

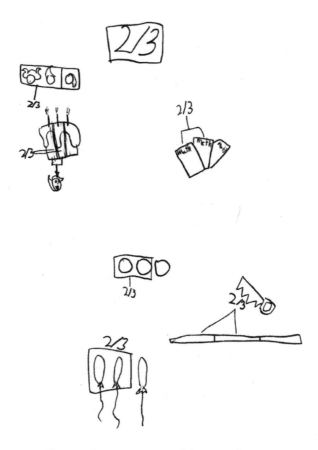

Fig. 5.7. Mary represents ²/₃ in several ways.

 DO YOU KNOW What the Elements of a Fraction Are?

One of the most common ways to think about a fraction is by considering its three key elements. You may remember from your school experiences that the number written below the fraction bar—representing the total number of equal parts in the whole—is called the *denominator* of the fraction. And the number written above the fraction bar—representing the number of parts to be considered—is called the *numerator*. And the resulting fraction represents *a number*.

When a child uses parts-of-a-whole ideas to show other fractions like ⁴/₉, he might arrange a collection of 4 red chips and 5 blue chips so that 4 of the 9 chips are red, or he might divide a rectangle (region) into 9 equal parts and color in 4 of them.

Whether children use numbers, words, or different kinds of models to show fractions, it is important that they realize that the parts are the same amount and that each of the parts represents a fractional amount of the whole. When students think about fractions in this way, they are using a *parts-of-a-whole interpretation*.

 READER'S CHALLENGE

How would you picture ⁴/₃ and ⁶/₂ using a parts-of-a-whole interpretation?

Does it concern you that the numerator of each fraction is larger than the denominator? It is tempting to think of fractions solely in terms of numbers between zero and one. However, there are numbers between one and two (e.g., ³/₂), two and three (e.g., 2¹/₄), and so on that can be represented with fractions. Because these numbers are between natural numbers, they can also be written as *mixed numbers* (1¹/₂ and 2³/₄) because they are composed of a natural number and a fraction between 0 and 1. You can also think about mixed numbers additively. For instance, 1¹/₂ can also be written as 1 + ¹/₂. Similarly, 2³/₄ can be written as 2 + ³/₄. Thinking about mixed numbers additively is useful for children as they begin making sense of addition and subtraction problems involving these numbers. And fractions like ⁴/₃ can be represented as the mixed number 1¹/₃. Four-thirds are four parts from two wholes, where each whole has three equal parts. Thus, the resulting picture would show one whole plus one-third of another whole. In general, any fraction in which the numerator is larger than the denominator represents a number larger than one.

Some fractions, such as ⁶/₂, are simply another way to write whole numbers. Using the parts-of-a-whole interpretation of fractions, ⁶/₂ means that the whole is divided into two equal pieces, or halves, and there are six of these one-half pieces. To make a diagram of this fraction, we could make three rectangles that are divided into halves. To depict the fraction, we label each of the whole rectangles as 1 and each part as ¹/₂. To show 6 parts, we shade all six halves of the rectangles. These six shaded parts also represent three whole rectangles. This is one possible way to explain why ⁶/₂ = 3 makes sense.

It is important for children to learn about different fractions using parts-of-a whole interpretation. They also use this interpretation to compare fractions and find equivalent fractions—two other ways they develop fraction number sense.

As an aside, there are also other ways to think about fractions. For instance, ²/₃ also means 2 ÷ 3—a division interpretation. Or ²/₃ can be represented as ¹/₃ x 2—an idea that is helpful when fifth graders explore multiplication with fractions. So your child will continue to build on these early ideas about fractions as they learn how to add, subtract, multiply, and divide fractions—a topic we address in the next chapter.

Strategies for Comparing and Ordering Fractions

Second and third graders first explore fractions such as $1/_2$, $1/_4$, and $1/_8$, followed by working with $1/_3$ and $1/_6$ to become familiar with these new numbers. Notice that each of these fractions has a numerator of 1. We refer to these types of fractions with a numerator of 1 as *unit fractions*. Typically, children have many experiences working with unit fractions before working with other types because they are the foundation for building understanding of other fractions.

One of the strategies children naturally use when exploring unit fractions is a *halving* strategy. Suppose a child wants to show one-fourth of a candy bar. To find one-fourth, she could divide each one-half into two equal parts. By cutting one-half of a candy bar into two equal parts, the whole candy bar now has four equal parts—fourths. Children also use a similar approach to show one-sixth by halving each one-third of a pizza into two equal parts. In this case, the whole pizza is made up of six equal parts or slices, each one-sixth of the whole pizza. Using a halving strategy, students can find different fractions that are half of the original fraction. And they can use unit fractions to represent other fraction numbers such as $2/_4$ as two $1/_4$ pieces, $3/_4$ as three $1/_4$ pieces, $5/_8$ as five $1/_8$ pieces, and so on. So working with unit fractions is a useful way for children to begin exploring how fractions are related.

Fourth and fifth graders often use a halving strategy to represent other unit fractions such as eighths, tenths, and twelfths. They also explore other less "friendly" unit fractions such as fifths, sevenths, and ninths.

When children investigate how different fractions are related, they are building an understanding of fractions as numbers. One of the important ways they do this is through comparing and ordering fractions—which fraction is larger or smaller. Recall that when children learn about whole numbers, they need to understand how numbers are related to each another. They need to have similar types of experiences looking into the relative magnitude of different fractions.

Children also use other strategies to compare fractions, particularly when using parts-of-a-whole interpretations, to determine how fractions with different denominators are related. As an example, take a moment and determine which fraction is larger, $2/_3$ or $2/_5$. Did you use what you know about the denominators to figure it out? Perhaps you found a common denominator, such as 15, for both fractions, and used this information to find the equivalent fractions $10/_{15}$ and $6/_{15}$, respectively. Then it is easy to see that $10/_{15}$ is larger, so $2/_3$ is larger than $2/_5$. Notice how DeSean, a fourth grader, shows that $1/_3$ is less than $2/_3$ (fig. 5.8).

Which number is larger 1/3 or 2/3? How do you know?

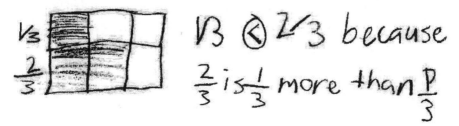

Fig. 5.8. DeSean explains why $1/3 < 2/3$.

Does his diagram make sense? What is the whole in his diagram? It appears he drew two rectangles, each representing a whole, and marked each into thirds. He then shaded one of the pieces in the top rectangle to show $1/3$ and two of the pieces in the bottom rectangle to show $2/3$. By stacking the two rectangles on top of each other, he could visually show that $1/3 < 2/3$. In fact, he explained that $2/3$ was exactly $1/3$ more. Because the fractions had the same denominator, he only needed to show that one fraction had more of the same size pieces than the other. His explanation also provides a glimpse of how he may think when comparing fractions with the same denominator.

Instead of comparing $2/3$ and $2/5$ using a common denominator strategy, let's use a *common numerator strategy*—a strategy that can easily be used when the numerators in both fractions are the same number. For $2/3$ and $2/5$, you know that you have two of the three equal pieces that make the whole and two of the five equal pieces that make up the same size whole. Although both fractions have two of these pieces, thirds are larger pieces, so $2/3$ is larger than $2/5$. Notice also that there was no need to perform any calculations to determine which fraction was larger. You only needed to think about the size of the pieces—using parts-of-a-whole ideas. Let's consider how DeSean determined that $2/3$ is greater than $2/5$ (fig. 5.9).

Which number is larger 2/3 or 2/5? How do you know?

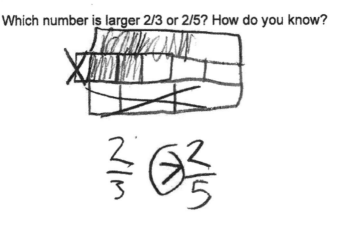

Fig. 5.9. DeSean shows that $2/3 > 2/5$.

Looking at his diagram, it seems DeSean struggled at first to show $2/_3$ and $2/_5$ with the same size wholes. Just as when he compared $1/_3$ and $2/_3$, he stacks the two rectangles, and then cuts the first rectangle into thirds and the second into fifths. He then shades two of the parts in each whole to show the fractional amounts. He appears to have visually compared the shaded parts to determine that $2/_3 > 2/_5$.

It is much more challenging for children to compare fractions with different numerators and denominators. For instance, how might a fourth or fifth grader determine which is the larger fraction, $3/_5$ or $2/_3$?

Sometimes children think that $3/_5$ must be larger than $2/_3$ because 5 is larger than 3. It is not uncommon for students to incorrectly apply ideas from their experiences with whole numbers when they work with fractions. Because of the tendency to confuse fraction ideas with whole number ideas, children are encouraged to draw and reason with pictures to understand that fractions are a new type of number.

We have already mentioned how children use a halving strategy to find smaller fractions such as $1/_2$ and $1/_4$. To show which fraction is larger, a child might draw a rectangle and mark a line down the middle to show two $1/_2$ parts, and then draw a line in one $1/_2$ portion to show two $1/_4$ parts to prove which fraction is larger (fig. 5.10). She can then easily use her drawing to explain that the $1/_4$ pieces are smaller pieces because it takes two of those pieces to make $1/_2$.

Fig. 5.10. Comparing $1/_2$ and $1/_4$

So how might a fourth or fifth grader compare $3/_5$ and $2/_3$? He could draw rectangles and shade in three-fifths of one rectangle and two-thirds of the other to prove that one amount is more than the other. But this approach is quite cumbersome and prone to error. For one thing, children sometimes overlook the fact that each rectangle (the whole) must be the same size, and for another, precise measurements are difficult to do. And in this case, using the halving method would only make it more complicated to compare the fractions. To determine which fraction is larger, children need to develop some other methods and strategies.

Although as a child you were probably steered to use a common denominator strategy to determine which fraction was larger, your children are encouraged to use *benchmark numbers*. They compare fractions by determining how they are related to whole numbers and fractions that are easy to think about, such as 0, $1/_4$, $1/_2$, $3/_4$, and 1.

READER'S CHALLENGE

To get an idea of how to use benchmark numbers, see if you can solve these two problems by comparing both fractions to a whole number or to a fraction that is easy to think about.

1. Place the appropriate symbol ([less than] <, [greater than] >, or =) between the fractions $\frac{7}{8}$ and $\frac{5}{6}$. Explain your solution.

2. Place the appropriate symbol (<, >, or =) between the fractions $\frac{2}{5}$ and $\frac{4}{7}$. Explain your solution.

While thinking about the first problem above, you probably noticed that the $\frac{7}{8}$ and $\frac{5}{6}$ are relatively close to 1 because $\frac{8}{8}$ is 8 parts out of 8, or one whole, and $\frac{6}{6}$ is 6 parts out of 6, which is also one whole. So the number 1 would be a good point of reference (or benchmark) from which to think about the relative size of the fractions.

The second problem can be solved by comparing each fraction to $\frac{1}{2}$. The fraction $\frac{2}{5}$ is less than $\frac{1}{2}$ because 2 is less than one-half of 5 (in fact $\frac{1}{2} = \frac{2\frac{1}{2}}{5}$). The fraction $\frac{4}{7}$ is greater than $\frac{1}{2}$ because 4 is greater than one-half of 7 ($\frac{1}{2} = \frac{3\frac{1}{2}}{7}$). In this way you can use $\frac{1}{2}$ to decide that $\frac{2}{5}$ is less than $\frac{4}{7}$.

Let's consider some of the ways that fourth graders solve these types of comparison problems using different strategies. In figure 5.11, Simeon uses a common numerator strategy to explain why $\frac{3}{5}$ is larger than $\frac{3}{8}$:

$\frac{3}{5}$ > than $\frac{3}{8}$.

An 8th is smaller than a 5th, so I think that $\frac{3}{5}$ is > than $\frac{3}{8}$.

Fig. 5.11. Simeon shows why $\frac{3}{5} > \frac{3}{8}$.

He uses his understanding of the size of the pieces of fifths and eighths to correctly explain why $\frac{3}{5}$ is larger. You can infer from his explanation that because fifths are larger than eighths, then $\frac{3}{5}$ of the whole will be larger than $\frac{3}{8}$ of the same whole.

To explain why $\frac{7}{8}$ is larger than $\frac{5}{6}$, Simeon uses a different strategy (fig. 5.12). As in the previous problem, he uses what he knows about the size of the sixths and eighths, but this time he applies a benchmark strategy for 1 to determine which is larger.

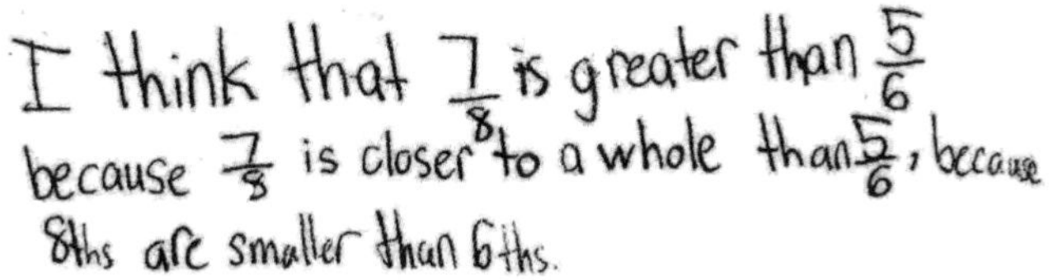

I think that $\frac{7}{8}$ is greater than $\frac{5}{6}$ because $\frac{7}{8}$ is closer to a whole than $\frac{5}{6}$, because 8ths are smaller than 6ths.

Fig. 5.12. Simeon describes why $^7/_8 > {}^5/_6$.

Simeon seems to imply that because eighths are smaller—$^1/_8$ is smaller than $^1/_6$—this means that the remaining $^7/_8$ pieces are closer to 1 than the $^5/_6$ pieces.

Shanetta uses parts-of-a-whole ideas to make a slightly different argument than Simeon did (fig. 5.13).

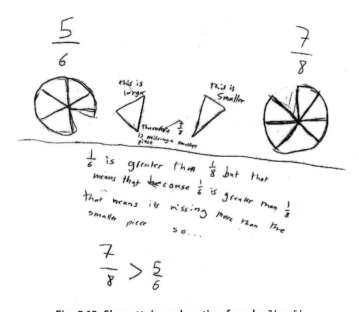

Fig. 5.13. Shanetta's explanation for why $^7/_8 > {}^5/_6$

Perhaps Shanetta's picture of the two wholes cut into eighths and sixths is not convincing to you because she made $^6/_7$ instead of $^7/_8$ in her picture. Her picture showing $^5/_6$ is correct, so you can assume that she simply forgot to mark one of the eighths in her picture to show $^7/_8$. And she does correctly explain that eighths are smaller pieces—a fact that she just knows. She also knows that $^1/_6$ is larger than $^1/_8$ because removing $^1/_6$ means more of the whole is missing. This means that the remaining $^7/_8$ of the whole is more than $^5/_6$ of the same whole. To give this kind of explanation, she needs to think about both the size of the individual pieces and the size of the remaining part of the whole—a fairly complicated way to reason about fractions. Taking both Shanetta's and Simeon's reasoning into account provides a clear and complete explanation for using 1 as a benchmark to determine why $^7/_8 > {}^5/_6$.

Their explanations are not so different from those of sixth graders solving the same problem. We provide these two examples to give you an idea of how your child's notions about fractions will continue to develop in middle school.

Notice that Darren and Tanya, sixth-grade students, like Simeon and Shanetta use 1 as the benchmark to compare the same fractions (figs. 5.14a and 5.14b).

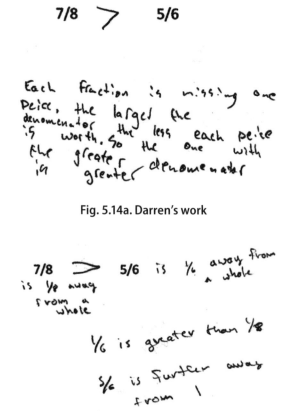

Fig. 5.14a. Darren's work

Fig. 5.14b. Tanya's work

Darren, like Shanetta, justified $7/_8$ as greater than $5/_6$ by comparing what "each fraction is missing." Tanya appears to have used similar reasoning. She notes the "missing" parts by writing "$7/_8$ is $1/_8$ away from a whole" and "$5/_6$ is $1/_6$ away from a whole," and then states, "$1/_6$ is greater than $1/_8$." Because $1/_6$ is greater than $1/_8$, Tanya concludes that $5/_6$ is further away from 1 than $7/_8$; therefore, $7/_8$ is closer to 1 and the larger number. Remarkably, without calculating common denominators or using formulas, all four children provide a clear justification for why $7/_8$ is larger than $5/_6$.

To make their cases, Darren and Tanya needed to figure out the difference between 1 and each fraction, and then decide which difference was smaller. In a sense, rather than comparing what was "there," they, like Shanetta and possibly Simeon, compared what was *not* there. The fraction with the smaller difference from 1 is the larger of the two fractions.

Going back to the problem posed earlier in this section, could you use one of these benchmark approaches to compare $^3/_5$ and $^2/_3$? One way is to compare each number with 1, noticing that $^3/_5$ is $^2/_5$ from 1 and $^2/_3$ is $^1/_3$ from 1. But determining whether $^2/_5$ or $^1/_3$ is larger is not an easier problem. Another approach is to compare the fractions to some other benchmark such as $^1/_2$. But both $^3/_5$ and $^2/_3$ are greater than $^1/_2$ and determining how far each number is away from $^1/_2$ is more cumbersome. You have already tried the strategies you know, so you might wonder if there is another way to make this comparison more manageable. Next, we explore a more general method for comparing fractions—working with equivalent fractions.

 DO YOU KNOW Why Fractions Are Infinite and Dense?

One of the important ideas your children encounter when working with fractions is that different fractions can be used to describe the same number. In fact, you can find an infinite number of equivalent fractions for $^1/_2$, $^1/_3$, or $^1/_9$, for example. You can also find an infinite number of equivalent fractions for all the other fractions too. Each fraction in its simplest form is unique. Equivalent fractions are different representations of this unique fraction (or rational number). Let's imagine placing each unique fraction and all of its equivalent fractions in the same bucket. You would never find $^2/_3$ in the $^1/_2$ bucket, for instance. And there is no end to the number of equivalent fractions you could have in each bucket because you could continue doubling, tripling, halving, and so forth, the numerators and denominators to place new equivalent fractions in their appropriate buckets.

You can always find a larger or smaller unique fraction too, and each can be represented in an infinite number of ways. Then there are the infinitely many fractions smaller or larger than each unique fraction—there are an infinite number of buckets. For these reasons, *rational numbers* (any number that can be written as a fraction) are what mathematicians call *dense*. The idea is more formally stated that between any two rational numbers there are infinitely many rational numbers. Although both rational numbers and whole numbers are infinite (they go on forever), one set of numbers is dense and the other is not. If you restrict yourself to thinking of whole numbers only, you cannot find another number between 23 and 24, for example. But if you include rational numbers, you find that there are an infinite number of other numbers between 23 and 24. Another way to think about this idea is that you can always determine the "next" whole number, but you can never determine a "next" rational number. For example, the next whole number after 3 is 4, and the next whole number after 4 is 5, and so on. Within the set of rational numbers, however, there is no "next" number that comes after the number 3 because there is no smallest rational number that comes after 3. So when children begin exploring equivalent fractions and finding new fractions, they are discovering a new set of numbers that is quite different. If the decimal and percent equivalents for each fraction are also included in these same buckets, the rational numbers seem incredibly more complicated than the set of whole numbers.

Equivalent Fractions

As we saw in the previous section, using diagrams or benchmark numbers as tools to compare fractions has limitations. In third grade, children also begin to study equivalent fractions as a more useful strategy for comparing fractions. *Equivalent fractions* describe the same rational number. For example, $^2/_4$ and $^5/_{10}$ are both equivalent to $^1/_2$. One of the important ideas that children explore is that fractions are equivalent to many, many other fractions. Initially, it is also very helpful for children to draw diagrams or use objects to show whether or not two fractions are equivalent.

Let's consider how Molly, our fourth grader, used a number line to explain that $^1/_2 = \,^4/_8$.

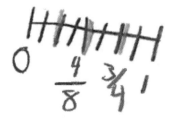

Fig. 5.15. Molly shows why $^4/_8 = \,^1/_2$.

Molly used a number line to make 0, $^4/_8$, $^3/_4$, and 1 (fig. 5.15). She then explained, "I know that 4 is exactly half of 8, so $^4/_8$ is $^1/_2$." Like Molly, children may use facts that they know, such as 4 is one-half of 8, 5 is one-half of 10, and so on, to determine if certain fractions are equivalent to one-half. They may use similar strategies to find equivalents for other fractions as well. For instance, to find an equivalent for $^1/_3$, the denominator needs to be three times that of the numerator because in the original fraction, the denominator is three times the numerator. Numbers for the equivalent fraction must follow this same relationship, or "multiplication rule." So $^3/_9$ is equivalent to $^1/_3$ because the denominator 9 is three times the numerator 3. As another example, $^2/_6$ is equivalent to $^1/_3$ because 6, the denominator, is three times the numerator 2. Can you think of other examples?

Referring again to Molly's picture, although she did not mention anything about fourths in her explanation, she also shows that $^2/_4$ is equivalent to $^1/_2$. Notice that she marked each fourth in a different color. Using her diagram, she also shows that $^2/_4$ is equivalent to $^4/_8$. Like Molly, children use rectangles or regions to make similar observations about equivalent fractions.

Children sometimes generate equivalent fractions by dividing a whole into a different number of parts. Figure 5.16 shows a representation of $^1/_2$ with shading in one of two parts of a rectangle.

Fig. 5.16. One of two parts of the region is shaded.

Children might divide the same rectangle into more and more equal parts using a halving strategy (fig. 5.17).

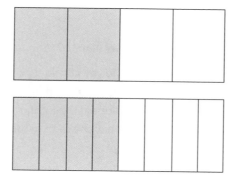

Fig. 5.17. One-half of one whole illustrated with different total numbers of parts, using a halving strategy.

When using a halving strategy like those above, children begin to notice that there is no limit to the number of equal parts they can make. What is important is that they become aware of the relationship between the number of shaded parts and the total number of parts. Using the example above, the total number of parts in the whole must be twice the number of shaded parts. If that relationship holds, then they have found a fraction that is equivalent to $^1/_2$. Children begin to see that there are an infinite number of fractions equivalent to $^1/_2$. They also may notice that they could divide each part into three equal pieces, four equal pieces, and so on, repeatedly, to find other fractions equivalent to $^1/_2$. In fact, they could go about this process forever to find more and more fractions equivalent to $^1/_2$. How would you partition the diagram to find fractions that are equivalent to $^1/_3$? $^2/_3$? Does this partitioning approach always work?

Eventually it is helpful for children to develop a more general approach to find equivalent fractions. During class discussions and with careful questioning, the teacher can lead his class to discover how to generalize the process pictured above by multiplying the numerator and denominator of a fraction by the same number. For example, you can find another fraction equivalent to $^1/_2$ by multiplying both the numerator and the denominator by 12:

$$\frac{1}{2} = \frac{1 \times 12}{2 \times 12} = \frac{12}{24}$$

Returning to the diagrams in figure 5.17, a child can also use a picture to explain why this procedure works. For example, she may notice that by multiplying the numerator and denominator by two, she doubles the number of equal parts in the whole and at the same time doubles the number of equal parts she is considering.

Finding equivalent fractions is a very useful strategy. In our discussion about adding and subtracting fractions in the next chapter, you will see how to use this strategy to complete a calculation more easily.

 READER'S CHALLENGE

Compare $8/_{25}$ with $4/_{13}$. Which is the larger number? How do you know?

How did you compare $8/_{25}$ and $4/_{13}$? Did you consider possible benchmarks? Maybe you observed that both numbers are less than $1/_2$ and seem relatively close to $1/_3$. Rewriting one of the fractions in the form of an equivalent fraction would be another approach. This is what one sixth grader did when working this problem (fig. 5.18).

$$\frac{8}{25} \quad > \quad \frac{4}{13}$$
$$\downarrow$$
$$\frac{8}{25} \longleftrightarrow \frac{8}{26}$$
$$1/_{26} < 1/_{25} \qquad 8 = 8$$

Fig. 5.18. A sixth grader uses an equivalent fraction when comparing fractions.

Following the arrows in her work, it looks as if she first determined that $4/_{13}$ is equivalent to $8/_{26}$. She doesn't show the multiplication of numerator and denominator by 2, but doubling is an easy computation for many students. By rewriting $4/_{13}$ as $8/_{26}$, she now has two fractions with the same numerator to compare. The student's next step is deciding that $1/_{26}$ is smaller than $1/_{25}$. Therefore, 8 of the smaller parts ($1/_{26}$) is smaller than 8 of the larger parts ($1/_{25}$). She uses this information to conclude that $4/_{13}$ is smaller than $8/_{25}$. In fact, she uses two techniques to solve the problem: finding an equivalent fraction (for $4/_{13}$) and a common-numerator strategy to explain why $8/_{25}$ is larger. Using these methods was much more efficient for her than finding a common denominator. To find the least common denominator, she would need to multiply $4/_{13}$ by $25/_{25}$ and $8/_{25}$ by $13/_{13}$—a much more cumbersome approach.

Working with Decimals

Decimals is a topic that can seem overwhelming. Why are decimals important? How does your child think about decimals? How are decimals related to fractions? More commonly used fractions such as $1/_2$ or $3/_4$ are oftentimes thought about, but when would you think about 0.50 (fifty hundredths) or 0.75 (seventy-five hundredths), the decimal equivalents for these fractions? Perhaps you are thinking that the context of money could be used to explain what 0.75 means? Seventy-five cents is the same as three quarters, or three of the four quarters that are needed to make one dollar; it is $3/_4$ of one dollar. Can this same context be used to think about $1/_{10}$? One-tenth is the same as one dime—one of the ten dimes needed to make one dollar. So 0.1 is $1/_{10}$ of a dollar. As these two examples illustrate, fractions and decimals can represent the same amount. You probably learned about fractions and decimals as separate topics when you were in school. Children today learn about fractions and decimals simultaneously and so are more comfortable thinking about both types of numbers interchangeably. A fourth grader, for instance, will learn that $1/_2$ is equivalent to 0.50. They may also learn that 50% is another way of representing the same amount. As when exploring whole numbers and fractions, it will be helpful for your child to work with diagrams and objects to develop an understanding of decimals and how decimals and fractions are related—a powerful idea they will continue to build on throughout their school experience.

Decimal and Place-Value Concepts

One of the important ideas related to working with decimals is they can be thought about by extending what is known about place value. In fact, when fourth and fifth graders work with decimals, they continue to build a more complete understanding of our base-ten numeration system. As these students were working with whole numbers in earlier grades, they began to understand that there were 10 ones in 1 ten, 10 tens in 1 hundred, and so on. Children extend these ideas when working with decimals. They learn that there are 10 one-tenths in one, 10 one-hundredths in one-tenth, 10 one-thousandths in one-hundredth, and so on. They also learn that $1/_{10}$ is the same as $10/_{100}$ and $10/_{100}$ is the same as $100/_{1000}$. And they can also use decimals to show these same relationships (0.1 = 0.10 = 0.100). And decimals are similar to fractions—they represent numbers that are either less than, equal to, or greater than 1 (e.g., 0.45 [forty-five hundredths], 0.034 [thirty-four thousandths], $4/_4$ [four-fourths], 1.0 [one], and 3.27 [three and twenty-seven hundredths]). Because we can represent some numbers as fractions and decimals, it makes sense to study these numbers at the same time. And sometimes it makes more sense to use one representation or another. For instance, it seems easier and more efficient to solve 7 x 2.4 than 7 x $2^4/_{10}$ or 7 x $2^2/_5$.

 READER'S CHALLENGE

Can you use more than one method to show that $3/_4$ is equivalent to 0.75?

Did you use a drawing or some other model as a strategy to solve the problem? Perhaps you rewrote $3/_4$ as an equivalent fraction by multiplying the 3 and the 4 by 25 to obtain $75/_{100}$. Or maybe you divided 3 by 4, using long division. Our point is that there is more than one way to correctly solve this problem.

The hundredths grid is a useful tool that fourth and fifth graders use to explore decimals and fractions. This grid may remind you of a flat base-ten block. The grid is similar. It is a 10-by-10 diagram with 100 squares; each square represents one-hundredth ($^1/_{100}$) of the entire grid. Recall that flats are also 10-by-10, but each square represents one (1) and the entire flat represents 100. To determine the decimal equivalent for $3/_4$, Student 1 might use a parts-of-a-whole interpretation of $3/_4$ and shade three of four equal parts of a 10-by-10 grid to show it (fig. 5.19).

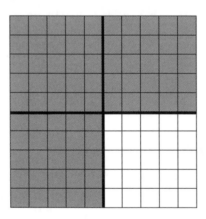

Fig. 5.19. A 10 x 10 grid is shaded to represent $3/_4$.

Because 75 parts out of 100 are shaded, she can use this information to explain that $3/_4$ is equivalent to $75/_{100}$. And $75/_{100}$ is equivalent to the decimal 0.75. Student 2 might shade the grid as three groups of 25 squares and color them as 7 columns of 10 squares plus 5 small squares (fig. 5.20). And Student 3 determines that because each column is $^1/_{10}$ of the whole grid and each small square is $^1/_{100}$ of the grid, he can represent the shaded parts as $7/_{10} + 5/_{100}$ of the 10-by-10 grid.

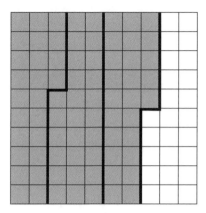

Fig. 5.20. A second way to shade ³/₄ of a 10 × 10 grid

Just as they did when learning about whole numbers, children make connections between fractions and their decimal equivalences using different strategies and methods.

Teachers can take note of various methods children use to help them make connections among equivalences too. For instance, in this case, the teacher might record the different approaches using both fractions and decimals:

$$\frac{3}{4} = \frac{75}{100} = \frac{7}{10} + \frac{5}{100} = 0.7 + 0.05 = 0.75$$

And displaying the children's pictures along with the extended number sentence is a natural spark for a classroom discussion about how the grid diagrams and the numbers are related.

Notice in the example above that each fraction has a denominator that is 10 or 100, or what we refer to as a *power of ten* ($10 = 10^1$ and $100 = 10^2$). For this reason, these are special types of fractions called *decimal fractions*. Any fraction that can be represented as a fraction with a denominator that is a power of ten is a decimal fraction. A simple and useful way for children to make connections between decimals and fractions is through working with decimal fractions.

Decimals, like fractions, can be formidable for children. While there are some similarities between fractions, decimals and whole numbers, decimals and fractions are different, and their differences in meaning and function from whole numbers and their relationship to each other can be challenging for elementary-aged children to grasp. Instruction in today's classrooms is geared to help children make sense of the mathematical concepts surrounding decimals and fractions much like instruction for whole numbers—a process that helps children build understanding of these new numbers using diagrams, manipulatives, and hands-on problem solving. By the time children reach middle school, they should be comfortable with the basics of fractions and decimals. It is then that children are introduced to complex concepts such as terminating and repeating decimals. concepts introduced in middle school. You may recall that fractions whose decimal representations have one or more digits that repeat over and over again with no end are repeating (and non-terminating) decimals. One common example is $1/_3$. It has a decimal representation of 0.33333 repeating; the digit 3 repeats indefinitely. Fractions like $1/_2$ and $1/_4$ and $2/_5$ have terminating decimals (0.5, 0.25, 0.4).

Earlier we mentioned that sometimes it is more useful to represent some amounts as fractions and others as decimals. As you can see above, for fractions like $1/_3$ that have decimal equivalents that never end, it can be more convenient to represent those amounts as fractions.

Strategies for Finding Decimal Fractions

Fifth graders learn that fractions such as $3/_4$ can also be thought of as $3 \div 4$. Thinking about fractions as dividing the numerator (dividend) by the denominator (divisor) introduces children to an entirely different approach to finding decimal equivalents by using the operation of division. In your school experiences, you might have been immediately guided to place the 3 inside a division box, put a decimal point after the 3, and append several zeros after the decimal point to solve $3 \div 4$. You then carried out the long division procedure to find that the decimal equivalent for $3/_4$ is 0.75 (fig. 5.21). But your child's teacher might ask the students to think about what the answer could be even before asking them to perform this operation. Could the answer to this problem be greater than 1? Less than 1? Why? By asking these types of questions, children can use their knowledge of fractions to consider what would be a reasonable answer.

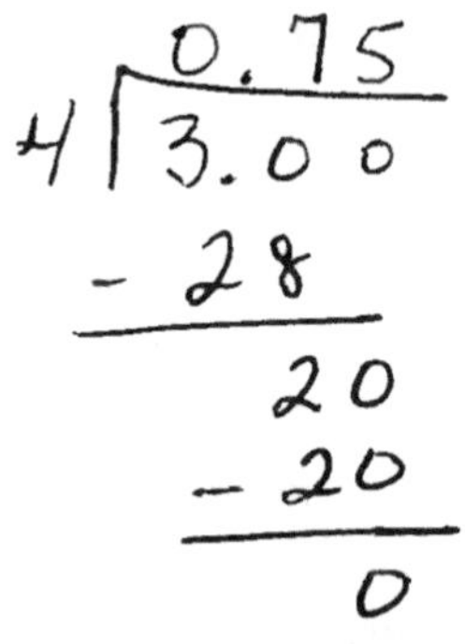

$$
\begin{array}{r}
0.75 \\
4\,\overline{)3.00} \\
-\,28 \\
\hline
20 \\
-\,20 \\
\hline
0
\end{array}
$$

Fig. 5.21. A student uses long division to determine the decimal form of $3/_4$.

Let's suppose a student uses a decimal fraction with a denominator of 10, 100, or 1000 to find the decimal equivalent of $3/_4$. Because this child knows that $4 \times 25 = 100$, she recognizes that $3/_4 \times 25/_{25} = 75/_{100}$. Because $75/_{100}$ is a decimal fraction, she knows she can represent it as its decimal equivalent 0.75, or she could use several multiplications to arrive at the same decimal fraction; for instance, $3/_4 \times 5/_5 = 15/_{20}$ and $15/_{20} \times 5/_5 = 75/_{100}$. What you see here is a child using a multiplication strategy to identify the decimal equivalent for a given fraction by finding the fraction's corresponding decimal fraction.

This approach does not always work, especially if the denominator has factors other than twos or fives, but this is a topic your child will explore in middle school.

Interestingly, you can use a hundredths grid to find these decimal equivalents without performing long division.

Decimals and Fractions: What's the Math?

Decimals provide a convenient way of writing fractions in terms of a denominator that is a power of ten. They are useful because children can use them to explore the structure of our base-ten system. As we discussed in chapter 3, our base-ten system is set up so that each place value is ten times that of the previous (and smaller) place value, that is, the tens place is ten times the ones place, and the hundreds place is ten times the tens place. When the direction is reversed, going from left to right, from a larger to a smaller place value, the place value is divided by ten. One hundred divided by ten is ten, and ten divided by ten is one. Continuing the pattern, when one is divided by ten, the value is one-tenth, which is, in fact, the name of the first place value to the right of the decimal point (fig. 5.22).

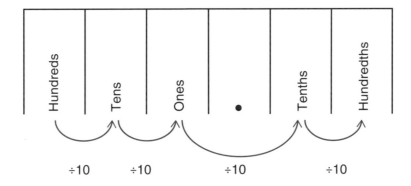

Fig. 5.22. The pattern of moving from larger to smaller place values by dividing by ten

A child might imagine a hundredths grid sliced into ten tiny slivers, each column or row having a value of one-tenth. By thinking this way, the student can make sense of why 0.1 is the same as 1 divided by 10 or $1/10$. Likewise, 0.01 represents $1/100$, 0.001 represents $1/1000$, and so on.

 TAKING A CLOSER LOOK at Children's Work with Decimals

Mr. Hernandez's class of fourth graders is comparing numbers and working with tenths, hundredths, and thousandths grids. A tenths grid (fig. 5.23), a hundredths grid (fig. 5.24), and a thousandths grid (fig. 5.25) are up on the board. He is pointing to the thousandths grid, a square representing one whole in which each small piece is $1/1000$, on the interactive board. He is curious to see what the students will come up with to represent the next place value to the right, which is the ten-thousandths place. We enter the discussion as he and the students talk about how tenths and hundredths are related.

Mr. Hernandez:	How do we get from hundredths to thousandths?
Grace:	We'd have to split each row in half.
Tomás:	Yeah. You need to divide each piece in half.
Mr. Hernandez:	Let me ask you this, then. To go from the tenths grid to the hundredths grid [figs. 5.23 and 5.24], did we divide each piece in half?

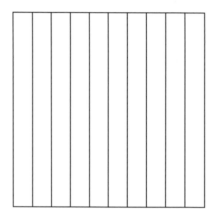

Fig. 5.23. A tenths grid

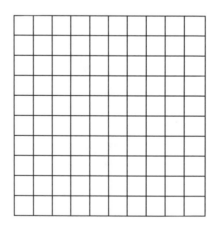

Fig. 5.24. A hundredths grid

Tomás and Megan:	Divide by ten!
Mr. Hernandez:	And from hundredths to thousandths?
Megan and Laura:	Divide by ten!
Mr. Hernandez:	And from thousandths to ten-thousandths?

Tomás, Megan, and Laura:	Divide by ten!
Grace:	That would be soooo tiny! I'd start with something big, like the whiteboard, so you could see it.
Tomás:	It's so weird. It seems the number should be getting smaller every time you write a digit there, but it's getting bigger.
Grace:	A digit that's not zero.
Tomás:	Yes. Like .723 and .7231.
Laura:	The pieces are getting smaller, but they're still adding something to it.
Tomás:	The pieces are getting smaller, but the numbers are getting larger. That's weird.

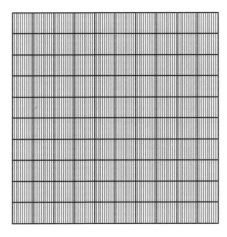

Fig. 5.25. A thousandths grid

These students are using what they know about our numeration system—not to mention ideas about how they might continue this process over and over. As they move from one place-value position to the next smaller position, they must divide each piece of the grid by ten. Initially they spoke of "splitting" or "halving" each small square, but with the teacher's help, decided they would need to divide the hundredths square ($^1/_{100}$) by ten for the next place value of thousandths. It's easy to imagine how the discussion might continue as the class thinks about dividing each square by ten repeatedly to get smaller and smaller decimals to show $^1/_{10,000}$, $^1/_{100,000}$, and so on. As their comments indicate, understanding place value is a complicated process, and it takes time and practice for children to fully grasp it for decimal numbers.

Things to Remember

♦ The simplest fraction for children to understand is one-half ($1/_2$). Even very young children have an intuitive idea of what this fraction means.

♦ Unit fractions, which have a numerator of one (1), for example, $1/_2$, $1/_3$, $1/_4$, and $1/_5$, are the building blocks for understanding and exploring relationships among different fractions.

♦ Typically, children have many experiences working with unit fractions before investigating more complicated fractions.

♦ As when learning about whole numbers, children use diagrams and draw pictures to understand and compare fractions and decimals.

♦ Benchmark numbers are whole numbers or fractions that are used as reference points when comparing fractions. Common benchmark numbers are 1 and $1/_2$.

♦ As children explore decimals, they extend their understanding of our base-ten numeration system and place value.

♦ Different fractions can be used to represent the same number or amount; for instance $1/_2 = 2/_4 = 4/_8 = 8/_{16}$.

♦ Learning about fractions and decimals at the same time helps children make stronger connections between these types of numbers.

Things to Do

♦ Capitalize on real-life situations, such as slicing pizza, sharing a candy bar, or counting coins, to talk with your child about fraction or decimal amounts.

♦ Encourage your child to draw pictures or use diagrams to think about fractions and decimals, especially if he or she is struggling with these concepts.

♦ Talk with your child's teacher to find out which fraction concepts your child will learn about during the school year.

♦ Revisit the "What's the Math" section or some of the "Reader's Challenge" boxes in this chapter to brush up on your skills with fractions and decimals.

♦ Review the discussion in chapter 3 about place value (pages 54–60).

Resources

We have tried to address many key ideas in this chapter, but we can only touch upon the topics. Additional resources you may find helpful and informative are listed below.

For Children

Adler, David A., and Edward Miller. *Fractions, Decimals, and Percents*. New York: Holiday House, 2010.

Dennis, J. Richard, and Donald Crews. *Fractions Are Parts of Things*. New York: Crowell, 1971.

Gifford, Scott, and Shmuel Thaler. *Piece=Part=Portion: Fractions=Decimals=Percents*. Berkeley, Calif.: Tricycle Press, 2003.

Leedy, Loreen. *Fraction Action*. New York: Holiday House, 1994.

McMillan, Bruce. *Eating Fractions*. New York: Scholastic, 1991.

Murphy, Stuart J., and Kevin O'Malley. *Jump, Kangaroo, Jump*. New York: HarperCollins Publishers, 1999.

More4U Online Resources

You can find a listing of additional helpful resources with links, including recommended games, by entering the access code on the title page of this book at NCTM's More4U page (nctm.org/more4u).

Chapter 6

Working with Fractions

Serena, a fourth grader, drew the picture in figure 6.1 to solve $3/_4 + 3/_4$.

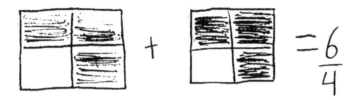

Fig. 6.1. Serena's drawing

What does Serena understand about fractions? Notice that she represented each $3/_4$ by shading three of four equal parts of a whole, in this case, a square. Her squares are not exactly the same size, but it is reasonable to assume Serena intended them to be so. She understands that addition with fractions, like with whole numbers, involves joining the parts from two collections (or sets) for a total of six parts. Because of her parts-of-a-whole understanding of fractions, she also knows that each of the six parts represents one-fourth of one, so she has six-fourths ($6/_4$) as her sum.

Children typically learn about adding and subtracting fractions in fourth grade, but even second and third graders informally explore these operations with fractions as they develop fraction number sense. They use the knowledge gained by representing and comparing fractions and determining equivalent fractions as well as by working with whole number operations to approach the operations with fractions.

You probably remember adding and subtracting fractions as a tedious process. It's likely you were taught the standard algorithms for which you often had to find equivalent fractions with common denominators before actually doing any adding or subtracting.

And because you learned fractions the way you did, you may not be completely satisfied with Serena's answer of $^6/_4$ for $^3/_4 + ^3/_4$. Shouldn't her answer be $1^1/_2$? Although she did not rename $^6/_4$ as $1^1/_2$, her answer is not incorrect. Sometimes it is more efficient to work with fractions that have not been rewritten as mixed numbers. Finding a common denominator is still a foundational process, but children in the upper (and lower) elementary grades can reason about these situations without looking for equivalent fractions or finding common denominators per se. Of course, if students are working with fractions that have common denominators like Serena was, their computations are easier because only the numerators need to be added or subtracted to find the total number of parts.

Just as they do when adding whole numbers, students often encounter combining and part-whole problem situations when adding fractions. Likewise, they face take-away and comparison subtraction situations when subtracting fractions. How do students make sense of these situations?

DO YOU KNOW about Pattern Blocks?

Elementary teachers like to use pattern blocks when teaching addition and subtraction with fractions. Children can use these blocks to make thinking about common fractional amounts easier. There are many ways to arrange different shapes to form whole units. For example, the hexagon can be made from two trapezoid pieces to depict halves; three rhombus pieces to show thirds; and six triangle pieces to indicate sixths (fig. 6.2a). Figure 6.2b illustrates how the rhombus and trapezoid can each be made with triangles. And of course, there are other combinations of different shapes that can be used to form a hexagon or a trapezoid.

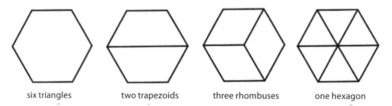

six triangles   two trapezoids   three rhombuses   one hexagon

Fig. 6.2a. Different ways to make one hexagon

1 rhombus = 2 triangles   1 trapezoid = 3 triangles

Fig. 6.2b. Relationships between pattern block pieces

Adding Fractions

Using pattern blocks, children can add (combine) fractional amounts to build a whole unit with different shapes. For example, a teacher might ask children to figure out various ways to make a hexagon (one whole) using triangles, rhombuses, or trapezoids. One child might figure out that she can make a hexagon using a trapezoid, a rhombus, and a triangle while another realizes that two rhombuses and two triangles also make a hexagon. With guidance from the teacher, children learn to write down these observations as number sentences involving the addition of fractions. Because a trapezoid, a rhombus, and a triangle make a hexagon, children observe $1 = \frac{1}{2} + \frac{1}{3} + \frac{1}{6}$. Similarly, because two rhombuses and two triangles make a hexagon, children can see $\frac{2}{3} + \frac{2}{6} = 1$.

Children can use pattern blocks and other materials to make observations about unit fractions, too. A case in point, a teacher may ask students to use only one type of shape to create a hexagon (one whole). A student might use six triangles or three rhombuses to make the hexagon (fig. 6.2a). Once students make their hexagon configurations, they can write number sentences to record the shapes they used. For instance, for six triangles, they would write $\frac{1}{6} + \frac{1}{6} + \frac{1}{6} + \frac{1}{6} + \frac{1}{6} + \frac{1}{6} = \frac{6}{6} = 1$; for three rhombuses, $\frac{1}{3} + \frac{1}{3} + \frac{1}{3} = \frac{3}{3} = 1$. The number sentences make sense to students because they can physically make the connection to the pattern blocks they used to create the hexagon.

These students are not working with equivalent fractions or common denominators, yet by engaging in the kinds of activities described above, these foundational ideas often surface naturally as children talk about why different combinations of blocks can represent the same whole unit. For instance, a child may realize that she could replace three triangles with one trapezoid and still have a hexagon. In this case, the child begins connecting $\frac{1}{2}$ and $\frac{3}{6}$ as she works with the pattern blocks. During discussions a teacher can lead children to making these connections by asking them to find other shapes to substitute for other pattern blocks. As you can see, working with patterns blocks helps children visualize and make sense of key ideas about how fractions are related.

When children begin to explore addition of fractions, they will often decompose one whole unit as well as fractional parts using various same-size unit fractions. By doing so, they begin to understand that when combining unit fractions, such as $\frac{1}{6}$, it takes exactly 6 one-sixths to make a whole unit. The parts-of-a-whole understanding fostered by experimenting with pattern blocks also comes into play as children investigate the other operations with fractions.

 READER'S CHALLENGE

Instead of one hexagon representing "one whole," suppose you use *two* hexagons to represent "one whole." In what ways can you fill this new type of whole unit? Do the values of the other pattern blocks change? You may want to determine the possible unit fractions for the pattern pieces first; for example, because two hexagons are the whole unit, a trapezoid represents $\frac{1}{4}$ of the whole.

What other unit fractions did you find for the various pattern blocks that could fill the one whole unit of two hexagons? The triangle is $1/_{12}$, the rhombus is $1/_6$, the trapezoid is $1/_4$, and the hexagon is $1/_2$. Lots of different combinations of these shapes are possible; for example, three trapezoids, one rhombus, and one triangle fill two hexagons. In terms of addition of fractions, this means $1 = 3/_4 + 1/_6 + 1/_{12}$. Or perhaps you realized that four rhombuses plus four triangles fill two hexagons. In that case, you have shown $1 = 4/_6 + 4/_{12}$. Alternatively, you might have noticed that one rhombus and ten triangles fill two hexagons, thus $1 = 1/_6 + 10/_{12}$.

As children's understanding of fractions and their relationships develops, they often use a parts-of-a-whole interpretation to solve fraction addition problems. Recall how fourth grader Serena solved $3/_4 + 3/_4$. She drew two squares (whole units) and shaded three of the four parts in each square to show three-fourths. Then she added the shaded parts to determine that the total number of parts is six (6, the numerator); she used the fact that each part was one-fourth of a whole to determine that the denominator is four (4). Looking at her work, the two collections being added together could be interpreted as each having 3 one-fourths. Can you see the 3 one-fourths in each square? Thus, when added together, the sum is 6 one-fourths or $6/_4$.

Children with fraction number sense are flexible in their thinking and can find other ways to add fractions. Andres, also a fourth grader, took a different approach to solve $3/_4 + 3/_4$ (fig. 6.3).

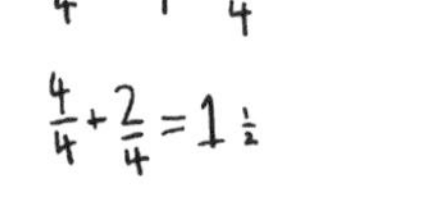

$$\frac{3}{4} + \frac{3}{4} = 1\tfrac{1}{2}$$

$$\frac{3}{4} + \frac{1}{4} = 1$$

$$\frac{3}{4} - \frac{1}{4} = \frac{2}{4}$$

$$\frac{4}{4} + \frac{2}{4} = 1\tfrac{1}{2}$$

Fig. 6.3. Andres adds $3/_4 + 3/_4$.

You might wonder why Andres didn't just add the numerators. Looking at the reasoning behind his approach, it appears Andres first shows how to make one whole unit by adding $1/_4$ to $3/_4$ (second line). His prior experiences with the parts-of-a-whole interpretation of fractions might have led him to recognize that $3/_4$ is exactly $1/_4$ less than $4/_4$, or one whole unit. Andres then indicates what remains to be added by subtracting $1/_4$ from $3/_4$ to get $2/_4$. Then he adds $2/_4$ to the one whole ($4/_4$) to get $1\tfrac{1}{2}$. Andres decomposed $3/_4$ into $2/_4$ and $1/_4$ to use a *making-one strategy*; he then broke one of the addends into $1/_4 + 1/_2$, and then combined the addends: $3/_4 + (1/_4 + 1/_2) = (3/_4 + 1/_4) + 1/_2 = 1 + 1/_2 = 1\tfrac{1}{2}$. He combines the fourths to make a whole unit and then adds the half to the unit to get $1\tfrac{1}{2}$.

If children are using pictures to solve the problem, they can still combine the fractional parts of each unit. A student might do this by showing how to fill one whole unit with 1 one-fourth from the other group of 3 one-fourths (fig. 6.4).

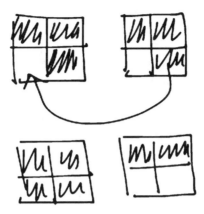

Fig. 6.4. A student shows how to make one whole with pictures.

Whether a child uses number sentences or another uses diagrams, they both use a making-one strategy to solve the problem. Interestingly, this strategy has some similarities to how children use *making ten* when solving whole number addition (page 49), but instead of decomposing whole numbers and combining them to make ten, children decompose and combine fractional parts to make one. In the examples above, students use what they know about the relationship between halves and fourths to find the total amount. Shifting from using a picture to find the sum of $3/4 + 3/4$, like Serena and the student above did, to writing equations to indicate how the sum of these two fractional parts is $1\frac{1}{2}$, like Andres, is one of many challenges children encounter when working with fractions.

 DO YOU KNOW How to Talk about Adding Fractions?

It may seem that your life doesn't present many chances to talk about addition of fractions, but when you think about it, events like driving to a football game, baking cookies, and other everyday events give you openings all the time. For instance, picking up a friend to go to a football game can open a conversation like this: "If it takes $3/4$ hour to drive to Peter's house, and then another $1\frac{1}{2}$ hours to drive to the stadium, how long will the drive be?" Cooking and baking can also provide great opportunities for fraction operations as you measure and mix: "If I give you the $1/3$-cup and the $1/2$-cup measuring cups, how much of 1 cup do you have?" When you think about ways to engage your children in everyday conversations about fractions, be sure to include fractions greater than one.

Before children can be asked to operate with fractions, they must understand what fractions mean; otherwise they may misapply what they know about whole number addition and "add across," adding both the numerators and denominators (fig 6.5).

$$\frac{3}{4} + \frac{3}{4} = \frac{6}{8}$$

Fig. 6.5 A student misapplies whole number addition.

But a child with fraction number sense knows that these fractions are both close to 1, and so the sum should be greater than 1. Because this child also understands equivalent fractions, she knows that $\frac{6}{8}$ is the same number as $\frac{3}{4}$. How could you add a nonzero number to itself and get the same number? That doesn't make sense. A child with fraction number sense knows that adding the numerators and denominators could not be correct. (See "Do You Know about Ratios?" (page 142) for an example of when answers like $\frac{6}{8}$ do make sense.)

But why is it incorrect to add the denominators? If addition involves combining parts, why not combine all of the parts? This is answered by using a parts-of-a-whole interpretation. You'll notice that the "adding across" process changes the size of the fractional parts being added; the parts go from being fourths to eighths. That's like saying $3 + 3 = \frac{3}{1} + \frac{3}{1} = \frac{6}{2} = 3$. The denominator tells you the size of the parts you are dealing with and can be thought of as a fractional unit. As such, it doesn't make sense to add them. Some teachers actually have their students write fractions in a way that demonstrates this idea; for this problem, that would be 3 fourths + 3 fourths = 6 fourths.

But how do students figure out sums of *unlike* fractions if not with common denominators? Consider this fourth-grader's illustration for $\frac{1}{2} + \frac{2}{3}$ (fig. 6.6). How did she represent each fraction? How did she do the combining?

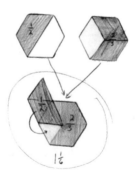

Fig. 6.6. A student uses a diagram to determine $\frac{1}{2} + \frac{2}{3}$.

She, like Andres, used a making-one strategy, using a hexagon to represent one whole unit. This is not an unusual choice. She drew her hexagons by tracing around a hexagon-shaped pattern block. She shaded half of one hexagon to show $\frac{1}{2}$ (or one trapezoid) and shaded two rhombuses on another hexagon to show $\frac{2}{3}$. To combine the fractions she drew the process of trying to fit the two fractional parts together into one whole unit (one hexagon). She filled in the available space in the hexagon depicting $2/3$ with the trapezoid ($1/2$). Notice how she outlined three triangles in the trapezoid and shows how one of the triangles neatly fits, leaving two triangles outside of the hexagon. Then she drew an arrow showing how another triangle (or $1/3$ of the half) fills the uncolored space in the hexagon depicting $2/3$. So she used two of three equal pieces (triangles) from the half hexagon to make one complete whole. Because six triangles make a hexagon, she knows she has $1/6$ of one whole remaining, so her answer is $1 1/6$.

Just like whole numbers, children decompose fractions and mixed numbers to make solving more challenging problems easier. Let's look at $4 1/7 + 5 1/5$ as an example. Because $4 1/7 = 4 + 1/7$ and $5 1/5 = 5 + 1/5$, a child might decide to add the whole numbers and the fractional parts separately, and then combine them to find the total. In this case, children would most likely find a common denominator to add the fractional parts $1/7$ and $1/5$. For a reminder on how that approach works, see figure 6.7.

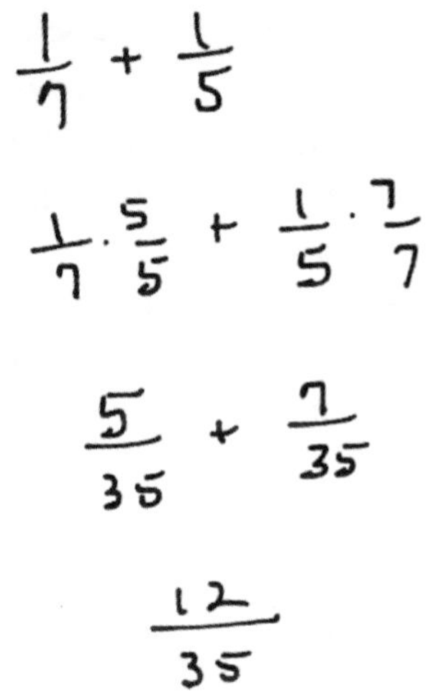

$$\frac{1}{7} + \frac{1}{5}$$

$$\frac{1}{7} \cdot \frac{5}{5} + \frac{1}{5} \cdot \frac{7}{7}$$

$$\frac{5}{35} + \frac{7}{35}$$

$$\frac{12}{35}$$

Fig. 6.7. Adding fractions using a common denominator strategy

In chapter 5 (page 124) we discussed how children learn to determine different equivalent fractions by multiplying the numerator and denominator by the same number. To find equivalent fractions in this case, the $1/7$ is multiplied by $5/5$ and the $1/5$ is multiplied by $7/7$. Because 7 and 5 don't have any common factors, the smallest common denominator is the product of 7×5, or 35. Once the equivalent fractions are formed with a common denominator, adding the fractions is simply a matter of adding the numerators. In this case the result is $1/7 + 1/5 = 5/35 + 7/35 = 12/35$, so $4 1/7 + 5 1/5 = 9 12/35$.

Children also have the option to *decompose fractions into friendlier numbers*. The challenge when doing this is finding appropriate equivalences and keeping what represents the whole (one unit) in mind as numbers are combined. Consider $4/6 + 11/12$. There are many ways a child could approach this problem using decomposition. A child who recognizes that $^{10}/_{12} = {}^5/_6$ may take the approach of decomposing $^{11}/_{12}$ as $^{10}/_{12} + {}^1/_{12} = {}^5/_6 + {}^1/_{12}$, and then adding $^4/_6 + {}^5/_6 = {}^9/_6 = 1{}^3/_6$, which is the same as $1{}^1/_2$. But there is still $^1/_{12}$ remaining to add to the partial answer. To add $^1/_2$ and $^1/_{12}$, the student rewrites $^1/_2$ as $^6/_{12}$ and then adds $^6/_{12} + {}^1/_{12}$ to get $^7/_{12}$. The final answer to $^4/_6 + {}^{11}/_{12}$ is $1{}^7/_{12}$. Another, perhaps more efficient, strategy would be to rename $^4/_6$ as $^8/_{12}$. The student could then decompose $^8/_{12}$ as $^7/_{12} + {}^1/_{12}$ and use a make-one strategy to find the sum $1{}^7/_{12}$.

Using sensible and efficient strategies to solve problems is always the goal in mathematics no matter what type of numbers children are working with.

 DO YOU KNOW Know about Ratios?

You know it is incorrect to add both numerators and denominators when adding fractions. But did you know there are situations when it seems as if that is exactly what happens; where, for example, "3 out of 4" plus "3 out of 5" *is* "6 out of 9"? Suppose Becky is a basketball player who made three out of four free-throw attempts in one game and three out of five in another. You can conclude that she has made six out of nine of her free-throw attempts in those two games. In this context, "3 out of 4" is not a fraction even though the words sound like the language of fractions. Instead, "3 out of 4" is a ratio of shots made to shots taken. You can interpret the ratio as a fraction by saying Becky has made three-fourths of her shots in one game, but to calculate her stats over both games, you must add the shots made *and* the shots taken. Figuring out how ratios and fractions are related yet different is complicated, and makes understanding fraction operations that much more difficult.

Adding Fractions: What's the Math?

Addition with fractions often involves rewriting one or more fractions in an equivalent form. Consider $^3/_4 + {}^1/_2$. To add $^1/_2$ to $^3/_4$, it is helpful to realize that $^1/_2$ is equivalent to $^2/_4$. To add these two numbers, you might first rewrite $^1/_2$ as $^2/_4$; then, to find the sum of $^3/_4 + {}^2/_4$, add the numerators so $^3/_4 + {}^2/_4 = {}^5/_4$. This problem can also be solved using a number line. The first jump is from 0 to $^3/_4$; the second is 2 one-fourth units ($^2/_4$) to the right from $^3/_4$. The resulting sum of $^5/_4$ is shown on the number line in figure 6.8.

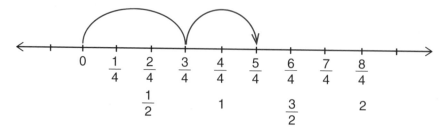

Fig. 6.8. A number line representation for $^3/_4 + {}^1/_2$

Recall that in figure 4.13 (page 82) we illustrated the decimal addition problem 0.2 + 0.5. In that example, the number line was marked by tenths. Although numbers may be written in a different form, children identify a common fractional unit to perform the addition (or do the combining). For the problem illustrated in figure 6.8, the common fractional unit was fourths. If you were adding $1/2$ to 0.3, the common fractional unit would be tenths because $1/2$ is the same as 0.5. In this case, $1/2 + 0.3 = 0.5 + 0.3 = 0.8$ or $5/10 + 3/10 = 8/10$. When children are comfortable working with equivalences, they can represent and solve a problem using different representations.

In chapter 4, we addressed a special situation that occurs when adding two numbers when one of the addends is zero (page 81). The same situation occurs when adding fractions. Consider $0 + 1/2$. Perhaps there are no chocolate chip cookies on Mark's plate, but $1/2$ of a cookie on Dan's plate. Combining the plates, there is $1/2$ cookie. The sum is simply $1/2$. Zero is called the *additive identity* because when adding a fraction to zero you always get that fraction. Adding zero does not change what you have!

Children learn that there are many ways to represent zero with a fraction. Fractions such as $0/1$, $0/35$, $0/1729$, and so on, are all equivalent to 0. Just as there are infinitely many fractions equivalent to $1/2$, so too are there infinitely many ways to express 0 as a fraction.

Subtracting Fractions

How do children make sense of take-away or other story problem situations that involve fractions? Essentially, they draw on many of the same ideas they use when making sense of fraction addition situations. As with addition of fractions, children often use a parts-of-a-whole interpretation of fractions to subtract them. Consider the following take-away subtraction situation:

Monique has $3^1/2$ candy bars. If she ate $1^1/2$ candy bars, how many bars does she have now?

To solve the problem, a child needs to think about removing $1^1/2$ candy bars from the $3^1/2$ Monique has. It is not only perfectly logical but also quite efficient for the student to first remove one candy bar. Now $2^1/2$ candy bars remain. Once the student has subtracted 1, she only needs to subtract $1/2$, and then count the remaining candy bars. In this case, the child did not need to find an equivalent fraction before subtracting $1/2$ to determine that the answer is 2 candy bars.

Let's look at a slightly different version of the candy bar problem:

Monique has $1^1/2$ candy bars. Jonah gives her more; now she has 3 candy bars. How many candy bars did Jonah give her?

The problem has been changed to a more challenging type of combining situation, which requires a child to perform different work than when solving a take-away situation. As one approach, the student could add on to the 1 whole and $1/2$ candy bar until he had 3 candy bars. He would then need to count the number of candy bars he added to answer the question. He could do this is by using a number line marked with halves. On the number line in figure 6.9 (following page), the child must determine what length a jump starting at $^3/_2$ and ending at 3 represents. Knowing that the number line is marked in halves, he can simply count the 3 halves between $^3/_2$ and 3. Jonah must have given Monique $^3/_2$ or $1^1/_2$ candy bars.

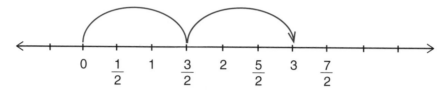

Fig. 6.9. A number line approach to determine $1^1/_2 +$ ___ = 3

Alternatively, another student could subtract $1^1/_2$ from 3 to arrive at the correct answer of $1^1/_2$. Take a look at Angela's work in figure 6.10 to see how a fourth grader might solve this situation as a subtraction problem using equations.

$$3 - 1\tfrac{1}{2} = \underline{\quad}$$
$$3 - 1 = 2 \qquad 2 - \tfrac{1}{2} = 1\tfrac{1}{2}$$

I minused the whole first.

Fig. 6.10. Angela's solution to $3 - 1^1/_2$

Angela first decomposed $1^1/_2$ into 1 and $^1/_2$; then she subtracted 1 from 3 to get 2. Her last step was to subtract the $^1/_2$ from the 2 to get her final answer of $1^1/_2$. To represent Angela's approach on a number line, the first jump is to 3; the second jump is a jump *back* of 1, landing on 2; then a third jump *back* of $^1/_2$, finally landing on the answer $1^1/_2$.

Whether they interpreted the problem as an addition or subtraction situation, the students arrived at the same answer. Understandably, using these approaches can be challenging for children who have incomplete ideas about equivalences ($1 = ^2/_2 = ^1/_2 + ^1/_2$).

What happens when we change the problem so that the initial amount is $1^1/_4$?

Monique has $1^1/_4$ candy bars. Jonah gives her more, and now she has 3 candy bars. How many candy bars did Jonah give her?

This time the child breaks apart one of the whole candy bars into fourths to solve $1^1/_4 +$ ___ = 3. The student must add $^3/_4$ to make 2 candy bars and then add 1 more candy bar to make 3 candy bars. In this case, as before, the student must count the parts he added to arrive at his answer of $1^3/_4$.

As you can see, students solve these types of subtraction problems using approaches similar to the ones they used when answering whole number problems. The difference here is the student grapples with concepts such as equivalent fractions and decomposition of fractions to solve these fraction subtraction problems.

When working out whole number subtraction situations, students often decide to decompose the numbers to make the problem more manageable. (In an example in chapter 4 on page 87, a student decomposed 100 as 70 plus 30 in order to subtract 30 from 100.) Students frequently use a similar strategy when solving fraction problems to make the numbers easier to work with. However, as the fraction problems become more complex with different denominators, such as $4^5/_{12} - 2^2/_7$, students must also have a thorough understanding of equivalent fractions, and must be extremely careful as they carry through the subtraction after decomposing the numbers. In this problem, a student might decompose the fractions by thinking of the problem as $(4 + {}^5/_{12}) - (2 + {}^2/_7)$. He may do that so he can subtract 2 from 4 and then $^2/_7$ from $^5/_{12}$. It can be confusing to know what to do with the resulting differences in the end. Should they be added or subtracted? Actually, the differences should be added together. It may be helpful to refer back to a whole number subtraction problem to understand why.

To subtract 25 from 87, you might think, "Take 20 from 80 to get 60; then 5 from 7 to get 2; therefore, the answer is 62." By doing so you have taken away $20 + 5$ from $80 + 7$. The sum of the differences between $80 - 20$ and $7 - 2$ is the total difference between 87 and 25. In a similar way, the sum of the differences between $4 - 2$ and $^5/_{12} - {}^2/_7$ is the total difference between $4^5/_{12}$ and $2^2/_7$. Of course, the most efficient way to determine the difference between $^5/_{12}$ and $^2/_7$ is to find a common denominator (84 works). The decomposition gets even more complex when subtracting fractions that require renaming.

 ## READER'S CHALLENGE

How would you approach the following subtraction problem?

$$4\frac{5}{12} - 2\frac{2}{3}$$

If you decompose the fractions based just on the whole number and fractional parts you would get $(4 + {}^5/_{12}) - (2 + {}^2/_3)$. Pairing up the whole numbers and the fractions leads to $(4 - 2) + ({}^5/_{12} - {}^2/_3)$, or $2 + ({}^5/_{12} - {}^8/_{12})$ because $^8/_{12}$ is equivalent to $^2/_3$ (multiply $^2/_3$ by $^4/_4$). But there is a slight problem because $^8/_{12}$ is greater than $^5/_{12}$. You might decompose the resulting 2 from $4 - 2$ into $1 + {}^{12}/_{12}$ because $^{12}/_{12} = 1$. If you take this approach, the next step is to add $^{12}/_{12} + {}^5/_{12}$ for $^{17}/_{12}$, from which you can now easily subtract $^8/_{12}$. The solution to the problem $4^5/_{12} - 2^2/_3$ is $1^9/_{12}$, or $1^3/_4$.

Alternatively, you might have chosen to rewrite the mixed numbers as fractions with a common denominator. Rewriting the mixed numbers as fractions also involves decomposition:

$$4\frac{5}{12} = 4 + \frac{5}{12} = \frac{48}{12} + \frac{5}{12} = \frac{53}{12}$$

$$2\frac{2}{3} = 2 + \frac{2}{3} = \frac{6}{3} + \frac{2}{3} = \frac{8}{3}$$

So the problem can be written as follows:

$$\frac{53}{12} - \frac{8}{3}$$

To solve the problem, you could decide to use twelfths as the common denominator and proceed as follows:

$$\frac{8}{3} \times \frac{4}{4} = \frac{32}{12}$$

$$\frac{53}{12} - \frac{8}{3} = \frac{53}{12} - \frac{32}{12} = \frac{21}{12} = 1\frac{3}{4}$$

Subtracting Fractions: What's the Math?

As with addition, subtracting fractions often involves rewriting one or more fractions in an equivalent form. Consider $3/4 - 1/2$. To subtract $1/2$ from $3/4$, knowing that $1/2$ is equivalent to $2/4$ is helpful; $1/2$ can be rewritten as $2/4$; then, to find the difference, subtract the numerators: $3/4 - 2/4 = 1/4$. As with the addition problem on page 142, the problem can also be solved using a number line. Instead of moving $2/4$ to the right of $3/4$ on the number line, the jump is $2/4$ to the *left* of $3/4$. The resulting difference is $1/4$. The solution can be written symbolically as the following:

$$\frac{3}{4} - \frac{1}{2} = \frac{3}{4} - \frac{2}{4} = \frac{3-2}{4} = \frac{1}{4}$$

Rewriting the fractions so they have like denominators makes subtracting (or adding) fractions much easier. As we have said before, mathematics is a consistent system. When adding or subtracting whole or rational numbers, essentially the same operation is performed, regardless of the type of numbers being added or subtracted.

Multiplying with Fractions

As children investigate the multiplication of fractions, they encounter many of the same types of situations they did when working with whole numbers. In chapter 4, whole number multiplication situations included repeated addition, area, and the counting principle, sometimes involving tree diagrams and arrays as tools for solving those problems. Multiplication of fractions is also introduced using repeated-addition situations. In our earlier discussions in this and the previous chapter, we mentioned that unit fractions are the building blocks for creating other fractions. You can think of $5/6$ as $1/6 + 1/6 + 1/6 + 1/6 + 1/6$ or as $5 \times 1/6$; in other words, you can think of fractions interchangeably as the result of repeatedly adding the same unit fraction or as multiplying the same unit fraction by a specific factor. So presenting repeated-addition situations to begin exploring multiplication of fractions is a helpful way for children to become accustomed to this operation. Children build on this idea as they encounter different types of multiplication situations that arise when working with fractions.

Let's look at an example of how fourth and fifth graders explore the multiplication of fractions and decimals by solving repeated-addition situations.

John wants to buy 5 packs of gum; each pack costs $1.25. How much will John have to pay for 5 packs of gum?

To determine the total cost for the gum, a student can either repeatedly add 1.25 five times (1.25 + 1.25 + 1.25 + 1.25 + 1.25) or multiply 1.25 by 5. To solve this problem, a student first decomposes $1.25 into $1 + $.25. She then multiplies the $1 by 5 for a total of $5. She starts to combine the five $.25 parts ($.25 + $.25 + $.25 + $.25 + $.25), but realizes that .25 (or $25/_{100}$) is equivalent to $1/_4$. She knows that 4 × $1/_4$ is 1 whole, so she adds that to the $5 to get a total of $6 plus $1/_4$ of a dollar more. Her answer is a total price of $6.25. Her method is summarized in figure 6.11.

```
5 x $1 = $5

5 x $0.25 = $0.25 + $0.25 + $0.25 + $0.25 + $0.25

        = $1/4 + $1/4+ $1/4+ $1/4 + $1/4

        = 4 x $1/4+ 1 x $1/4

        = $1 + $1/4

Total is $5 + $1 + $1/4= $6.25
```

Fig. 6.11. One possible approach to the gum problem

Sonja, a fourth grader, uses repeated addition, separating the whole number parts and the fraction parts (fig. 6.12). Notice how each whole dollar is drawn along the top of her solution. How does she determine 5 × $.25?

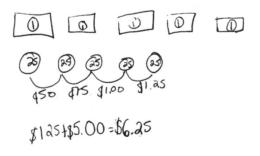

Fig. 6.12. Sonja's solution to the gum problem

To determine 5 × $.25, Sonja represents each $.25 as a quarter, and then counts by twenty-fives to add 25 five times. She also changes units, recognizing that $.25 is 25¢. She writes each intermediate sum under her drawing of the quarters. The first two quarters are worth 50¢, the third makes 75¢, and the fourth makes 100¢, but notice that here she returns to the dollar unit and writes $1.00. After adding the fifth quarter, she writes $1.25. She concludes the total is determined by adding the $1.25 to $5.00 for $6.25.

There are other types of multiplication situations too:

At the grocery store, nuts are sold by the pound. Roasted walnuts cost $9.00 per pound. How much will 2/3 of a pound of roasted walnuts cost?

The student must determine what $2/_3$ of $9.00 is (i.e., $6.00). Notice how the word "of" is used here. The $2/_3$ is acting on the $9.00, which is our "whole" amount. Finding the fractional portion of an amount, in this case, $9.00, is referred to as an *operator-multiplication situation*.

Calculating sales tax, determining how much is saved with a 20% off coupon, and enlarging a 3-by-5-inch photo 150% on a photocopier are all examples of operator situations because finding a fractional portion of a quantity is the objective. In fact, many multiplication problems involving fractions are operator situations.

Before students are taught a standard algorithm for multiplying fractions, they often draw upon the strategies they used for whole number multiplication. Henry, a sixth grader, is solving the operator multiplication problem, "What is $3/_4$ of $2/_3$?"

$$= \frac{6}{12} = \frac{1}{2}$$

Fig. 6.13. Henry's diagram for $3/_4 \times 2/_3$

He began by partitioning a rectangle into thirds horizontally and coloring two of the rows to show $2/_3$ (fig. 6.13). Then he partitioned the whole again, this time vertically, into fourths. He started coloring in three of the four columns to represent the $3/_4$, but he did not color the three columns all the way to the bottom of the rectangle. "I knew I wanted $3/_4$ of the $2/_3$, and I could already see that the whole was in twelfths." Henry also indicated with the double shading that only the portions colored on both the $2/_3$ and $3/_4$ parts was his answer; he literally colored $3/_4$ of $2/_3$. The $2/_3$ is represented by two of the three rows in his rectangle; think of these two rows as the whole unit. To find $3/_4$, this new "whole" needs to be partitioned into four equal parts. Henry accomplishes this by making four columns. Three of the columns within the $2/_3$ represent $3/_4$ of $2/_3$. This strategy resembles the problem about the throw rug in chapter 4 (p. 96). In fact, the model Henry is using is often referred to as an *area model of fraction multiplication*. Indeed, you can think of Henry's diagram in terms of area. Although his rectangle is not drawn to scale, the dimensions of the whole rectangle are 1 by 1, giving an area of 1 square unit. The diagram illustrates how much of a whole unit is filled by a rectangle with the dimensions $^3/_4$ by $^2/_3$. As we see from Henry's work, the smaller rectangle fills $^1/_2$ of the unit rectangle.

 DO YOU KNOW What Is Different?

As students gain experience with fractions, they make connections between working the operations with fractions and working them with whole numbers. They may also notice some distinct differences. A case in point is multiplication. Multiplying any two natural numbers greater than one results in an answer that is larger than each factor. But when multipying fractions, the answer does not always produce a result that is larger than either of the factors. For instance, $^1/_2$ x 5 is $^5/_2$, which is less than 5, the number on which the $^1/_2$ operates. Students need to make a significant shift in their understanding of multiplication when working with fractions.

Multiplying Fractions: What's the Math?

In chapter 4 we addressed the meaning of multiplication in terms of repeated addition. Repeated addition can also be used to make sense of a fraction multiplied by a whole number, such as 6 × $^2/_3$. It is easy to imagine six groups of $^2/_3$. To do this, we use copies of Sarah's drawing for $^2/_3$ from page 112 (fig. 6.14).

Fig. 6.14. Six groups of $^2/_3$

To determine the answer, first think about how many full jugs can be made by transferring the milk from some of the jugs. Imagine picking up the first jug to fill the neighboring jugs. Because exactly $^1/_3$ of each jug is empty, the first jug can completely fill the next two jugs (fig. 6.15).

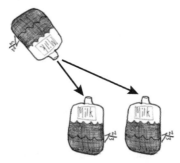

Fig. 6.15. One jug is used to fill two other jugs.

Similarly, the fourth jug can fill the fifth and six jugs. The result is four full jugs; therefore, $6 \times {}^2/_3 = 4$.

Interestingly, $6 \times {}^2/_3$ can also be approached using the operator interpretation of multiplication. To do this, think about how to determine ${}^2/_3$ of 6 (or ${}^2/_3 \times 6$). Begin with 6 whole units, and then partition the 6 units into three equal groups (or thirds of 6) using two vertical lines (fig. 6.16).

Fig. 6.16. Six whole units partitioned into thirds

As you can see, ${}^1/_3$ of 6 is 2 whole units, and ${}^2/_3$ of 6 is 4. So the product of 6 and ${}^2/_3$ can be thought of in terms of either repeated addition or as an operator situation.

For more complex problems such as ${}^3/_5 \times {}^4/_9$, it is more efficient to use the standard algorithm, which is sometimes introduced by grade 5. The standard algorithm involves multiplying the numerators together and then multiplying the denominators (fig. 6.17).

$$\frac{3}{5} \times \frac{4}{9} = \frac{3 \times 4}{5 \times 9} = \frac{12}{45}$$

Fig. 6.17. Using the standard algorithm to multiply fractions

The number 1 plays a large role in children's work with fraction multiplication. Just as with whole numbers, 1 is the multiplicative identity for fractions because any fraction multiplied by 1 is just that fraction; for example, ${}^3/_5 \times 1 = {}^3/_5$ and ${}^{99}/_{1000} \times 1 = {}^{99}/_{1000}$. This is true even if the fraction is zero because ${}^0/_5 \times 1 = {}^0/_5$. (Remember that zero multiplied by a number is always zero.) And because every fraction has infinitely many fractions that are equivalent to it, you can write 1 in many ways, such as ${}^5/_5$, ${}^{13}/_{13}$, ${}^{59}/_{59}$, and so on. As long as the numerator and denominator are the same, the fraction is equivalent to 1. This concept plays a special role in multiplication problems when students discover common factors in the numerators and denominators of fractions they are multiplying.

To illustrate how children might work with common factors , let's consider ${}^3/_5 \times {}^{10}/_9$. Using the standard algorithm, the student multiplies numerator by numerator and denominator by denominator to get ${}^{30}/_{45}$. He notices that the numbers 30 and 45 have a common factor of 15. That common factor, written as ${}^{15}/_{15}$, is just another way of representing 1, and it can be used to write the product in a simpler form, in this case as ${}^2/_3$ (fig. 6.18).

$$\frac{30}{45} = \frac{15 \times 2}{15 \times 3} = \frac{15}{15} \times \frac{2}{3} = 1 \times \frac{2}{3} = \frac{2}{3}$$

Fig. 6.18. Using common factors to write a fraction in simpler form

Of course, some children may notice that 30 and 45 have common factors of 3 and 5:

$$\frac{30}{45} = \frac{(2 \times 3 \times 5)}{(3 \times 3 \times 5)} = \frac{2}{3} \times \frac{3}{3} \times \frac{5}{5} = \frac{2}{3} \times 1 \times 1 = \frac{2}{3}$$

Children and teachers sometimes say that the common factors "cancel each other." What they are expressing is that the $^3/_3$ and the $^5/_5$ are both 1.

Identifying and eliminating common factors can also be thought of as the reverse of the process used in determining equivalent fractions when adding or subtracting fractions. Both processes involve finding equivalent fractions. To create a common denominator, the child needs to multiply by 1; when simplifying a fraction, the child recognizes a factor of 1. To find an equivalent fraction to $^4/_7$, for example, children multiply by a fraction equivalent to 1:

$$\frac{4}{7} = \frac{4}{7} \times 1 = \frac{4}{7} \times \frac{5}{5} = \frac{20}{35}$$

To simplify a fraction, such as in the example below, children look for fractions equivalent to 1 by identifying factors that the numerator and denominator have in common:

$$\frac{20}{35} = \frac{4}{7} \times \frac{5}{5} = \frac{4}{7} \times 1 = \frac{4}{7}$$

Dividing with Fractions

In the fourth and fifth grades, children begin to investigate division with fractions through solving sharing and repeated-subtraction situations. When working with sharing situations like "How many cookies does each person get if 3 people share 5 cookies?" teachers want students to partition the whole (5 cookies) into equal-size groups (3) and determine the size of each group. In cases of repeated subtraction such as "How many $^1/_2$ hours are in 5 hours?" teachers want students to think about how many groups of a given size ($^1/_2$ hour) are in the whole (5 hours). When solving either of these situations, students must adjust their thinking about the quantities involved when working with fractions. The teacher needs to carefully structure problems so children develop meaningful connections between whole number division and division with fractions. How are these connections built?

Children in second and third grades begin developing ideas about fractions as they work with sharing situations. Take a look at the second grader's work in figure 6.19 (following page). What ideas about sharing does this student understand? Which ideas appear to be missing?

Fig. 6.19. A second grader partitions a cookie into three pieces.

The student understands that he needs to break the cookie into three pieces—he may even think his pieces are the same, but may not know how to write the amount as a number (i.e., $1/3$). The student sems to have difficulty, like most younger children, partitioning a circle into three equal parts.

Consider Aaron's work in figure 6.20. Aaron, a fourth grader, used a sharing division situation to show $2/3$.

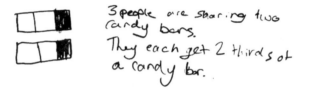

Fig. 6.20. Aaron's work for a sharing division situation

This is a typical problem that students are asked to solve. How is this problem different from whole number problems children solved earlier? Here, although the two candy bars are shared by three people, the answer will be fractional parts of a candy bar. Notice how Aaron solved this problem. He divided the bars into thirds to get 6 candy-bar pieces, and then determined that each friend gets $2/3$ of a candy bar. In his diagram, the amount is $2/3$ of one candy bar, not $2/3$ of the two candy bars. It is hard to tell exactly how he assigned parts of the candy bars to each of the three people. However, he has clearly demonstrated how to solve a division situation that results in a fraction. Additionally, Aaron has brought many different ideas into play, such as sharing equally (dividing), determining the whole, dividing a collection to make equal parts, and combining parts of wholes to determine the total.

Let's look at a similar sharing situation:

There are 4 brownies to be shared among 6 people. How much will each person get?

To solve this problem, children have to think about ways to determine equal parts so the brownies can be distributed equally among 6 people (fig. 6.21).

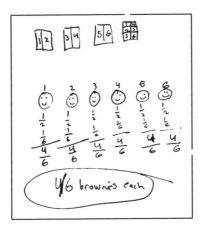

Fig. 6.21. One solution to the Brownie problem

This fourth grader drew a picture to help her figure out the situation. She assigns the brownie parts to each of the six people by numbering the parts. She initially gives each person $1/2$ brownie, using 3 of the 4 brownies. Then, she gives each person $1/6$ of the remaining brownie. Looking at her picture, she sees that each friend will receive exactly $1/2 + 1/6$ of a brownie. The student adds the fractional quantities to find the total amount (notice that she knows that $1/2 = 3/6$) and concludes that each friend will receive $4/6$ of a brownie. The student partitioned the brownies into different size parts and added unlike fractions to determine the total amount for each person (or each group). Given that she added $1/2$ and $1/6$, it is curious that she did not rewrite her answer of $4/6$ as $2/3$. Did you simplify the answer to $2/3$? If so, did you notice which factor of 1 you used? It was $2/2$: $4/6 = 2/3 \times 2/2 = 2/3$. The answer can be written as $2/3$ of a brownie.

 DO YOU KNOW How Teachers Introduce Fractions?

Teachers often introduce fractions by asking children to solve sharing division story problems. Rather than posing problems such as sharing 6 cookies among 3 friends, the teacher changes the numbers in the problem, for example, sharing 6 cookies among 4 friends, resulting in leftover objects (cookies) that must be accounted for. To solve this problem, children must evenly break apart the leftover cookies so each person gets the same amount.

Determining what to do with the leftovers can be challenging for younger children. First graders might decide not to share the two leftover cookies, but older children usually divide the leftover cookies fairly.

Teachers also pose problems in which children will only receive part of a whole unit. By changing the problem from sharing 6 cookies among 4 friends to sharing 4 cookies among 6 friends, children explore fractional amounts. It is important for children to solve these types of problems as they learn about fractions.

Repeated-subtraction problems like the following are another type of situation that children encounter when dividing fractions:

Megan has 2 yards of ribbon that she wants to cut into ½-yard-long strips. How many ½-yard strips will she be able to get out of 2 yards of ribbon?

Because this problem involves linear measures, the student could either use actual yardsticks or draw rectangular regions. If using yardsticks, the student could start by cutting a half-yard piece of string or ribbon; then with two yardsticks end-to-end, she could measure out half-yard pieces in the two yardsticks. After doing so, the student decides that Megan can get a total of 4 strips because there are 4 half-yards in 2 yards.

Alternatively, children might draw a rectangle to represent the two yards of ribbon (fig. 6.22).

| ½ yard | ½ yard | ½ yard | ½ yard |

Fig. 6.22. A student draws a picture of the Ribbon problem.

A child can simply count to determine there are 4 half-yard strips in 2 yards. If she counts, she can determine how many groups of $1/_2$ are in 2, and can conclude that 2 yards ÷ ½ yard = 4 strips. In both approaches the child is repeatedly adding $1/_2$ until she gets to 2. Using repeated subtraction to solve the problem is somewhat similar; however to do that, the child would start with 2 and repeatedly subtract $1/_2$ until reaching 0:

$$2 - \frac{1}{2} = 1\frac{1}{2}$$

$$1\frac{1}{2} - \frac{1}{2} = 1$$

$$1 - \frac{1}{2} = \frac{1}{2}$$

$$\frac{1}{2} - \frac{1}{2} = 0$$

The answer is 4 because $1/_2$ was subtracted four times.

Problems can be made more complex by using numbers that are harder to represent with physical materials. In a sharing situation, the harder it is to represent the number of people who are sharing, the more difficult the problem becomes. For example, the Brownie problem above could be changed so that 2 brownies are to be shared among 10 friends. The student would need to partition 2 wholes into 10 equal parts, or in parts that are $1/_5$ of 1 whole. For children, showing fifths is typically more challenging than working with halves and fourths.

In middle school, repeated-subtraction problems are made more complex by choosing fractions that are more difficult to represent. For example, the Ribbon problem could be presented as, "How many $2/_3$-yard strips of ribbon are in $4^1/_3$ yards?" or "How many $2/_5$-yard strips are in $8^3/_4$ yards?" When problems become even more challenging, it is the ideal time for teachers to encourage children to develop formal procedures for division with fractions.

The Invert-and-Multiply Algorithm for Dividing Fractions: What's the Math?

Most adults learned the invert-and-multiply algorithm for dividing fractions in the upper elementary grades or in middle school. As you might remember, the process involves rewriting the division problem in terms of multiplication. For example, to divide $1/_2$ by $3/_4$, invert $3/_4$ to $4/_3$ (called the reciprocal), and then multiply $1/_2$ by $4/_3$. Because the product $1/_2 \times 4/_3 = 2/_3$, we know that $1/_2 \div 3/_4 = 2/_3$. Why is this true? How does the process work?

In chapter 2 (page 32) we addressed the reasoning behind this algorithm by describing one way to think about the following problem:

> *Sally has $2 \, 2/_3$ feet of ribbon and she wants to cut the ribbon into ½-foot pieces to make bows. How many bows can she make?*

We used this problem to show why it makes sense to solve a division problem by using multiplication. Here, we provide a more formal explanation of why the standard algorithm works.

Paying attention to the patterns that emerge when similar division problems are posed is the key to making sense of this algorithm. Let's take a look at a simple example, $1 \div 1/_3$. This division can be interpreted as "How many groups of $1/_3$ are in 1 whole?" Further, because $1/_3$ is one of three equal parts of a whole, you know that there are exactly three groups of $1/_3$ in 1 (fig. 6.23).

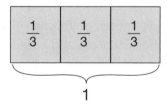

Fig. 6.23. Three groups of $1/_3$ in 1 whole

You can also reason through corresponding problems such as $1 \div 1/_4$ and $1 \div 1/_n$ in the same way. The result is always straightforward. There are exactly four groups of $1/_4$ in 1; therefore, $1 \div 1/_4 = 4$. In general, for a natural number n, $1/_n$ is defined as one of n equal parts of one unit. So there are exactly n groups of $1/_n$ in 1. Thus, $1 \div 1/_n = n$ for any natural number n. See these relationships in table 6.1 on the following page.

Table 6.1. Patterns in division problems of the form $1 \div 1/n$

Division Problem	Interpretation	Answer
$1 \div 1/2$	How many groups of $1/2$ are in 1?	2
$1 \div 1/3$	How many groups of $1/3$ are in 1?	3
$1 \div 1/4$	How many groups of $1/4$ are in 1?	4
$1 \div 1/5$	How many groups of $1/5$ are in 1?	5
$1 \div 1/n$	How many groups of $1/n$ are in 1?	n

Let's consider $10 \div 1/3$. Because there are three groups of $1/3$ in 1, there must be ten times as many groups of $1/3$ in 10 units; that is, there are 30 groups of $1/3$. Let's look at the thinking involved. You wanted to know how many thirds are in 10, but to determine that you used what you knew about how many thirds are in 1. Because you know that there are three groups of $1/3$ in every 1 (whole), there are a total of $10 \times 3 = 30$ groups of $1/3$. The reciprocal gives you a rate (how many groups of $1/3$ per 1) that you can then use to determine how many groups of $1/3$ are in 10—or any other amount you choose.

This reasoning applies to more complex fractions as well. In general, the reciprocal of a fraction tells exactly *how many* of that fraction is in one whole. So, when we invert the second fraction in the algorithm, we rewrite the problem as a multiplication problem. The reciprocal gives us the number of fractional parts that are in one whole and the first fraction tells us how many groups.

READER'S CHALLENGE

The relationship between multiplication and division is fundamental but often misunderstood, particularly when working with fractions. As you've seen, each division of a fraction number sentence can be rewritten as a unique multiplication number sentence, and you've seen why it works. Can you solve $13/4 \div 1/2$ by showing how division and multiplication ideas are connected? (See the "Taking a Closer Look" section below for the explanation.)

TAKING A CLOSER LOOK at Fifth- and Sixth-Graders' Division with Fractions

How do children divide fractions without using the invert-and-multiply algorithm? What challenges do they face when doing so? We suggest you work on the problem above before reading the students' solutions.

Sam has a minibike that holds $1/2$ gallon of gas. If he has a gas can containing $13/4$ gallons of gas, how many times will he be able to fill his minibike?

One challenging aspect of this problem is determining what to do with the leftover gas after counting the $1/2$ gallons. Take a look at Student 1's work in figure 6.24.

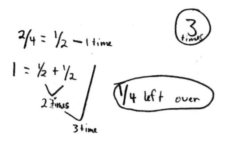

Fig. 6.24. Student 1's solution to the Minibike problem

Student 1 determined the number of $1/2$ gallons in $13/4$ gallons by first noting that $2/4$ is $1/2$ gallon, so it can be used to the fill the minibike one time. She also recorded that $1 = 1/2 + 1/2$ and so the 1 gallon can be used to fill the minibike two more times. Finally, she writes down the total number of times the tank can be filled and circles her answer (3 times) and writes how much gas will be left over—exactly $1/4$ gallon.

Figure 6.25 below illustrates a similar approach taken by Student 2. On the left, you see how he measured two groups of $1/2$ in the 1 whole gallon of gas. The 1 and the 2 on either side of the diagonal in the box denote the two times that the minibike can be filled with 1 gallon of gas. On the right, this student illustrated how $3/4$ is the same as $1/2$ plus $1/4$. He uses this fact to show that he can fill up the minibike one more time with $1/4$ gallon of gas left over.

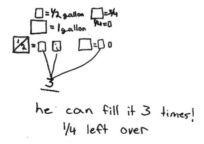

Fig. 6.25. Student 2's solution to the minibike problem

In this problem, the students are determining the number of full half gallons there are in $13/4$ gallons. There are three half gallons—they can fill up the tank three times. Suppose you encountered a slightly different version of this problem—how many $1/2$ gallons are in $13/4$ gallons? You know there are 3 half gallons in $13/4$ with $1/4$ gallon left over. But what do you do with the $1/4$ gallon of gas left over? You must determine how many $1/2$ gallons are in $1/4$ gallon. In other words, what is $1/4$ divided by $1/2$? To answer this question, teachers encourage students to change their reference point and think about "How much of $1/2$ is in $1/4$?" because $1/2$ is greater than $1/4$. And because $1/2$ of $1/2$ is $1/4$, you know that $1/4$ divided by $1/2$ is $1/2$. Therefore, another way to answer the original question is to say, "The tank can be filled $3^1/2$ times."

Things to Remember

- Children build number sense for adding and subtracting fractions using strategies that mirror those they used for solving whole number addition and subtraction situations. They decompose numbers, work with friendlier numbers, and use a *making-one* strategy to solve problems.
- Thinking about fractions as parts of a whole is a fundamental understanding that enables children to make sense of and solve addition, subtraction, multiplication, and division problems using fractions.
- Understanding and working with equivalent fractions are crucial skills. Children can use these skills to devise efficient strategies for solving problems involving the four operations.
- Children continue to make diagrams and use manipulatives as they add, subtract, multiply, and divide fractions.
- Children expand their understanding of multiplication as they explore working with fractions. Multiplication with fractions introduces a new situation—the operator situation.
- Sharing situations are used to develop students' understanding of fractions and division with fractions.

Things to Do

- Look for fraction situations around the home to initiate conversations about fraction operations with your child, such as measuring ingredients for a double batch of cookies or soup or finding the center of a picture frame that measures $9^1/2$ inches wide.
- If you are having trouble with the invert-and-multiply algorithm for dividing fractions, it might be helpful if you read the section "Do You Know Why We Multiply to Divide Fractions?" in chapter 2 (page 32).
- Go back and review your work from the Reader's Challenges.

Resources

We have tried to address many key ideas in this chapter, but we can only touch upon the topics. Additional resources you may find helpful and informative are listed below.

For Children

Calvert, Pam, and Wayne Geehan. *Multiplying Menace: The Revenge of Rumpelstiltskin*. Watertown, Mass.: Charlesbridge Publishing, Inc., 2006.

————. *The Multiplying Menace Divides*. Watertown, Mass.: Charlesbridge Publishing, Inc., 2011.

Leedy, Loreen. *Fraction Action*. New York: Holiday House, 1994.

Napoli, Donna Jo, and Anna Currey. *The Wishing Club: A Story About Fractions*. New York: Henry Holt, 2007.

Pallotta, Jerry, and Rob Bolster. *The Hershey's Milk Chocolate Bar Fractions Book*. New York: Scholastic Inc., 1999.

More4U Online Resources

You can find a listing of additional helpful resources with links, including recommended games, by entering the access code on the title page of this book at NCTM's More4U page (nctm.org/more4u).

7

Mathematics at Home

> Luis, a preschooler, came to school one morning eager to tell his teacher,
> Ms. Luongo, about an exciting event. *"I did math last night at home!"* She asked,
> *"Really? What did you do?"* Luis replied, *"I helped set the table, and I had to make
> sure I had enough forks."*

When you think about doing math at home, what is the first thing that comes to
mind? "Homework" pops up for many parents and caregivers. But as Luis discovered,
opportunities to think mathematically are everywhere. Daily household activities
such as folding napkins, sorting clothes, helping cook a meal, or wondering how long
until bedtime can lead to meaningful mathematical conversations with your child.
Mathematical thinking involves raising questions and searching for patterns—in essence,
it is about figuring things out. Perhaps that night at Luis's house, there were guests for
dinner. Did someone tell him how many forks to put on the table or did he figure that out
himself? Everyday life presents numerous situations for problem solving.

Talking about mathematics is a worthwhile practice you can do to help your children
see the connections math has to "real life." These conversations can be sparked by
homework problems, grocery shopping, browsing in a toy store, or other activities in
daily living. Mathematics can and should be a regular subject that you talk about with
your children.

Before setting out to make math a routine part of your conversations, it is helpful
to know what to expect from your children as they make sense of what they're learning
in school. For example, it is important to realize that mathematical thinking does not
always progress in a straight line; sometimes a child will temporarily revert back to a less
sophisticated approach when learning something new. To start the discussion, we revisit
some ideas about what it means for children to make sense of procedures.

Making Sense of Procedures

What does it mean for children to do meaningful mathematics? Earlier in this book, we discussed the importance of understanding not only how to use procedures but also why those procedures work. How can parents help their children make sense of the methods and procedures they're learning and using in school?

One of the crucial goals of elementary school is for children to develop mathematical methods and strategies that eventually become automatic. The procedures should make sense to children, and they should be able to explain why the procedures work. To help your children achieve this goal, you may need to take on a new role when you work and talk together. But you may not know the inner workings of these procedures, although you may easily solve the problem. It was not until recently that understanding why procedures work has been emphasized in school mathematics, so like many others, you may find some processes difficult to explain. For instance, there are few individuals who can clarify the underpinnings of the invert-and-multiply method when dividing fractions. (See page 155 to find one way to do this.)

If you did not have many opportunities to explore mathematical reasons for different procedures in your own education experience, you may find it challenging to work with your children as they do their math homework. So you and your children may need to collaborate to make sense of the mathematics they are learning.

Whether you are playing a math game or helping your child with her homework, keep these few cautionary notes in mind, and you will both be happy with the experience:

Although the ultimate goal is that children develop efficient and fluent skills, strategies, and methods, these approaches may look markedly different for each child. For instance, a young child may need to rely on counting strategies for some time before using non-counting strategies. Using non-counting strategies is one of the goals for students in the primary grades, but students also need time to develop these skills and concepts. Not all students will develop these skills and concepts at the same time in the same way. And do not assume that a child who uses counting strategies is not being efficient. Children should count objects, including their fingers, early on. As they develop new methods over time, they will no longer need to count by ones to solve problems.

Sometimes children return to simpler methods when they encounter new, more challenging ideas. Recently, a colleague reported that her first-grade students, who had demonstrated mastery of counting by fives and tens, began counting by ones when determining how many tennis balls a large bucket could hold. Reverting to that method could be related to the quantity or type of items involved. It could even be associated with the children wanting to be accurate. It is not uncommon for children to temporarily use less efficient strategies when exploring new ideas. But you'll be fascinated to see how quickly they develop efficient methods as they become comfortable with those new ideas.

You should support the notion that mathematics makes sense. Your children may use certain procedures, but do not know why they work. You can ask them to talk about the problem(s). You might work together to understand why the procedures work. There are few content areas that are more logically structured than mathematics. Encourage your children to figure out the meaning of the mathematics they are learning. If it seems that your children's math instruction in school is focused on memorizing formulas without enough opportunities to make sense of the mathematics, you may need to make it a point to talk with them about their work.

Talking About Mathematics

Children learn a great deal by watching adult behavior, so it's important that your child observe you reasoning mathematically in everyday situations. It's simple to do what's called a "think aloud." Our example is a parent thinking aloud while shopping for cupcakes for a party:

> *"Wait a minute. I need to get cupcakes for twenty-seven kids, and these cupcakes come in packs of twelve." The parent then places the packs in the cart, one by one. "So that's twelve ... um ... twenty-four ... not enough ... I need three more cupcakes ...oh yeah, there are at least three more cupcakes in this pack. Okay. That's enough, and there are some left over too."*

Depending on her age and readiness, the daughter might join in the sense making. What is important is that her parent is being a good role model for mathematical thinking. The parent is not embarrassed or nervous, and takes the time to figure out the right number of cupcake packs to buy. Subtle displays like this bring math "home" and help safeguard against math anxiety or math avoidance in children. The key is to make the invisible math you do every day visible to your child.

Talking about Mathematics with Your Child

The counterpoint to your display of everyday math is your child's conversation about the mathematics he or she is learning in school. Just as you might discuss a book that your child is reading, encourage him or her to talk to you about math class. If you show interest in the mathematics, your child may follow your lead and show more interest in it, too.

While your child may describe activities that do not sound like those in the math classroom of your childhood as you talk about math, you may discover something you never realized before, and the joy and playfulness of mathematics can become a shared experience. For example, one mother commented that as she and her third grader talked about arrays and drew pictures, she finally realized why the numbers 4, 9, 16, 25, and so on are called square numbers. Figure 7.1 on the following page represents 4 and 9 with arrays and reveals why they are called square numbers—the arrays are square shaped.

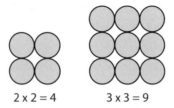

2 x 2 = 4   3 x 3 = 9

Fig. 7.1. The numbers 4 and 9 represented with square arrays

The mother said, "It had never dawned on me before, but they actually make squares. I also never realized that they increase the way they do, +5, +7, +9, and on and on. My child showed me why that was true too." How did her child do this? One possibility is by drawing nested square arrays (fig. 7.2).

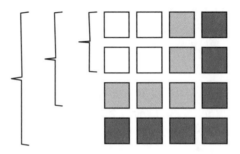

Fig. 7.2. Nested square arrays

The 2 × 2 array, made with white squares, is nested within the 3 × 3 array and the 3 × 3 array is nested within the 4 × 4 array. Notice how the number of lilac squares (5) illustrates the difference between 9 and 4, and the number of purple squares (7) illustrates the difference between 16 and 9; that is, 4 + 5 = 9 and 9 + 7 = 16. Using this diagram, a child might explain that to get the next square number, he must add squares around two edges of the 4 × 4 array. He determines that he must add four to each of the two edges plus one more for the corner, adding a total of nine squares. Therefore 16 + 9 = 25 represents the next square number. This pattern continues; to generate the square number after 25, you must add the next odd number, which is 11.

 DO YOU KNOW What Figurate Numbers Are?

Square numbers are one example of what mathematicians call *figurate numbers*—numbers that can be represented as a geometric shape. In addition to square numbers, there are triangular, pentagonal, and hexagonal numbers as well as other figurate numbers. There are even numbers associated with three-dimensional shapes like cubic and pyramidal numbers. The triangular numbers are frequently a topic of study in elementary school that carries forward into the study of algebra and functions. The first four triangular numbers are illustrated in figure 7.3.

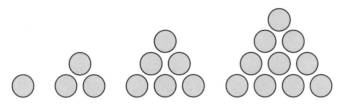

Fig. 7.3. The first four triangular numbers are 1, 3, 6, 10.

Triangular numbers are generated by adding consecutive natural numbers; that is, the first triangular number is 1; to find the next, you add 1 + 2. To find the third triangular number, you add 1 + 2 + 3, and so on. Another way of generating triangular numbers is to add another row of dots along the bottom edge to form a new larger triangle. That new row of dots will have exactly one more dot than the previous row. So, to find the next triangular number using triangles, a row of 5 more dots is added to the 10 for 15, or you could find the sum of 1 + 2 + 3 + 4 + 5. To see how to use algebra to represent these numbers, read the discussion about the staircase problem in chapter 8, page 184.

Let's look at the square numbers. The list of square numbers begins with 0, 1, 4, 9, 16, 25, 36, and continues forever. (In fact, any set of figurate numbers continues forever.) In algebra, these square numbers are referred to as *perfect squares*. Each perfect square can be represented by writing a whole number multiplied by itself or by writing the number with an exponent of two as follows:

$0^2 = 0 \times 0 = 0$; $1^2 = 1 \times 1 = 1$; $2^2 = 2 \times 2 = 4$

It may seem impossible to have a 0×0 array, but zero multiplied by itself is zero, and so it fits the pattern of a square number.

Following the logic of the patterns for figurate numbers reminds us how mathematics' consistent structure can be used to make sense of new mathematical situations and concepts.

When you engage in conversations about math with your child, keep these rules of thumb in mind:

- Let your child drive the conversation.
- Ask your child to explain his or her thinking with words, pictures or diagrams, and numbers.
- Remember that your child's strategy may be different from your own.
- Be patient. Explaining ideas can take time.
- Expect the unexpected. Math is a strong web of deeply interconnected ideas. The conversation could expand your child's understanding—and your own.

The vignette about buying cupcakes at the supermarket is an example of a parent being a good role model for mathematical reasoning. The parent is relaxed and demonstrates that making sense of problems is an everyday phenomenon. But what if you are a parent who is highly anxious about math? Children are remarkably perceptive and able to intuit others' feelings about matters—including mathematics—sometimes merely from body language. You may be all too aware of this and worried that you're sending the wrong messages to your children about math. There are techniques and activities you can use to de-escalate your anxiety and reduce the chances that your children pick up on it (see "Taking a Closer Look at Math Anxiety" below). Remember, we are *all* mathematical thinkers whether we are working out if we will be late for an appointment or if we have enough cash to purchase an item.

 TAKING A CLOSER LOOK at Math Anxiety

Some people experience tension and worry when doing math. Math anxiety is "a feeling of intense frustration or helplessness about one's ability to do math" (Smith and Smith 1997, p. 1). It can negatively impact many facets of life including education, personal finance, and career opportunities. Even though they may not realize it, adults with math anxiety may be passing on negative feelings about math to children.

Researchers B. Sidney Smith and Wendy Hageman Smith (1997) have suggested that "math myths," such as the ones listed below, may contribute to the feeling of many people that they are simply not good at math:

MATH MYTH 1: Math requires logic, not intuition.

MATH MYTH 2: Mathematicians do problems quickly in their heads.

MATH MYTH 3: Men are better at doing math than women.

MATH MYTH 4: Mathematicians don't make computational errors.

MATH MYTH 5: There is only one correct answer.

MATH MYTH 6: Math is not a creative endeavor.

MATH MYTH 7: Some people have a math brain and others do not.

Do any of these statements sound familiar? If so, can you remember how old you were when you started to deduce these messages? Perhaps you can think of a few more. It may surprise you to know that only in the United States do people generally believe that learning mathematics depends on special ability (Mathematical Sciences Education Board 1989). It's no wonder that so many of us grew up thinking, "I'm not a math person."

If you do have math anxiety, what can you do? Our first recommendation is to slow down. When you are doing math—either in real-life situations or helping a child with homework—*take your time.* You may have painful memories of doing timed fact drills, but the truth is when you are at the store estimating how much something will cost, no one is timing you! And it's a great opportunity to model sense making for children. You may also find that relaxation techniques such as deep breathing really help. Slowly take in a breath of air, fill your lungs, hold your breath for a few seconds, and then slowly let your breath out.

If you're concerned that your own math anxiety may be "catching," here are some tips for preventing math anxiety in children:

◆ Be aware of messages you may be sending about math. This may be in the form of verbal or nonverbal communication.

◆ Allow children to use all types of reasoning to make sense of math.

◆ Maintain the expectation that everybody can do math, even you.

Homework

Debate continues about the role and usefulness of homework. In some countries, very little homework is assigned, and in others, homework is a cultural norm. Opinions vary from family to family, school to school, and teacher to teacher. However, in our experience, homework is a crucial issue for many parents.

Homework can serve many purposes, depending on the teacher's goals. At times, a homework assignment is given to provide students with additional practice. Other times, a teacher may want students to go home and write up an explanation for an observation that was made in class. In general, many teachers think of homework as an opportunity for students to stay engaged with the important ideas currently being addressed in class. And that comes in many forms.

One benefit of homework is that it gives parents and caregivers information about the math concepts students are exploring. Whatever the homework expectation is in your child's math classroom, it is important to understand that an activity focusing on practicing a specific skill may provide some benefit, but repeating a procedure *incorrectly* many times can be detrimental in the long run.

Where homework is completed determines, in part, how easy it is for you to monitor your child's progress. Ideally, homework is completed in a place where the parent can easily check in and be available when questions arise. Being in the same room is helpful just so you can have a sense of how your child is handling the task. Watching your child's body language can give this away. Making yourself visible, and more important, your child visible to you is crucial to knowing how things are going.

Homework can also be an opportunity to have a good math conversation. Remember to first listen to your child's reasoning and then encourage him with good questioning. The goal is not to do the assignment for him, but to help him figure it out for himself.

Good questions are those that guide children's mathematical thinking without giving away the solution to a problem. Teachers are masterful at this skill. With practice, you can learn how to do the same as you work with your children. And if you need assistance, you can always talk with your child's classroom teacher. Most teachers are eager to connect with parents and offer assistance and suggestions about the best way to help your child. This said, it can be very difficult to ask questions that encourage your child to try a different approach, consider other possible approaches, or revise an answer.

 TAKING A CLOSER LOOK at Asking Questions

The primary "rule" of asking "good" questions is to pose more open-ended questions than questions with single-word answers. For example, asking "How do you know?" is likely to generate a response that reveals more about your child's understanding than asking "Is that true?" The questions you ask may also depend somewhat on the stage your child is in the problem-solving process. For example, if your child gets stuck when starting a problem, then you may want to ask him to reread the problem aloud. Sometimes children get stuck with a calculation or procedure while at other times they find errors with the solution they came up with. Because of this, we have organized a sample list of questions you can ask at critical junctures in the problem-solving process (see also https://connectedmath. msu.edu/families/homework-support/).

When your child is getting started, these are good questions to ask:

◆ Can you read the problem to me?

◆ What do you need to figure out?

◆ What do you already know?

◆ Have you solved a problem that was similar to this one?

◆ What parts make sense to you?

◆ What parts do not make sense to you?

If your child gets stuck while working on a problem, these are helpful questions to ask:

◆ Do you see any patterns or relationships?

◆ Can you try drawing a picture to make sense of the problem?

◆ What do you mean by …?

◆ What would happen if …?

◆ How do you know?

◆ Can you explain it in a different way?

◆ What other math does this remind you of?

After your child has found a solution, these questions are useful:

◆   Have you answered the question?

◆   Is your solution reasonable? How do you know?

◆   What worked?

◆   What did not work?

When Homework Is a Struggle

If your child is struggling with a homework assignment and has spent a reasonable amount of time and effort on it, it might be a good time to stop. Make sure you communicate with the teacher about what happened and give as much information as possible. By third grade, you might encourage your child to take on this responsibility by coaching him on what to say and what to write about the difficulties he encountered. It is important to communicate exactly what mathematical struggles your child had. Be specific and focus the communication on the mathematical ideas. It is also reasonable to expect a fifth grader to tell her teacher that she couldn't do the homework and explain why. She might write on her homework paper something like, "I got stuck when dividing these two decimal numbers because I didn't know how to divide a smaller number by something bigger with decimals." Communication with their teachers should continue as students move on to middle school, too. We know one eighth-grade math teacher who asks his students to write down how much time they spent on a problem and to note exactly "where they were in their thinking." Eventually students can take responsibility for and monitor their own learning. But no matter who communicates with the teacher about homework difficulties, always keep in mind that teachers want and need this type of information to support students as best as possible.

What If You Just Can't Help?

Even with an abundance of online tutorials and help forums, there may come a time when you feel you cannot help your child with her math homework. This is an opportune time to contact the teacher and ask what other resources or help are available. Remember, even frustrating homework experiences keep parents and teachers aware of a student's progress. Continue to talk about math with your child, ask him to show you what he is learning, find out what he likes best about his math class, and so on.

Creating Other Opportunities to Talk About Mathematics

Being a good role model for mathematical thinking and supporting your child's homework routine are not the only avenues to conversations about math. There are other activities, all with an element of fun, that provide an opening for math talk.

✳ **DO YOU KNOW** How to Choose Math Activity Books?

Math activity books for children are sold in many places—at bookstores, school fairs, supermarkets, toy stores, and so on. Be cautious when choosing these books. Unfortunately, many that are available can be used in ways that contradict the message of this book—that mathematics is about making sense of problems and figuring things out. In general, we recommend books that engage children in solving puzzles, whether they are number puzzles or word puzzles. Books that offer pages and pages of practice with a particular operation can be helpful if used appropriately. See "The Role of Practice" section in chapter 2 (page 40) for more insight on this issue. But such books can be detrimental if a child is not ready for such work. A far better approach is giving your children a blank piece of paper and having them make up their own problems to solve. You will learn a lot about where your children are in their thinking, both what they are comfortable with and how they might be challenging themselves to move ahead.

Games

When adults describe the math classroom of their childhoods, some may not recall *ever* playing games in school. But modern educators recognize the importance of playing math games. Games are fun and very motivating, and they have many benefits for children. Games—

- ◆ reinforce mathematical objectives;
- ◆ are repeatable and sustain interest and engagement;
- ◆ can be open-ended, allowing for multiple approaches;
- ◆ increase curiosity and motivation;
- ◆ reduce anxiety about math;
- ◆ build strategy and reasoning skills;
- ◆ lead students to talk about mathematics; and
- ◆ compel players to work mentally. (Adama Britt 2014, p. 7)

If your child's teacher sends a game home, find time to play it with him. If the game is too easy or too difficult for your child, you may think of ways to adapt the game or to adjust the difficulty level. For example, the game "Close to 100" can be made more challenging by changing the game to "Close to 1,000" (mentioned in chapter 3) or by using wild cards (in which a player assigns a digit to the card when it is drawn). For students who are ready to work with decimals, try playing "Close to 1" instead. Children will also come up with their own ways of increasing a game's difficulty level.

Quality math games do not have to be expensive: Many age-appropriate math games may be played with a simple deck of playing cards. You may have played *Go Fish* as a child, and it is still a very popular game. There is a wonderful variation of this game called *Tens Go Fish*. Recall that with *Go Fish*, a player asks a partner for a card that matches one of the cards she is holding in her hand. Each time the child finds a match, she removes that card from her hand and makes a pair with the card that she receives from her partner. If the partner does not have the card that she asks for, the partner says, "Go fish," and she must pick up a card from the deck. As play continues, it becomes the partner's turn and he asks for cards to make matches with cards that he is holding. The game ends when players can no longer make pairs.

Tens Go Fish is played using similar rules. Two simple changes in the game make this an excellent game for practicing addition facts for ten (0 + 10, 1 + 9, 2 + 8, 3 + 7, 4 + 6, and 5 + 5). First, the game is played with only forty-four instead of fifty-two cards—only the numbers 0 through 10 are played (aces can stand for one and some other face card for zero). Second, matches are made when players make pairs that sum to ten.

This game is a very popular game with first and second graders. As they play, they have many opportunities to make sums of ten. And they have chances to practice different methods for finding sums if they do not know these basic facts. For instance, a child might have a 6 card in her hand. She does not know the number she needs to make 10, but she can use a counting-on strategy to determine that she must ask her partner for a 4 card. Later in the game, if she has another 6 in her hand, she may not need to use this counting strategy—she knows that she needs a 4 card. If she does not remember, then she has another occasion to figure out that she must ask her partner for a 4 card. By its very nature, the game provides players repeated openings to figure out the card needed to make a sum of ten. Moreover, as children play the game, they can write number sentences to record the pairs they have made. This is an important way to practice writing the different facts for ten. The players can also discuss which facts they are missing on their papers and talk about how they know they have all the different ways to make ten. As you see, this is a multilayered game that helps children think about some complex ideas surrounding the facts for ten; for example, 6 + 4 = 10 and 4 + 6 = 10. Knowing these facts becomes very important as children develop chunking strategies to make sense of problems (see page 49).

There are many other card games that can be found on the Internet that are appropriate for reinforcing elementary math skills. We list a few more card games in table 7.1. You may come across these games—or very similar ones—when searching for games online. If you do not have a deck of playing cards, you can also make number cards to play these games.

Table 7.1. Card games using a deck of playing cards

.	Brief Description
Compare and **Double Compare** Grades 1–3	**The Game:** To play "Compare," divide the playing deck into two equal piles. The players turn a card faceup and determine which card has the larger number. The player with the larger number wins the cards. "Double Compare" is played the same way, but each player places two cards faceup and the sums are compared. **The Math:** Children think about the relative size of numbers, solve addition problems, and practice basic addition facts.
Salute Addition Grades 1–3	**The Game:** This game requires three players, one "adder" and two "saluters." Saluters each take one card from the deck and hold the card, face out, on their forehead so that they can only read the card of the other saluter. The adder, who can see both cards, announces the sum of the cards. The first saluter to determine what his or her card is wins the round. Players rotate positions. **The Math:** Children use part-whole reasoning, think about the relationship between addition and subtraction, and practice basic addition and subtraction facts.
Salute Multiplication Grades 3–5	**The Game:** This game is played just like the addition version described above, only there is a "multiplier" instead of an "adder." That player announces the product of the numbers of the two cards held by the saluters. The first saluter to determine what his or her card is wins the round. Players rotate positions. **The Math:** Children identify the missing factor in a multiplication statement, think about the relationship between multiplication and division, and practice basic multiplication and division facts.
Make 100 Grades 3–4	**The Game:** Players are dealt six cards. Each player chooses four cards to create 2 two-digit numbers. The goal is to make two numbers whose sum is as close to 100 as possible. Aces stand for 1, queens stand for 0, and kings and jacks are wild cards. Draw four new cards each round. Score each round by finding the difference between 100 and each player's sum. Total scores from five rounds to determine the winner. Low score wins. **The Math:** Children think about addition of two-digit numbers, addition and subtraction strategies for making 100, and place value.
Make the Most of It Grades 4–5	**The Game:** Remove kings and jacks. Aces stand for 1 and queens stand for 0. Players draw one card at a time for a total of five cards. Each card is placed in the ones, tens, hundreds, thousands, and ten thousands positions and cannot be moved. Players draw a sixth card and replace one of the five cards. High number wins the round. **The Math:** Children practice reading numbers and think about place value.

While there are some excellent commercial games available, the difficulty is in knowing which ones to choose. We discuss some of our favorites below.

24® Game (grade 4 and up). This game helps both children *and* adults develop fluency with numbers and operations. Players use the four numbers on the card in play exactly once to obtain the number 24. Players can use any combination of the four basic operations during play. The order in which the numbers are used in the operations does not matter. The game can be played independently or with up to four players. Some elementary schools host official 24 Game tournaments that are open to students across the region. For more information about this game, including rules for tournament play, see More4U and the resource list at the end of this chapter.

Let's consider the thought process a child might go through when faced with a particular card; the card in figure 7.4 has the numbers 3, 4, 11, and 13 and is similar to one from the 24 Game. Notice that the numbers are oriented around the center square. This is important to know when distinguishing a 6 from a 9 on a card!

In what ways can the child combine these numbers using any of the four operations to get a total of 24? First, she might immediately notice that she can multiply 4 by 3 to get 12. Then she may think that if she could only add 12 or multiply by 2, she would get to 24. Studying the numbers, she realizes that 13 – 11 is 2—the very number she needs to make 24. Now she can multiply the 12 she got from 4 × 3 by 2 and get 24. Symbolically, her solution can be written as (4 × 3) × (13 – 11).

Fig. 7.4. A card similar to a 24 Game card

The cards are marked according to level of difficulty. The card in figure 7.4 has a single white dot in each corner. A single dot indicates the easiest level of difficulty. There are two other more challenging levels, indicated by two and three dots respectively. Cards with one dot usually have several different solutions. The number of possible solutions decreases as the difficulty increases. The numbers on easier cards include more factors of 24. More difficult cards also tend to involve more subtraction. Because the card in figure 7.4 is from the "easiest" category, there should be additional solutions.

→ READER'S CHALLENGE

Try to find at least one more solution to the 24 Game card in figure 7.4. Your goal is to use each of the numbers 3, 4, 11, and 13 exactly once to make 24.

How did you play with the numbers? Children quickly learn that it is a good idea to simply add the numbers on the card—that sometimes works! In this case, the sum of the numbers is 31, which is too much. Perhaps you tried multiplying other pairs of numbers besides 3 and 4. A child might try multiplying 3 by 11 to get 33, and then think about how he can work backwards to make 24. Since $33 - 24 = 9$, he may try to make 9 with the other numbers. This works out neatly because $13 - 4 = 9$, so he has, indeed, found a solution. His solution can be written as $(3 \times 11) - (13 - 4)$. The expression $(13 \times 3) - (4 + 11)$ also works. When multiple players play the game, the one who shares a correct solution first keeps the card.

Interestingly, the 24 Game can be used to address more than fluency with numbers and operations. By comparing written solutions to a card, you and your child can have conversations about equivalence, the order of operations, and properties of operations. Just having your child write his or her solution down is an important mathematical activity. And writing the solution down in a way that accurately reflects the process involves considering the use of parentheses to indicate the order in which he or she worked. All written solutions to a particular card should be equivalent mathematical expressions that use the same four numbers.

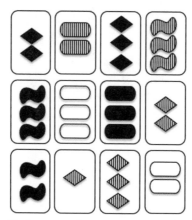

Fig. 7.5. A group of cards similar to SET cards

SET® (age six and older). The game is usually played with twelve cards lying faceup in a three-by-four array on a table (fig. 7.5). In figure 7.5 we show three of the four attributes—the shapes (squiggle, diamond, and oval), the shading (solid, stripes, and no shading), and quantity (one, two, or three shapes). Actual SET cards are also one of three colors (red, purple, or green). When younger children are learning the game, it is helpful to play with cards of only one color. Finding matches using all four attributes can be very challenging and overwhelm beginners. Children can ease into working with all four attributes as they become comfortable playing the game.

There are no turns in this game. Each player tries to identify a set, three cards that are either all the same or all different for a particular feature. If the set has the same feature, it must have that feature on all three cards in the set (for example, all three cards must have two shapes on them). If the set is of a different feature, this feature must be different for each of the cards in the set (for example, solid, stripes, and no shading).

When a player sees a set, she removes those three cards from the table. Three more cards are then laid out and play resumes. Can you find a set in figure 7.5? One possible set is one in which the shapes are different but each card has the same number of shapes and same shading (fig. 7.6).

Fig. 7.6. A set with the same number of shapes, same shading, but different shapes

Generally, the more features cards share, the easier it is to see the set. When three or four features are all different, seeing the set can be a challenge. One example of this type of set is pictured below in figure 7.7. Notice that the shapes, shading, and quantities are all different in this set.

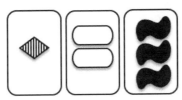

Fig. 7.7. A set in which three features are different.

Another way to use the cards is to draw two cards and then think about what type of card is needed to make a set. There are also online daily puzzles at four levels of difficulty (http://www.nytimes.com/crosswords/game/set/). The play in the daily puzzles is a little different in that some of the cards must be used in more than one set.

BLINK® (*age five and older*). This two-player card game is similar to SET. Players try to find a match in their stack of thirty cards to a card that is visible. To make a match, the card played must be the same color or the same shape or the same number (of shapes) as the visible card. Figure 7.8 shows three cards from the deck. To make a match with any of these cards, a player must place a card with the same color, the same shape, or the same number of shapes as one of these cards. The game ends when one of the players has played all of his thirty cards.

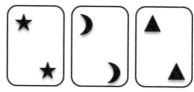

Fig. 7.8. Cards similar to those in the *BLINK* card game

This game is lots of fun for children. They love playing games that require them to be "fast," and, like SET, there are no turns. More important, they are also rapidly considering how the cards are alike or different from the three cards held in their hands. A child may first focus on the color of the cards. If none of the colors matches with one of her cards, she will switch her focus to another attribute, such as the number of shapes or the type of shape. Remarkably, a player is constantly and speedily making decisions about which card to play in which pile at the same time her partner is playing.

This game is much less taxing than SET, yet there are many similarities between the two. If children have difficulty playing SET, you might try *BLINK* instead. They will still have many of the same opportunities to compare attributes among different sets, and at the same time have a grand time playing the game.

 DO YOU KNOW about After-School Events?

Schools sometimes host "Math Nights" or "Math Fairs." These are wonderful events where families learn new math games and activities to play at home. They are also great opportunities to show interest in your child's math learning, to stay connected to the school community, and, perhaps most important, to have fun learning with your child.

Computer Activities

One big difference between your schoolroom and your children's is the presence and acceptance of computers and calculators as learning tools. Some education researchers have turned their attention to how computer activities can enhance the learning experience. Researchers Julie Sarama and Douglas H. Clements (2002) found that software should relate to children's experiences and interests. They also found that it is important for children to use more open-ended computer tools as they explore math concepts. Many of the ideas we discuss here were suggested or influenced by these researchers' work.

Whether it is educational software, online games, or apps, there is a superabundance of computer activities available today. If you allow your child computer time and are looking for activities that promote understanding and fluency, keep the following recommendations in mind:

◆ Always try an activity yourself first before your child tries it. Are the images and reading level appropriate? Are the directions clear?

◆ If the resource is a drill and practice game, first determine if your child has had enough time and experience making sense of the concept or skill. When used too early in the learning process, drills may threaten a child's view of himself as a mathematical learner. Is your child ready for a drill?

◆ Does the game provide time and opportunity for the child to use reasoning?

◆ Does the game allow you to adjust the difficulty level?

◆ Does the game have a "free explore" component? (For example, does the software provide opportunities for the child to make designs with geometric shapes?)

◆ Is the game competitive or noncompetitive? Both can be helpful.

◆ Ask your child's teacher for recommendations, and be sure to share your success stories.

Below are a few computer activities that we like along with brief descriptions of how they might be used. (You can find the links to these activities on NCTM's website by entering the access code on the title page of this book at nctm.org/more4u.)

Meteor Multiplication (grades 3 and up). This is a good game for improving fluency with basic math facts—and children enjoy it. The premise for this game is a meteor shower. These meteors, marked with multiplication problems, are moving toward the spaceship in the middle of the screen. The spaceship is marked with the product associated with the problem on one of the meteors. The player must rotate the spaceship toward the correct meteor and blast it off the screen. Then a new number appears on the spaceship, and the player again searches to find the matching meteor as they hurtle towards the spaceship. The content range and game speed are both adjustable, making this game appropriate for grades 3 and up. There is one minute of play each round.

Factorize (grades 3 and up). Illuminations is a K–12 resource developed and maintained by the National Council of Teachers of Mathematics (http://illuminations. nctm.org). In the "Factorize" activity, children use a grid to make rectangular arrays that represent the area of a rectangle for the given number. There is a text box for the child to record all possible multiplication combinations that match the given product. For instance, if 12 is the given number, the player would make as many different rectangles with an area of 12 as she can (i.e., rectangles with dimensions 1 by 12, 2 by 6, or 4 by 3). Children can use this game to explore multiplication ideas (arrays and area) or to practice basic facts (to read more about arrays, see chapter 4, page 96). They can also investigate factors for different numbers.

READER'S CHALLENGE

Consider again the possible rectangle dimensions for a rectangle of area 12 using only whole number dimensions (1 by 12, 2 by 6, or 4 by 3). Do you see any interesting relationships among the three factor pairs? Children may notice that if the first factor in a factor pair is doubled and the second factor halved, you get the next factor pair. So 2×6 becomes 4×3, and both of these products are 12. This "doubling and halving" strategy may also be physically apparent in the dimensions of the corresponding rectangles on the screen.

Base Blocks (grades 2 and up). The National Library of Virtual Manipulatives (http://nlvm.usu.edu/en/nav/vlibrary.html) project began more than twenty years ago, and its many Java applets function as "virtual manipulatives." The Base Blocks activity may be used as a free-explore activity, or children may choose to quiz themselves by representing given numbers with the virtual base-ten blocks. The difficulty level is adjustable.

Factor Dazzle (grades 3 and up). To play games on the Calculation Nation® website (http://calculationnation.nctm.org), students must first assign themselves a screen name and password. After choosing a game, players decide if they want to challenge themselves or challenge other players from around the world. To play the game "Factor Dazzle," a player begins by selecting a number from a list of given numbers. Suppose the player chooses the number 36. Her opponent must find all the factors for 36. The player would collect 36 points; however, her opponent would collect the sum of all of the other factors of 36, so the opponent would get a score of $1 + 2 + 3 + 4 + 6 + 9 + 12 + 18$ for a total of 55 points. Not only do students practice factoring and learn more characteristics of specific numbers, they improve their strategies with repeated play. What would be a good number to choose if you were selecting first from the set of whole numbers from 1 to 36 ?

Fraction Flags (grades 2 to 4). The school district of Oswego, New York, has available on its website a list of interactive games for families to explore, including two "Fraction Flag" activities that even second graders can do. Players must design a flag using the appropriate number of colors, and each color must exactly cover the correct portions of the array (the "flag"). There is no one "right" way to complete the flag. For instance, if the player designs a flag using halves, she fills half the squares using one color and the other half using a different color. It does not matter which squares are one or the other color as long as half of the squares are filled using each color.

Monster Squeeze (ages four to seven). This is an app from Everyday Mathematics® available for purchase on the publisher's website (https://www.mheonline.com). Two players take turns guessing the other player's number. Each time the player makes a guess, the monster's arms move closer and closer to the target number along a number line. This "guess my number" activity helps children become familiar with the relative size of numbers by comparing numbers and helps them to visualize the position of numbers on a number line.

Counting with the Very Hungry Caterpillar (up to five years old). This is an app for young children available for purchase on iTunes (https://itunes.apple.com). To play, the child counts pictures of different food items that the Hungry Caterpillar might eat. There are five different levels in the game. At each level, the child is prompted by a voice-over to select one or more food items to count. If the child correctly or incorrectly selects the number of items in the picture, that game continues. Once an item is selected, a hole appears where the caterpillar has eaten through the food item. At each level, the child may be asked to count the items for different situations. For level five, for instance, the child is prompted to choose the number of a particular type of food item to eat. As the child selects the number of items from a screen with several different types of foods, a voice-over counts the item(s) that the child selects. The child has repeated experiences counting small collections of food items. Apps such as these may help children build counting strategies because they reinforce one-to-one correspondence; one touch means one count.

These are just a few of the many computer resources available today. As you know, technological assets are continually being created and revamped. This can be a challenge for parents, but it is also exciting to explore new games and other programs as they become available. Get your child involved in the review process too. For example, you might ask, "What's the math?" to emphasize the importance of the mathematical aspects of the game.

 DO YOU KNOW How to Use Math Games?

Games must be fun for children. If they're not, children won't want to play. Children won't like every game, so expect some trial and error as to what works for your child. Although it is important that your child be mentally stimulated, your child should enjoy these challenges and be eager to become more successful as she or he plays the game. What makes for a good game? Games should not be cumbersome. Sometimes the simplest of math games can be the most fun; think of card games such as "War" or "Compare." Certainly the game should be engaging for your child and allow your child to make different choices and decisions during play. And play competitive as well as noncompetitive games. Most important, games should offer opportunities for your child to reason about math ideas.

Final Thoughts

Even if you "hated math" as a student, you can still be a successful mathematics role model for your children: Talk to your kids about what they're learning in math class; be an attentive helpmate as they grapple with their homework; join in the fun of math games; let your child see you make sense of mathematics in everyday situations, whether it's calculating the tip for the server at a restaurant or figuring out how long to cook the turkey (maybe he or she will help you solve these problems!). As your children move through the elementary grades into middle school and then high school, your role will change, but the goal is the same—that your children be successful math learners and can make sense of mathematics whether they are working on school assignments or curious about the rock ripples in water or how birds fly. By focusing on the ingenuity of your child's mathematical thinking, you may begin to find elementary mathematics a captivating and inviting subject after all.

Throughout *It's Elementary*, we've discussed the importance of making connections between and among mathematical concepts as well as "laying foundations" and "building on skills and processes." In the final chapter, we discuss the continuing development of these connections in middle school and high school by focusing on one problem that morphs from grade to grade, starting in first grade and continuing through high school.

Things to Remember

- Children's mathematical development doesn't follow a straight line. They may revert to simpler techniques when confronted with new concepts, or they may understand one idea but not how it is related to another.

- If your child has been assigned math homework, don't do it for them. Do be supportive and offer assistance when you can.

- Let your child drive the conversation.

- Remember that your child's strategy may be different from your own.

- Be patient.

- Expect the unexpected.

- Have fun.

Things to Do

◆ Play math games with your child. It is a wonderful way to help your child practice and use different skills. You can also brush up on some of your skills too, an added benefit.

◆ Try working some of the logic and math-related puzzles such as Sudoku or Ken-Ken in your local newspaper to review skills and to challenge your thinking. You might work these puzzles with your children too.

◆ Reread the section on practice in chapter 2, pages 40–41.

◆ Attend family math nights with your child at school. If your school does not offer this type of event, suggest that the PTA or the principal host one.

◆ If you are anxious about helping your child with math assignments, pick out one of the resources on math anxiety to read.

◆ Talk with your child's teacher to learn more about how you can effectively help your child with homework.

Resources

For Adults

Boaler, Jo. *What's Math Got to Do with It? How Teachers and Parents Can Transform Mathematics Learning and Inspire Success*. New York: Penguin Books, 2015.

Britt, Bonnie Adama. *Mastering Basic Math Skills: Games for Kindergarten through Second Grade*. Reston, VA: National Council of Teachers of Mathematics, 2014.

Britt, Bonnie Adama. *Mastering Basic Math Skills: Games for Third through Fifth Grade*. Reston, VA: National Council of Teachers of Mathematics, 2014.

Connected Mathematics Project. "Homework Support." Michigan State University. May 2015. https://connectedmath.msu.edu/families/homework-support/

National Council of Teachers of Mathematics. "Math homework due tomorrow. How can I help?" Figure This! May 2015. http://figurethis.nctm.org/fc/family_corner_homework.htm

National Council of Teachers of Mathematics. "What can I do to help my child get the most out of math?" Figure This! May 2015. http://figurethis.nctm.org/fc/family_corner_support.htm

TERC. "Doing Math Together." *Investigations in Number, Data, and Space*. 2013. https://investigations.terc.edu/families/doing_math/index.cfm

TERC. "Finding and Using Mathematical Children's Literature with Elementary Students." Investigations in Number, Data, and Space. 2013. https://investigations.terc.edu/library/mathactivities/children_lit2.cfm

Tobias, Sheila. *Overcoming Math Anxiety*. New York: W. W. Norton, 1993.

More4U Online Resources

You can find a listing of additional helpful resources with links, including recommended games, by entering the access code on this book's title page at NCTM's More4U page (nctm.org/more4u).

8

Connections to Middle School and Beyond

Students in middle school and upper grades should have the same opportunities to share, examine, and justify mathematical ideas as students in elementary school. They, too, are faced with the same challenge as younger students—to make sense of the mathematics they are learning. Like their elementary school counterparts, older students may work individually or in small groups, perhaps consulting sophisticated handheld technology or using computers as tools for exploring mathematical concepts. Likewise, teachers have a similar role in middle and high school classrooms to that of elementary teachers— selecting challenging problems intended to bring important concepts to the fore and managing discussions in a way that establishes respectful yet critical consideration of students' ideas. So while students and teachers may be discussing different topics and using more sophisticated technology to support their reasoning, the classroom culture in the middle and upper grades can be very similar to that of elementary classrooms.

Even though the mathematical topics of the middle and upper grades are necessarily different, many of these topics originate from concepts that are addressed in the elementary curriculum. Elementary children have had a wide range of meaningful mathematical experiences; the task of the middle and high school teacher is to build on and continue to develop these skills and processes.

At this point, it is probably no surprise to you that mathematical concepts continue to develop and build on one another throughout the K–12 curriculum. For instance, what students learn about multiplication extends from working with whole numbers and fractions in the early grades to multiplication of integers, irrational numbers, and algebraic expressions in the middle grades. In high school, students learn to multiply matrices, complex numbers, and functions. Students make sense of these ideas, in part, by thinking about how these new concepts are related to previous experiences with multiplication throughout their school careers. By doing so, students expand their methods of mathematical reasoning along the way.

In this chapter, we present an example of how elementary mathematical sense making develops into the reasoning of the middle and high school years. We start with a pattern-finding task that is posed at various grade levels and use it to illustrate how students might explore and develop mathematical ideas about patterns from different vantage points, showing how students' ways of reasoning about mathematics develop over time. Perhaps more important, you can see how the mathematical insights of younger children are crucial in forming the basis for the more advanced approaches that students develop in the upper grades.

Pattern-finding tasks such as the one in figure 8.1 (Thompson 1985) are common in the elementary and middle school curriculum. For younger students, the goal might be to verbally describe the pattern and demonstrate how to build staircases with different numbers of steps. In the middle grades, this pattern task might be used to motivate students to develop some general claims about relationships. In fact, students explore similar tasks in high school (and even college) when engaged in creating formal proofs.

Ten blocks are needed to make a staircase of four steps as shown below. How many blocks are needed to make ten steps? How many blocks are needed to make fifty steps?

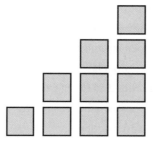

Fig. 8.1. The Staircase problem

First Grade

Some first graders were working on a problem similar to that in figure 8.1. They were determining the number of creatures arranged in this staircase-like pattern. (The problem is based on the children's book *Rooster's Off to See the World* by Eric Carle.) The work of two students, Zelia and Jessica, is shown in figures 8.2a and 8.2b.

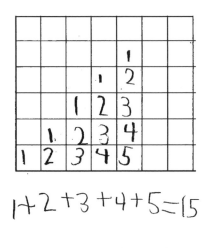

$$1+2+3+4+5=15$$

Fig. 8.2a. Zelia's work

$$1+2+3+4+5=15$$

Fig 8.2b. Jessica's work

The way these students have documented their work illustrates two equally valid ways of explaining a "growing" pattern: Zelia used squares from a sheet of grid paper to count the number of the blocks in her staircase while Jessica sketched the blocks in hers and drew a particular type of animal in the blocks of each row. Both of the students have appropriately represented the problem and have determined that the total number of blocks is 1 + 2 + 3 + 4 + 5 = 15. For Zelia, it appears that to make the next size staircase (that is, add a step), she would add a sixth *column* and write the numerals 1, 2, 3, 4, 5, and 6 in order from top to bottom. Jessica seems to be building her staircases by adding *rows* of animals; to create the next size staircase, she would need to add a bottom row of six animals. Either way, both of these first graders would be able to tell you how to build a staircase with six steps and how to determine how many blocks (or creatures) would be used. Because they already know how many blocks are in a staircase with five steps, the students may notice that they just need to add six to fifteen to determine the total. They might then double-check by counting all the blocks. In response to the question about the number of blocks in a staircase with ten steps, we would expect either student to count the blocks in each new step until they had counted all the blocks for ten steps. Or perhaps they would explain, "All you have to do is add all the numbers from one to ten."

Middle School

How would a middle school student determine the number of blocks for a staircase with fifty steps? How would he think about the relationship between the number of steps and the number of blocks? First, he might create several examples of staircases using images of blocks as in figure 8.3 on the following page.

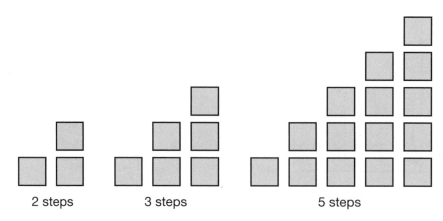

2 steps   3 steps   5 steps

Fig. 8.3. Different size staircases

He might also draw different staircases and record the number of blocks and steps for each staircase. With some guidance from his teacher, he might then organize the information from his drawings in a table like the one below (table 8.1).

Table 8.1. Data for particular size staircases

Number of Steps	Number of Blocks
1	1
2	3
3	6
4	10
5	15
6	21

As the student considers the number of steps in his various staircases, he notices that the number of blocks he uses is related to the number of steps in the staircase. His work here is different from that of the first graders. He would explain that he added another row each time he added steps. The middle school student also explains the pattern he notices—he needs to add the first fifty counting (natural) numbers $1 + 2 + 3 + 4 + ... + 50$ to determine how many blocks are used in a staircase with fifty steps. But because adding these numbers to find the total number of blocks is not an efficient strategy, the middle school student is challenged to find a more effective way to determine the number of blocks.

When searching for a more efficient method of determining the number of blocks for large staircases, many students at all grades find it helpful to manipulate the blocks to create other shapes to make it easier to calculate the total number of blocks. A student might observe, for example, that two staircases of the same size fit together to form a rectangle. Figure 8.4 shows two pairs of staircases; each pair has one staircase built with light purple blocks and the other with dark purple blocks. Notice that both pairs of staircases form a rectangular array and that the four-step staircases form a 4-by-5 array and the three-step staircases form a 3-by-4 array. By making these arrays, the student has used another idea that is addressed in the elementary school curriculum.

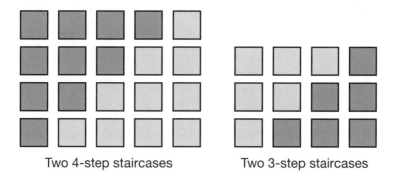

Two 4-step staircases   Two 3-step staircases

Fig. 8.4. Pairs of staircases form rectangular arrays.

After making this connection between pairs of staircases and arrays, the student may use different staircases to make additional arrays. And because the teacher regularly reminds him and other students that it can be helpful to record this type of information in a table, he decides to write down information about each of the arrays. He expands his first table (table 8.1) to include this new information, and records the total number of blocks in each array and the dimensions of the array (table 8.2).

Table 8.2. Data from different size staircases and corresponding arrays

Number of Steps	Number of Blocks in Staircase	Number of Blocks in Array	Dimensions of Array
1	1	2	1 × 2
2	3	6	2 × 3
3	6	12	3 × 4
4	10	20	4 × 5
5	15	30	5 × 6
6	21	42	6 × 7

As the student explores different staircases and examines data in the table, he may notice that the number of blocks in the staircase is exactly one-half the number of blocks in the array. This makes sense to the student because the arrays were made with two staircases of the same size. In addition, he may see that because the array is in the form of a rectangle, he can determine the total number of blocks in the array by multiplying its dimensions. Algebraically, he notices that the dimensions of the array are always the number of steps (n) by the number of steps plus one ($n + 1$). That is, the number of blocks (B) for a staircase with n steps is determined by multiplying the number of steps (n) by one more than the number of steps ($n + 1$) and then dividing by 2. This can be written symbolically as the following:

$$B = \frac{n(n+1)}{2}$$

After arriving at this general formula, the middle school student will likely test it out by trying different values for n for additional verification that it is true. For example, for a staircase with seven steps ($n = 7$), the formula indicates there should be twenty-eight blocks (fig. 8.5).

$$\frac{7(7+1)}{2} = \frac{56}{2} = 28$$

Fig. 8.5. A middle school student tries a different value to verify his "staircase" rule.

Knowing how the blocks for a seven-step staircase compare to a six-step staircase, the student can also add seven to the total of blocks needed in a six-step staircase and get $21 + 7 = 28$. Alternatively, the student might imagine his array diagrams more generally, offering a visual proof for his formula (Alsina and Nelsen 2006). Figure 8.6 represents one way a middle grade student could visually show how this formula works for a staircase with n steps. Notice that even though the diagram has a specific number of steps (7), the student can look at it more generally and see it as any number of steps n.

What the middle school student has done is to develop a rule using the number of steps to find the total number of blocks. (Note that he has used an array, a concept from the elementary school curriculum, to develop his case.) In other words, he has described the relationship between the number of steps and the number of blocks. By doing so, the student has touched upon a more advanced idea, the concept of *function*. The number of blocks is a function of the number of steps!

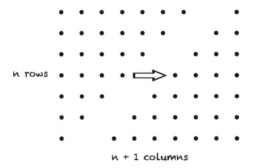

When you put two staircases of the same size together, you get a rectangular array that has one more column than the number of rows. I used dots to build my staircases instead of blocks because they are easier to draw.

n rows

$n + 1$ columns

There are $n \times \frac{(n+1)}{2}$ blocks in one staircase.

Fig. 8.6. A middle school student gives a visual proof for his formula.

DO YOU KNOW What a Mathematical Function Is?

It has probably been a while since you've encountered the concept of *function* in mathematics. Simply put, it is a relationship between two sets in which each object from one set is assigned to exactly one element from the other set. In the Staircase example, one of the sets is composed of the natural numbers, 1, 2, 3, 4, and so on, representing the number of steps in each staircase. The other set contains the numbers 1, 3, 6, 10, 15, and so forth, representing the number of blocks in each staircase. The rule derived by the student assigns each natural number to a particular number of blocks. Check the links in More4U if you would like to know more about this mathematical concept.

High School

What might a high school or college student do with the Staircase problem? Students in the upper grades may learn how to prove that this same formula works for all possible cases, that is, all natural numbers. One such method is called *proof by mathematical induction*. The concept behind this particular proof is similar to the ideas addressed by the middle school student's observations about his table of blocks; the total number of blocks changes as the number of steps increases by one. The high school student notices, for instance, that a staircase with eleven steps will have exactly eleven more blocks than a staircase with ten steps. The student might describe this idea algebraically "as a staircase with $k + 1$ steps will have exactly $k + 1$ more blocks than the staircase with k steps." The student uses this idea to explore proof by mathematical induction.

The Staircase Problem and Mathematical Induction: What's the Math?

The process of mathematical induction requires the student to first check that the formula works for the smallest possible size staircase ($n = 1$). This part of the proof process is referred to as the *base case*.

$$\text{If } n = 1, \text{ then } \quad B = \frac{1(1+1)}{2} = \frac{1 \times 2}{2} = 1$$

Because the result of applying the formula matches the number of blocks needed for a staircase with one step, that is, 1 block, the student is confident the formula works for the first case. Next is the inductive part of the proof. For this part, the student assumes the formula works for a staircase with an arbitrary number of steps (call it k) and determines whether or not this assumption leads to the truth of the formula for a staircase with $k + 1$ steps. If the formula is true for $k + 1$ steps based on the assumption that it is true for k steps, then, together with the information that it is true for the first natural number, the student knows that the formula is true for all natural numbers.

The inductive part of this proof involves a fair amount of algebraic work. Below are the details of the proof:

If a staircase with k steps has $\dfrac{k(k+1)}{2}$ blocks, the student must algebraically demonstrate that a staircase with $k + 1$ steps will have $\dfrac{(k+1)(k+2)}{2}$ blocks.

The $k + 2$ comes from adding 1 to the number of steps, $k + 1$. To show that this formula is true for a staircase with $k + 1$ steps, the student first observes that the number of blocks for a staircase with $k + 1$ steps is $k + 1$ more than the number of blocks for a staircase with k steps:

$$\frac{k(k+1)}{2}+(k+1)$$

Algebraically, this can be rewritten by getting a common denominator. To do this, the student multiplies $(k + 1)$ by $^2/_2$ (another way to write the number 1):

$$\frac{k(k+1)}{2}+(k+1)\text{x}\frac{2}{2}$$

The student then writes $(k + 1)$ x $^2/_2$ as a single fraction with $2(k + 1)$ in the numerator:

$$\frac{k(k+1)}{2}+\frac{2(k+1)}{2}$$

Now that both fractions have the same denominator of 2, the numbers can easily be combined into a single fraction by adding the numerators:

$$\frac{k(k+1)+2(k+1)}{2}$$

The next step is a bit tricky. It is tempting to use the distributive property to multiply $(k + 1)$ by k and $(k + 1)$ by 2. And it does work to do that. However, a more efficient approach is for the student to notice the common factor of $(k + 1)$. Thus the student can rewrite the sum of $k(k + 1)$ and $2(k + 1)$ as the desired result, the product of two consecutive numbers $(k + 1)$ and $(k + 2)$ divided by 2:

$$\frac{(k+1)(k+2)}{2}$$

Notice that the observation made by the first graders, Zelia and Jessica, as to how the staircase grows from one size to the next, is an idea that the high school student needs to use to develop the proof. The student must use the fact that the staircase with $k + 1$ steps will have exactly $k + 1$ blocks more than a staircase with k steps. Additionally, to successfully work through the algebra, the student applies more general principles related to concepts learned in elementary school, finding common denominators and identifying common factors.

Final Words

To sum up, the Staircase problem is one that younger children approach and solve by noticing the pattern in how the staircase "grows." Middle grades students build on that idea by developing a formula that determines the number of blocks based on the number of steps in the staircase. In the process, they may also establish a visual proof for their formula. Students in the upper grades continue to examine these ideas as they explore formal proof. Amazingly, high school students develop an algebraic approach to the problem by using those ideas they unraveled as younger students about how the number of blocks increased with each additional step.

You can have a part in your children's success with mathematics. And their successes can even come in the form of mathematical challenges that they invent for themselves just for the joy of doing mathematics. Our hope is that this book inspires you to launch your family as its own community of mathematical learners where everyone's ideas are appreciated and mathematics is valued as a life-enhancing discipline worthy of time and effort.

And so we close with one last story that illustrates one way parents can participate in their children's mathematical worlds.

During a back-to-school evening event for parents, Mr. Gonzalez, a fourth-grade teacher, presented parents with the following division problem:

$$56 \div 14$$

Mr. Gonzalez asked parents to think about how they would solve the problem without using the standard algorithm for division. After a few minutes, parents began offering various ways to think about the problem. Some of their solutions were very creative.

A few parents came up with the idea of doubling the divisor and then doubling again. They explained that because 14 and 14 is 28, and 28 and 28 is 56, the quotient must be 4.

Some of the parents took a totally different direction by halving the numbers. These parents explained that because half of 56 is 28 and half of 14 is 7, that means $56 \div 14 = 28 \div 7$. Remembering their basic math facts, the quotient had to be 4.

One father said he knew that $52 \div 13$ was 4 because there are 4 suits in a deck of cards and 13 cards in each suit. He realized 56 was exactly 4 more than 52, so $56 \div 14$ would have the same quotient as $52 \div 13$.

All the approaches engendered rumblings among the parents, who wondered if approaches other than their own always worked. The parents were engaged in an enthusiastic and meaningful discussion that mirrored their children's experiences in school. They went home with a much better idea of what their children encounter every day in math class. They also discovered for themselves that there is usually more than one "right" way to the correct answer. Perhaps many were also inspired to ask their child just how they would make sense of the problem. We hope so.

Resources

We have tried to address many key ideas in this chapter, but we can only touch upon the topics. Additional resources you may find helpful and informative are listed below.

For Adults

Conway, John Horton, and Richard K. Guy. *The Book of Numbers.* New York: Copernicus, 1996.

Gardiner, Martin. *The Colossal Book of Mathematics.* New York: W. W. Norton & Company, Inc., 2001.

Garland, Trudi Hammel. *Fibonacci Fun: Fascinating Activities with Intriguing Numbers.* Parsippany, N.J.: Dale Seymour Publications, 1997.

Merzbach, Uta C., and Carl B. Boyer. *A History of Mathematics.* Hoboken, N.J.: Wiley, 2011.

Peterson, Ivars. *The Mathematical Tourist: Snapshots of Modern Mathematics.* New York: W. H. Freeman and Company, 1988.

Pickover, Clifford A. *The Math Book: From Pythagoras to the 57th Dimension, 250 Milestones in the History of Mathematics.* New York: Sterling Publishing, 2009.

For Older Children

Enzensberger, Hans Magnus. *The Number Devil: A Mathematical Adventure.* New York: Henry Holt and Company, 1998.

Garland, Trudi Hammel. *Fascinating Fibonacci: Mystery and Magic in Numbers.* Parsippany, N.J.: Dale Seymour Publications, 1987.

Reimer, Luetta, and Wilbert Reimer. *Mathematicians Are People, Too.* Parsippany, N.J.: Dale Seymour Publications, 1990.

More4U Online Resources

You can find a listing of additional helpful resources with links, including recommended games, by entering the access code on this book's title page at NCTM's More4U page (nctm.org/more4u).

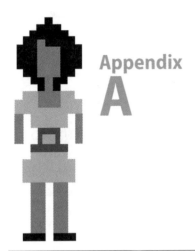

Solution to the Handshake Problem

Using a circle diagram, we can illustrate the handshakes between *Person 1* and the five other people in the room with the following diagram. Each of the five segments represents a handshake that involves *Person 1*.

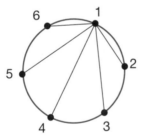

To avoid over-counting, we now consider the ***other*** handshakes that involve *Person 2*. Using the diagram we see that *Person 2* will shake hands with exactly four ***other*** people in the room (the handshake between Person 2 and Person 1 has already been counted). Those additional handshakes are illustrated below with the four gray segments.

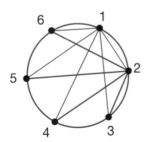

Continuing in this manner, we see that *Person 3* will make three other handshakes, *Person 4* will make two more, and *Person 5* will make one more handshake. By the time we get around the circle to *Person 6*, all the handshakes have been counted.

In total, there are 5 + 4 + 3 + 2 + 1 = 15 handshakes when there are six people, assuming each person shakes hands with every other person exactly once. Notice that 15 is exactly half of 5 x 6, the initial guess of the students.

Now consider the case where there are 7 people shaking hands. Using our strategy above, we get 1 + 2 + 3 + 4 + 5 + 6 = 21, which is half of 6 x 7. For 8 people, the sum is 28, which is half of 7 x 8. Continuing in this way, we can consider the general case where there are n people shaking hands. In that case there are 1 + 2 + 3 + ... + (n − 1) handshakes. But how many is that? Based on the patterns we have observed, we might guess that the total number of handshakes can be written as follows:

$$\frac{(n-1)\,n}{2}$$

For 7 people, $n = 7$ and $n − 1 = 6$, so if we insert this information into our formula, the results are as follows:

$$\frac{(7 \times 6)}{2} = \frac{42}{2} = 21$$

This problem is a classic mathematics problem that has connections to important ideas in probability and statistics as well as geometry and number theory. We can formally prove this general result using a technique called *proof by mathematical induction*. You will notice that we present an analogous problem in Chapter 8 (the Staircase problem), along with details about proof by mathematical induction.

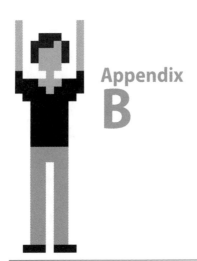

Division with Zero

Case 1: What happens when you try to divide 0 ÷ 1? Using the definition of division, if $0 \div 1 = c$ for some number c, then $0 = c \times 1$. To determine the solution, think about what number when multiplied by 1 will result in a product of 0. The only number that results in a zero product when multiplied by 1 is 0. Thus, $c = 0$ and $0 \div 1 = 0$. This result is the same any time you divide 0 by a nonzero number. That is, $0 \div b = 0$, for any nonzero number b. This is because $0 \times b = 0$ for any number b.

Case 2: What happens when you try to divide 0 ÷ 0? As in the case discussed in chapter 4, you might first temporarily abandon part of the definition to see what happens. If $0 \div 0 = c$ for some number c, then $0 = c \times 0$. In this case, there are many numbers that satisfy the second equation since any number multiplied by zero is zero. Thus, c can be any number. When this type of situation occurs in mathematics, we say that the solution is indeterminate—you quite literally cannot determine a unique solution. Thus $0 \div 0$ is indeterminate.

Glossary

absolute value. The distance between a number and zero on a number line. It is always a positive number.

addend. In addition, a number that is to be added to another number.

addition. One of the four elementary operations of arithmetic. It can be thought of in terms of combining (putting additional objects into a given collection) or in terms of part-whole (putting two different types of collections together to form a new type of collection). When adding two or more numbers (addends), the result is called the sum.

additive identity. See *identity element.*

algorithm. A sequence of steps that can be used to solve every problem within a specific category of problem. A student may, for example, come up with a strategy for adding two three-digit numbers that involves adding the hundreds places first, then the tens, and then the ones. Because this strategy can be used in every problem involving the addition of two three-digit numbers, the sequence of steps the student used is called an algorithm.

algebraic thinking. Knowledge about numbers and operations that includes understanding properties of number operations, connections among operations with different sets of numbers, and the ability to use properties to solve problems as well as explain and justify generalizations about number operations.

argument. A statement or series of statements given to support a mathematical claim.

assessment. The process by which a teacher attempts to determine what students know and understand about a particular topic.

automaticity. Automatic recall of information.

basic fact fluency. The ability to recall mathematical facts, for example $5 + 3 = 8$, $7 - 4 = 3$, $2 \times 2 = 4$, and $10 \div 2 = 5$, in three to four seconds.

cardinality. The number of elements in a set.

collaborative learning. A method of instruction in which the teacher arranges students in groups of two to four children and monitors students' progress as each group works together to solve a problem.

collection. See *set.*

combining. See *addition.*

computational fluency. Using a sensible strategy to compute efficiently and accurately.

conceptual knowledge. Understanding ideas in connection with several other ideas.

conjecture. A statement of a mathematical claim. The statement could be true or false. For example, "multiplication always results in a larger number" is a conjecture that is false. Take, for instance, 6 x 1/2 = 3, which is less than 6.

decompose. To think of a number in terms of the addition or multiplication of two or more numbers.

denominator. The part of the numerical representation of a fraction that represents the size of the fractional part. In the fraction 3/4, 4 is the denominator.

direct instruction. In mathematics classrooms, a method of instruction in which the teacher provides information to students on how to solve particular types of problems.

diagram. A drawing used to represent one or more mathematical ideas.

difference. The result of subtracting one number from another. For example, in the equation 7 – 3 = 4, 4 is the difference.

dividend. In division, the amount to be divided. For example, in 15 ÷ 3, the number 15 is the dividend.

division. One of the four elementary operations of arithmetic. It can be thought of in terms of repeated subtraction (counting the number of groups of a certain size) or in terms of sharing (equal distribution of objects among a certain number of groups). When dividing two numbers, the result is called the quotient.

divisor. In division, the number by which you are dividing. For example, in 20 ÷ 6, the number 6 is the divisor. It is also defined as an integer that leaves remainder zero upon division. For example, 4 is a divisor of 20 because 20 ÷ 4 = 5. See also *factor.*

element. A member of a set or collection of objects.

equality. This is a special mathematical relationship in which mathematical expressions represent the same number or quantity.

equation. A statement of equality about mathematical expressions that may or may not be true. The equation 12 + 3 = 5 + 10 is true because 12 + 3 is 15 and 5 + 10 is also 15. The equation 5 + 7 = 12 + 8 is not a true statement of equality because 5 + 7 is 12 and 12 + 8 is 20.

factor. In multiplication, a number that is to be multiplied by another number. It is also defined as a number (usually a natural number) that leaves remainder zero upon division. For example, the factors of 12 are 1, 2, 3, 4, 6, and 12. See also *divisor.*

figurate numbers. Numbers that can be represented as a particular geometric shape. For example, the number 16 is a "square" number because 16 objects may be arranged in the shape of a square, and the number 10 is a "triangular" number because 10 objects may be arranged in the shape of a triangle.

fraction. In elementary mathematics, a fraction is a number represented as *a/b*, where *a* and *b* are whole numbers and *b* is not zero. The number *a* is the *numerator* and the number *b* is the *denominator*. More broadly, a fraction is a number represented as the division of two other numbers.

fraction bar. A symbol that indicates division of two numbers.

function. A relationship between two sets where each member of one set is assigned to exactly one member of the other set.

identity element. A number from a set associated with a particular operation that has no effect when the operation is applied. For example, 0 is the additive identity of the set of rational numbers because 0 added to any other rational number c is just that number c. The number 1 is the multiplicative identity.

integers. The set of numbers that consists of the number zero and the natural numbers and their opposites.

interpretation. A way of thinking about a number or operation.

invented strategy. An approach to solving a problem created by an individual or group of individuals.

inverse element. A number from a set associated with a particular operation and a particular number that results in the identity element when the operation is applied. In the set of rational numbers, the number –2 is the *additive inverse* of 2 because –2 + 2 = 0. The number $^1/_2$ is the *multiplicative inverse* of 2 because $^1/_2$ x 2 = 1. See also opposite and reciprocal.

justify. The act of providing mathematical reasons for a solution process or mathematical claim. Similar to argument.

manipulatives. Materials students can physically move around to explore mathematical ideas. Teachers use both homemade and manufactured materials. Virtual manipulatives are computer images of physical manipulatives that students can move around on a computer screen to explore mathematical ideas.

mathematical induction. Proof by mathematical induction is a type of logical deductive argument. In general, this type of argument demonstrates the truth of a formula for an unbounded subset of the natural numbers.

model. This word has two meanings in mathematics classrooms: 1) A diagram or arrangement of manipulatives used to illustrate of a way of thinking about a mathematical idea. For example, a rectangular array is a model for thinking about multiplication. 2) A mathematical description of a relationship between quantities in a real-world situation that is often used to make decisions. For example, the volume of dirt in a rectangular garden box can be modeled with the expression length x width x height and used to determine how much soil should be purchased to fill the box.

multiplication. One of the four elementary operations of arithmetic. There are many ways to think about multiplication, including *repeated addition* (combining a certain number of same-size collections of objects), as a *rectangular array* (arranging objects into rows of the same number of objects), or as *scale factor* (stretching or shrinking an amount by a certain factor). When two numbers are multiplied, the result is called the *product*. The numbers being multiplied are called *factors*.

multiplicative identity. See **identity element.**

natural numbers. A natural number is any number that can be generated by repeatedly adding 1, starting at 1.

number sense. Conceptual knowledge about numbers that includes understanding how numbers are related, connections among different sets of numbers, and the ability to use number relationships to solve problems.

numeration. A system for counting and representing numbers.

numerator. The part of the numerical representation of a fraction that represents the number of fractional parts. In the fraction 3/4, 3 is the numerator.

operation. A process for acting on pairs of numbers (such as addition and multiplication) or pairs of other mathematical objects (in advanced mathematics).

opposite. The additive inverse of a number. See also **inverse element.**

prime number. A natural number larger than 1 with exactly two natural number divisors (or factors). The set of prime numbers begins with 2, 3, 5, 7, and so on.

procedural knowledge. Knowing how to perform a set of steps to solve a problem.

procedure. A sequence of steps used to solve a problem.

process. A way of thinking about and solving a mathematical problem.

product. The result of multiplying two or more numbers.

property. A mathematical claim that is true for an entire set of numbers.

quantity. Finding an amount of something either by counting (e.g., there are 6 cars) or by measuring (e.g., she is 5 feet tall).

quotient. The result of dividing two numbers.

rational numbers. The set of numbers that can be represented as a fraction where both the numerator and denominator are integers, with the exception that the denominator cannot be the number 0.

reciprocal. The multiplicative inverse of a number. For example, 3 is the reciprocal of 1/3 and vice versa. See also **inverse element.**

region. An area defined by some geometric shape such as a rectangle.

remainder. The amount left over after dividing two numbers. For example, 23 divided by 5 is 4 with remainder 3.

repeated subtraction. See **division.**

sense making. Using ideas to reason about a mathematical problem.

set. A group of objects often called a *collection*. Members of a set are called *elements*.

sharing. See **division.**

situation. A story problem or context that invites a particular interpretation of an operation.

skill. A process that is automatic or routine.

sociomathematical norms. Accepted ways of doing and talking about mathematics in the classroom. These norms could be different from classroom to classroom.

standard algorithm. A procedure or a set of procedures that is widely known and used.

story problem. A real-world scenario posed as a question that can be solved using mathematics.

strategy. A particular process used to solve a mathematical problem.

subtraction. One of four elementary operations of arithmetic. It can be thought of in terms of *take-away* (removing objects from a given collection) or *comparison* (examining how much more or less one collection is in relation to another). When two numbers are subtracted, the result is called the *difference*.

sum. The result of adding two or more numbers.

undefined. A quantity or operation that does not have mathematical meaning. For example, $1/0$ is undefined because in the equation $1/0 = a$, there is no solution for a.

variables. Symbols, letters, or words used to represent one or more numbers in equations, formulas, inequalities, and in other instances when a name is needed for a quantity that is either known, unknown, or for which there are a range of values.

virtual manipulatives. See **manipulatives.**

whole numbers. The set of numbers that consists of the number 0 and the natural numbers.

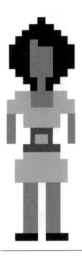

Bibliography

Adama Britt, Bonnie. *Mastering Basic Math Skills: Games for Kindergarten through Second Grade.* Reston, Va.: NCTM, 2014.

Alsina, Claudi, and Roger B. Nelsen. *Math Made Visual: Creating Images for Understanding Mathematics.* Washington, D.C.: Mathematical Association of America, 2006.

Ball, Deborah Loewenberg, and Hyman Bass. "Making Mathematics Reasonable in School." In *A Research Companion to Principles and Standards for School Mathematics*, edited by Jeremy Kilpatrick, W. Gary Martin, and Deborah Schifter, pp. 27–44. Reston, Va.: NCTM, 2003.

Ball, Deborah Loewenberg. "With an Eye on the Mathematical Horizon: Dilemmas of Teaching Elementary School Mathematics." *Elementary School Journal* 93, no. 4 (1993): 373–97.

Barnett-Clarke, Carne, William Fisher, Rick Marks, Sharon Ross, and Rose Mary Zbiek. *Developing Essential Understanding of Rational Numbers for Teaching Mathematics in Grades 3–5*, edited by Rose Mary Zbiek. Reston, Va.: NCTM, 2010.

Bass, Hyman. "Computational Fluency, Algorithms, and Mathematical Proficiency: One Mathematician's Perspective." *Teaching Children Mathematics* 9 (February 2003): 322–27.

Bastable, Virginia, and Deborah Schifter. "Classroom Stories: Examples of Elementary Students Engaged in Early Algebra." In *Algebra in the Early Grades*, edited by James J. Kaput, David W. Carraher, and Maria L. Blanton, pp. 165–84. New York: Lawrence Erlbaum Associates, 2008.

Boaler, Jo. *What's Math Got to Do with It? How Teachers and Parents Can Transform Mathematics Learning and Inspire Success.* New York: Penguin Books, 2008.

Burns, Marilyn. *About Teaching Mathematics.* Sausalito, Calif.: Math Solutions Publications, 2000.

Carpenter, Thomas P., Elizabeth Fennema, Megan Loef Franke, Linda Levi, and Susan B. Empson. *Children's Mathematics: Cognitively Guided Instruction.* Portsmouth, N.H.: Heinemann, 1999.

Carpenter, Thomas P., Megan Loef Franke, and Linda Levi. *Thinking Mathematically: Integrating Arithmetic and Algebra in Elementary School.* Portsmouth, N.H.: Heinemann, 2003.

Cavey, Laurie O. and Margaret T. Kinzel. "From Whole Numbers to Invert & Multiply." *Teaching Children Mathematics* 20, no. 6 (2014): 374–83.

Chapin, Suzanne H., and Art Johnson. *Math Matters: Understanding the Math You Teach, Grades K–8.* 2nd ed. Sausalito, Calif.: Math Solutions Publications, 2006.

Chapin, Suzanne H., Catherine O'Connor, and Nancy Canavan Anderson. *Classroom Discussions in Math: A Teacher's Guide for Using Talk Moves to Support the Common Core and More, Grades K–6: A Multimedia Professional Learning Resource.* 3rd ed. Sausalito, Calif.: Math Solution Publications, 2013.

Clements, Douglas H., and Julie Sarama. "Young Children and Technology: What's Appropriate?" In *Technology-Supported Mathematics Learning Environments.* 2005 Yearbook of the National Council of Teachers (NCTM), edited by William J. Masalski, pp. 51–74. Reston, Va.: NCTM, 2005.

Cobb, Paul, and Grayson Wheatley. "Children's Initial Understanding of Ten." *Focus on Learning Problems in Mathematics* 10, no. 3 (1988): 1–28.

Cobb, Paul, Ada Boufi, Kay McClain, and Joy Whitenack. "Reflective Discourse and Collective Reflection." *Journal for Research in Mathematics Education* 28, no. 3 (1997): 258–77.

Cobb, Paul, and Graceann Merkel. "Thinking Strategies as an Example of Teaching Arithmetic through Problem Solving." In *New Directions for Elementary School Mathematics.* 1989 Yearbook of the National Council of Teachers of Mathematics (NCTM), edited by Paul Trafton, pp. 70–81. Reston, Va.: NCTM, 1989.

Common Core Standards Writing Team. "Progressions Documents for the Common Core Math Standards." Institute for Mathematics and Education, University of Arizona, 2013, http://ime.math.arizona.edu/progressions/.

Connected Mathematics Project. "Homework Support." Michigan State University, May 2015. https://connectedmath.msu.edu/families/homework-support/.

Conway, John Horton, and Richard K. Guy. *The Book of Numbers.* New York: Copernicus, 1996.

Cotter, Joan. *Math Card Games.* 3rd ed. Hazelton, N.D.: Activities for Learning, 2000.

Eisele, Rita. "Math Anxiety: A Hindrance to Equity." Paper presented at the Annual Meeting of the National Council of Teachers of Mathematics, Washington, D.C., April 2009.

Falkner, Karen P., Linda Levi, and Thomas P. Carpenter. "Children's Understanding of Equality: A Foundation for Algebra." *Teaching Children Mathematics* (December 1999): 232–36.

Fosnot, Catherine Twomey, and Maarten Dolk. *Young Mathematicians at Work: Constructing Number Sense, Addition, and Subtraction.* Portsmouth, N.H.: Heinemann, 2001.

———. *Young Mathematicians at Work: Constructing Multiplication and Division.* Portsmouth, N.H.: Heinemann, 2001.

———. *Young Mathematicians at Work: Constructing Fractions, Decimals, and Percents.* Portsmouth, N.H.: Heinemann, 2002.

Fuson, Karen C. "Conceptual Structures for Multiunit Numbers: Implications for Learning and Teaching Multidigit Addition, Subtraction, and Place Value." *Cognition and Instruction* 7 (1990): 343–403.

———. "Developing Mathematical Power in Whole Number Operations." In *A Research Companion to Principles and Standards for School Mathematics,* edited by Jeremy Kilpatrick, W. Gary Martin, and Deborah Schifter, pp. 68–94. Reston, Va.: NCTM, 2003.

———. "Toward Computational Fluency in Multidigit Multiplication and Division." *Teaching Children Mathematics* 9 (February 2003): 300–05.

Guedj, Denis. *Numbers: The Universal Language.* New York: Harry Abrams, 1997.

Hiebert, James S., Thomas P. Carpenter, Elizabeth Fennema, Karen C. Fuson, Diana Wearne, Hanilie Murray, Alywyn Olivier, and Piet Human. *Making Sense: Teaching and Learning Mathematics with Understanding.* Portsmouth: N.H.: Heinemann, 1997.

Jackson, Philip W. *Life in Classrooms.* New York: Holt, Rinehart and Winston, 1990.

Kamii, Constance. *Young Children Reinvent Arithmetic: Implications of Piaget's Theory.* 2nd ed. With Leslie Baker Housman. New York: Teachers College Press, 2000.

Kamii, Constance, and Rheta DeVries. *Physical Knowledge in Preschool Education: Implications of Piaget's Theory.* New York: Teachers College Press, 1993.

Kamii, Constance, and Ann Dominick. "The Harmful Effects of Algorithms in Grades 1–4." In *The Teaching and Learning of Algorithms in School Mathematics.* 1998 Yearbook of the National Council of Teachers of Mathematics (NCTM), edited by Lorna J. Morrow and Margaret J. Kenney, pp. 130–39. Reston, Va.: NCTM, 1998.

Kilpatrick, Jeremy, Jane Swafford, and Bradford Findell eds. *Adding It Up: Helping Children Learning Mathematics.* Washington, D.C.: National Academy Press, 2001.

Lampert, Magdalene. "When The Problem Is Not The Question and the Solution Is Not The Answer: Mathematical Knowing and Teaching." *American Educational Research Journal* 27, no. 1 (1990): 29–63.

———. "Choosing and Using Mathematical Tools in Classroom Discourse." In *Advances in Research on Teaching,* vol. 1, edited by Jere Brophy, pp. 223–64. Greenwich, Conn.: JAI Press, 1989.

Lamon, Susan J. *Teaching Fractions and Ratios for Understanding Essential Content Knowledge and Instructional Strategies for Teachers.* 3rd ed. New York: Routledge, 2012.

Lanin, John, Amy Ellis, Rebekah Elliot, and Rose Marie Zbiek. *Developing Essential Understanding of Mathematical Reasoning for Teaching Mathematics in Prekindergarten–Grade 8.* Reston, Va.: NCTM, 2011.

Lappan, Glenda, James T. Fey, William M. Fitzgerald, Susan Friel, and Elizabeth Difanis Phillips. *Connected Mathematics 2: Parent Guide.* Boston, Mass.: Pearson/Prentice Hall, 2006.

Lester, Jill Bodnar. "Establishing a Community of Mathematics Learners." *In What's Happening in Math Class? Envisioning New Practices Through Teacher Narratives,* edited by Deborah Schifter, pp. 88–102. New York: Teachers College Press, 1996.

Litwiller, B., and George Bright, eds. *Making Sense of Fractions, Ratios, and Proportions.* 2002 Yearbook of the National Council of Teachers of Mathematics (NCTM). Reston, Va.: NCTM, 2002.

Lloyd, G. M., B. A. Herbel-Eisenmann, and J. R. Star. *Developing Essential Understanding of Expressions, Equations, and Functions for Teaching Mathematics in Grades 6–8.* Reston, Va.: NCTM, 2011.

Lobato, Joanne, and Amy B. Ellis. *Developing Essential Understanding of Ratios, Proportions, and Proportional Reasoning for Teaching Mathematics in Grades 6–8,* edited by Rose Marie Zbiek. Reston, Va.: NCTM, 2010.

Ma, Liping. *Knowing and Teaching Elementary Mathematics: Teachers' Understanding of Fundamental Mathematics in China and the United States.* New York: Routledge, 2000.

Mack, Nancy K. "Connecting to Develop Computational Fluency with Fractions." *Teaching Children Mathematics* 11 (November 2004): 226–32.

Masalski, William J., ed. *Technology-Supported Mathematics Learning Environments.* 2005 Yearbook of the National Council of Teachers of Mathematics (NCTM). Reston, Va.: NCTM, 2005.

Mason, J., Alan Graham, and Sue Johnston-Wilder. *Developing Thinking in Algebra.* Thousand Oaks, Calif.: SAGE Publications, 2005.

Mathematical Sciences Education Board, Board on Mathematical Sciences, National Research Council. *Everybody Counts: A Report to the Nation on the Future of Mathematics Education.* Washington, D.C.: National Academy Press, 1989.

Michigan State University. *Connected Mathematics 2, Bits and Pieces II: Using Fraction Operations.*

Upper Saddle River, N.J.: Pearson Prentice Hall, 2006.

Miura, Irene T., Yukari Okamoto, Chungsoon C. Kim, Marcia Steere, and Michael Fayol. "First Graders' Cognitive Representation of Number and Understanding of Place Value: Cross-National Comparisons—France, Japan, Korea, Sweden, and the United States." *Journal of Educational Psychology* 85, no. 1 (1993): 24–30.

National Council of Teachers of Mathematics. *Principles and Standards for School Mathematics.* Reston, Va.: NCTM, 2000.

National Council of Teachers of Mathematics. *Rich & Engaging Mathematical Tasks: Grades 5–9.* Reston, Va.: NCTM, 2012.

National Governors Association Center for Best Practices (NGA Center) and Council of Chief State School Officers (CCSSO). *Common Core State Standards for Mathematics.* Washington, D.C.: NGA Center and CCSSO, 2010. http://www.corestandards.org.

Nebesniak, Amy, and Ruth Heaton. "Student Confidence & Student Involvement." *Mathematics Teaching in the Middle School* 16, no. 2 (2010): 96–103.

O'Connell, Susan. *Introduction to Problem Solving: Strategies for the Elementary Math Classroom.* Heinemann: Portsmouth, N.H., 2000.

Parker, Ruth. *Helping with Math at Home.* Portsmouth, N.H.: Heinemann, 2006.

Reys, Barbara J., Robert E. Reys, and Oscar Chávez. "Why Mathematics Textbooks Matter." *Educational Leadership* (February 2004): 61–66.

Russell, Susan Jo. "Developing Computational Fluency with Whole Numbers." *Teaching Children Mathematics* 7 (November 2000): 154–58.

Sarama, Julie, and Douglas H. Clements. "Learning and Teaching with Computers in Early Childhood Education." In *Contemporary Perspectives in Early Childhood Education*, edited by Olivia N. Saracho and Bernard Spodek, pp. 71–219. Greenwich, Conn.: Information Age Publishing, 2002.

Schifter, Deborah. "Learning to See the Invisible: What Skills and Knowledge Are Needed to Engage with Students' Mathematical Ideas?" In *Beyond Classical Pedagogy: Teaching Elementary School Mathematics,* edited by Terry Wood, Barbara Scott Nelson, and Janet Warfield, pp. 109–34. Mahwah, N.J.: Lawrence Erlbaum Associates, 2001.

Schifter, Deborah, Virginia Bastable, and Susan Jo Russell, eds. *Building a System of Tens Facilitator's Guide.* Boston: Pearson, 2010.

———. *Making Meaning for Operations Facilitator's Guide.* 2nd ed. Boston: Pearson, 2010.

Schoenfeld, A. H. "Learning to Think Mathematically: Problem Solving, Metacognition, and Sense Making in Mathematics." In *Handbook of Research on Mathematics Teaching and Learning*, edited by D. A. Grouws, pp. 334–70. New York: Macmillan, 1992.

Smith, B. Sidney, and Wendy Hageman Smith. "Coping with Math Anxiety." *Studying Math: Pathways to Success.* Math Academy Online, 1997. http://www.mathacademy.com/pr/minitext/anxiety/.

Smith, David A., Deborah Schifter, Virginia Bastable, and Susan Jo Russell. *Number and Operations: Calculating with Whole Numbers and Decimals.* 2nd ed. Boston: Pearson, 2010.

Sowder, Judith, Larry Sowder, and Susan Nickerson. *Reconceptualizing Mathematics for Elementary School Teachers.* 2nd ed. New York: Freeman, 2013.

Steffe, Leslie P., Ernest von Glasersfeld, John Richards, and Paul Cobb. *Children's Counting Types: Philosophy, Theory, and Application.* New York: Praeger Scientific, 1983.

Stein, Mary Kay, Barbara W. Grover, and Marjorie Henningsen. "Building Student Capacity for Mathematical Thinking and Reasoning: An Analysis of Mathematical Tasks Used in Reform Classrooms." *American Educational Research Journal* 33, no. 2 (Summer 1996), 455–88.

Stein, Mary Kay, and Margaret Schwan Smith. *5 Practices for Orchestrating Productive Mathematics Discussions.* Reston, Va.: NCTM, 2011.

Stenmark, Jean Kerr, Virginia Thompson, and Ruth Cossey. *Family Math.* Berkeley, Calif.: Lawrence Hall of Science, 1986.

TERC. *Investigations in Number, Data, and Space.* 2nd ed. Glenview, Ill.: Pearson Scott Foresman, 2008.

Thompson, Alba G. "On Patterns, Conjectures, and Proof: Developing Students' Mathematical Thinking." *Arithmetic Teacher* 33 (September 1985): 20–23.

Van de Walle, John A., Karen Karp, and Jennifer M. Williams. *Elementary and Middle School Mathematics: Teaching Developmentally.* 7th ed. Boston: Allyn & Bacon, 2010.

Whitenack, Joy Wright. "Modeling, Mathematizing and Mathematical Learning as It Is Situated in the Mathematics Classroom." PhD diss., Vanderbilt University, 1995.

Whitenack, Joy W., Nancy Knipping, Ok-Kyeong Kim, and Gay Ragan. "The Dialectical Role of Purposeful Play, Emerging Mathematical Practices, and Instructional Design Theory." Paper presented at the Annual Meeting of the American Educational Research Association, Seattle, April 2001.

Whitenack, Joy W., Nancy Knipping, Sue Novinger, Linda Coutts, and Scott Standifer. "Teachers' Mini-case Studies of Children's Mathematics." *Journal of Mathematics Teacher Education* 3 (2000): 101–23.

Whitenack, Joy W., and Erna Yackel. "Making Mathematical Arguments in the Primary Grades: The Importance of Explaining and Justifying One's Ideas." *Teaching Children Mathematics* 8 (May 2002): 524–27.

Wright, Robert J., Jim Martland, and Ann K. Stafford. *Early Numeracy: Assessment for Teaching and Intervention.* London: Paul Chapman Publishing Ltd, 2000.

Yackel, Erna. "A Foundation for Algebraic Reasoning in the Early Grades." *Teaching Children Mathematics* 3 (February 1997): 276–80.

———. "What We Can Learn from Analyzing the Teacher's Role in Collective Argumentation." *Journal of Mathematical Behavior* 21, no. 4 (2002): 423–40.

Yackel, Erna, and Paul Cobb. "Sociomathematical Norms, Argumentation, and Autonomy in Mathematics." *Journal for Research in Mathematics Education* 27 (July 1996): 458–77.

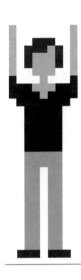

Index

Note: Page numbers in *italics* indicate glossary terms.